CLIMBING AND HIKING
IN ECUADOR

"We came again
into the Land of the
Butterflies, and saw the great
Morphos sailing to and fro,
with myriads of attendant
satellites in chrome,
carmine and vermilion"
Whymper

CLIMBING AND HIKING IN ECUADOR

Rob Rachowiecki
and
Betsy Wagenhauser

BRADT PUBLICATIONS, UK
HUNTER PUBLISHING, USA

DEDICATION

To my parents, Alec and Rene Rachowiecki, with love and gratitude

Engravings from *Travels Amongst the Great Andes of the Equator* by Edward Whymper, originally published in 1891 by John Murray.
Maps by Hans Van Well
Front cover photos by Matt Dickinson (ascending Cotopaxi) and Betsy Wagenhauser (Podocarpus)
Back cover photo (Chimborazo) by Betsy Wagenhauser
Typeset by Patti Taylor, London NW8 ORJ
Printed by the Guernsey Press, Channel Islands

ACKNOWLEDGEMENTS TO THE FIRST EDITION

Many people in Ecuador helped me in researching and writing this book. I am particularly grateful to Mike Hooper, who not only gave me his house to stay in, but also managed to nearly demolish two 4WD vehicles in his attempts to get me up the mountains and, when all else failed, accompanied me to the top of several on foot.

Other hikers and climbers who accompanied me on my many mountaineering fiascos and occasional successes were Susan Alexander and Paul Dutch (Chimborazo area hikes and Carihuairazo ascents); Geof Bartram of the American Alpine Institute with Chris Curry (Cotacachi, Las Cajas and the Inca Trail to Ingapirca); Ivan Castaigne (Iliniza Norte, Cayambe and useful verbal information); Myles Conway and Dave (Reventador and various foolish ventures into the jungle); Jim Desrossiers and Roberto Fuentes (El Altar); Alan Klingenstein (Andes to Jungle Hike and verbal abuse); Steve McFarland, ex-president of the now defunct International Andean Mountaineering Club (various excursions); Michael Orr (Cotopaxi, Cayambe, Imbabura, El Altar, Iliniza Sur); Carol from the US who walked around Cotopaxi; Big Al who climbed Tungurahua and ate 20 boiled eggs in a weekend; and various other people whose names I've misplaced but who helped in many adventures.

It's more than just support in the mountains that helps get a book written. Many people helped me in Quito and elsewhere with hospitality and information. Thank you to Pieter von Bunningen, Alan Cathey, Carol Dennison, Dr Minard "Pete" Hall, Elaine Hooper, Helena Landázuri of the Fundación Natura, Alan Miller, and various Peace Corps volunteers, especially Tom in Mulaló and the gang in Tena.

Licenciado Gabriel Pazmiño and Isabel Oviedo both helped tremendously with obtaining my visa extensions in Quito — without their help this book would never have been started.

Michael Kelsey and Michael Koerner, whose books are listed in the bibliography, reviewed and criticized my manuscript in its early stages, and Pieter Crow and Kevin Healey wrote useful letters about various aspects of Ecuadorian mountaineering.

Mike Shawcross read the proofs, and Dr Cathy Payson checked the health section.

My parents provided me with work space and a typewriter during the two all too short months I spent in England transcribing my field notes into the finished product.

For some reason, the person who deserves the greatest thanks and praise always gets left until the end. Adequate acknowledgement cannot be given to Hilary Bradt, editor, publisher, and good friend, who never flagged in supporting me in this venture.

Sincere thanks to you all.

Rob Rachowiecki

ACKNOWLEDGEMENTS TO THE SECOND EDITION

A great number of people deserve special thanks for all the advice, information, companionship, and support that helped put this newest edition in print.

I am grateful to many members of the South American Explorers Club who assisted with updates during their travels in Ecuador, especially Peter Heebink and Sally Wright for the Atillo to Achupallas hike; and Bruce Roberson, Ted Hughes and Grant Sible for updates on Sangay and Reventador. Saoirse McClory expertly managed the SAE Clubhouse in Quito so that I could hide away and devote time toward this new edition, and Alex Newton shared with me his beautiful hiding place.

Professional climbers Freddy Ramirez and Hugo Torres came through with superb advice and new route descriptions for several climbs and hikes, and Juan Rodriguez and Juan Currasco were great sources for rock climbing in the country, especially around the Cuenca area.

Jean Brown was a wealth of information and provided several new hikes including Sigchos, Apuela, and Machalilla; Val Pitkenthly, intrepid guide, shared with me her Piñan Lakes hike.

I am grateful to the readers who took the time to report changes and offer advice, especially Geert Cromphout and John and Christine Myerscough.

Among those who braved the bitter elements and soaring heights with me, I'd especially like to thank Vicky Longland, Clarice Strang, John Kurth, Eric Lawrie, Petra Schepens and, again, Alex, all of whom brought along a wonderful sense of adventure and a great capacity for fun.

Most importantly, I would like to thank Rob Rachowiecki and Hilary Bradt for their friendship over the years and for their support and encouragement during the production of this newest edition. I am grateful to them for giving me the opportunity to contribute.

Betsy Wagenhauser

PREFACE TO THE SECOND EDITION

Two authors' names appear on this book but we have decided not to credit each piece with either Betsy or Rob — it's too distracting for the reader who is more concerned with climbing or hiking. If you have any queries or comments send them to me, indicating the page number, and I will make sure it is forwarded to the right person.

Readers' letters have always played an important part in updating our books so please let us know if there have been any changes or new information which should go into the next edition.

¡Vaya Bien!

Hilary Bradt

INTRODUCTION ... WHY ECUADOR?

Though one of the smallest countries in South America, Ecuador offers an incredible diversity of scenery, wildlife, and people. The mountaineer and adventurous traveller have a choice of the ice-clad Andes, tropical rainforest, mountain trails leading to Inca ruins, and quiet beaches; all these attractions lie within a day's journey of Quito, the capital city. This accessibility makes Ecuador an attractive destination for climbers and hikers of all abilities, and avoids the long approaches and expedition planning often necessary in other high mountain ranges.

Mountaineers find Ecuador well suited as a high altitude training ground. There are many technically straightforward ascents of 5000-metre peaks. Climbers can gain technical experience in the lower ranges of Europe and North America and then learn about how the body functions at high altitudes in the Ecuadorian Andes. A combination of these abilities will produce climbers ready to challenge some of the world's most difficult high peaks.

Superb mountain scenery is only one of Ecuador's attractions. It has some of the best beaches in South America, colourful Indian markets, and plenty of wildlife, especially birds. Come and see for yourself.

ABOUT THE AUTHORS

Rob Rachowiecki, who is British, has been exploring wilderness areas in various parts of the world since the age of sixteen. He has travelled overland from Alaska to Tierra del Fuego, and now lives in Arizona with his wife and daughters Julia, aged 4, and Alison aged 2. He still manages to visit the Andean countries for a couple of months each year, leading groups for Wilderness Travel of California. He is the author of the Ecuador, Peru and Costa Rica travel survival kits published by Lonely Planet.

Betsy is originally from Texas, but has lived in South America for the last five years aiding and abetting travellers through her work at the South American Explorers Club in Lima and Quito. While setting up the club in Ecuador she found time to climb and hike extensively, as well as leading treks for Wilderness Travel. A keen mountaineer and photographer, she has contributed photos and articles to several guidebooks to South America and is currently working on a resource guide to the continent.

THE HIGHLANDS
OF ECUADOR

COLOMBIA

CHILES ▲

Tulcán

COTACACHI
▲

Ibarra

IMBABURA ▲

Olavalo

CAYAMBE
▲

REVENTADOR ▲

PICHINCHA ▲

QUITO

ATACAZO ▲

PASOCHOA
▲

Baeza
ANTISANA ▲

CORAZÓN ▲

SINCHOLAGUA ▲

SUMACO ▲

RUMIÑAHUI ▲

ILINIZAS ▲

COTOPAXI ▲

Latacunga

Ambato
Baños

CARIHUAIRAZO ▲

TUNGURAHUA ▲

CHIMBORAZO ▲

EL ALTAR ▲

Riobamba

SANGAY ▲

Guayaquil

N

0   20   40   60
km

Macas

∴ Ingapirca
   (ruin)

CUENCA

↓ Loja & PERU

CONTENTS

CHAPTER 1

Ecuador:
General Information

A traveler. I love his title. A traveler is to be reverenced as such. His profession is the best symbol of our life. Going from-toward; it is the history of every one of us.

Henry David Thoreau

GEOGRAPHY

Geographically, Ecuador is one of the most varied countries in the world, despite its small size (283,520 sq km, only a little larger than Great Britain).

The Andean range is at its narrowest here and divides the country into three distinct regions. To the east of the Central Sierra lies the tropical rainforest of the upper Amazon basin (known as the Oriente) and to the west are the more accessible but equally hot and humid coastal lowlands. It is barely 200 km from the western lowlands to the eastern jungle, yet within this narrow area are found peaks to 6310 m forming two major *cordilleras* or mountain ranges.

The two cordilleras run north-south and are 40 to 60 km apart. Between them lies the fertile Central Valley which is about 400 km long and contains Quito and most of Ecuador's major cities as well as almost half of the country's inhabitants. It is this Central Valley that was called "The Avenue of the Volcanoes" by the famous German explorer and scientist, Alexander von Humboldt, who visited Ecuador in 1802.

GEOLOGY

Ecuador has one of the world's greatest concentrations of volcanoes. There are over thirty, of which at least eight are considered to be active.

The Eastern Cordillera, sometimes known as the Cordillera Real, is older and (on average) higher and larger than the Western Cordillera. Base rock is mainly gneiss, mica-schist and other crystalline rocks, but constant and heavy volcanic activity has covered the area with plenty of volcanic material and resulted in several classically cone shaped volcanoes of which Cotopaxi (5897 m) is particularly famous. Several smaller peaks, not of volcanic origin, are found on the eastern slopes of this *cordillera* pushing their way out of the jungles of the Oriente, and further to the east other isolated mountains are completely separated from the Eastern Cordillera by jungle, The most important are Reventador (3485 m) and Sumaco (3900 m) both of which are active and relatively inaccessible volcanoes.

The Western Cordillera range is not generally as massive as the Eastern, despite the presence of Ecuador's highest peak, the dormant volcano Chimborazo (6310 m). The range is made of porphyritic eruptive rocks of the Mesozoic age, and intense volcanic activity has covered it with volcanic material to an even greater extent than the Eastern Cordillera.

HISTORY

Very little is known of the earliest history of the area. In the early 1400s at least six linguistic groups were recognized in the highlands alone (the Pasto, Cara, Panzaleo, Puruhá, Cañari, and Palta) and by the middle of the century the Caras had gained a dominant position. They overpowered a minor tribe, the Quitus (hence Quito), forming the kingdom of the Shyris which was the major presence in the area at the time of Inca expansion from the south. Despite several years of resistance, the Shyris and nearby lesser groups were integrated into the Inca empire by about 1490.

In 1525 the Inca Huayna Capac died, dividing his empire between two sons. Atahualpa, of Shyri descent on his mother's side, became ruler of the northern part of the empire, whilst Huáscar received the rest. Violent civil war between the two brothers followed and Atahualpa won. Thus when the Spanish conquest began in 1532 the Inca Empire had been severely weakened by the civil war. Atahualpa was captured and paid a huge ransom in gold and silver for his release; despite this he was murdered by Pizarro and the Inca Empire effectively came to an end.

In 1534 Sebastián de Benalcázar founded Quito on the ruins of the old Shyri city. After the success of the Spanish conquest the area became known as the Audiencia de Quito, and (except for a period of 6 years) remained under the viceroy of Peru until 1740 when it became part of the Viceroyalty of Nueva Granada. The sixteenth to eighteenth centuries were characterized by peaceful colonialism. Agriculture was developed, the Indians were exploited, and Spain profited.

By the nineteenth century, in common with other parts of South America, a strong independence movement had developed. From 1809 several unsuccessful attempts were made at independence but it was not until May 24 1822 that Mariscal Sucre finally defeated the royalist forces at the Battle of Pichincha. Although free of the Spanish, the area now became part of Gran Colombia and it took over eight more years before Ecuador became completely independent under the leadership of the first president, General Juan José Flores.

The rest of the nineteenth century was a continuous struggle between conservatives and liberals. By the end of the 1800s Ecuador was under the military rule of General Eloy Alfaro and much of the twentieth century has been a succession of unstable military governments. A civilian leader, President Jaime Roldós, was elected in 1979 and after his untimely death in an air accident was succeeded in 1981 by his Vice-President, Osvaldo Hurtado Larrea. The country has continued to democratically elect civilian governments with León Febres Cordero serving from 1984-1988, and Rodrigo Borja Cevellos in office from 1988 to the present.

PEOPLE

A census held in 1990 revealed that Ecuador's population had reached 10,400,000. This is approximately thirteen times the number of Indians estimated to have been living in the area at the time of the Spanish conquest. The population density of about 37 people per sq km is the highest in South America.

About 40% of this total are Indians and an equal number are *mestizos* (mixed Spanish/Indian stock). About 10% are white and the remainder black or Asian.

The majority of the Indians are Quechua speaking and live in the highlands; they are the direct descendants of the inhabitants of the Inca Empire. There are also several small groups living in the lowlands and speaking their own distinct languages. These tribes include, among others, the Shuar (Jívaro), Auca, Cofan, and Secoya of the Oriente and the Cayapa and the Colorado Indians of the coastal plain. The highland Indians are often bilingual, although Spanish is a second language and not much used in remote areas. Until land reforms of the 1960s the majority of the Quechua Indians were little more than slaves to the big *hacienda* owners. Nowadays they are developing co-operatives and own land but nevertheless live at a subsistence level in many cases.

Some groups, notably the Otavalo Indians and to a lesser extent the Salasacas and Cañars, have made a reputation as excellent weavers and craftsmen (and women) and their goods are in great demand. After some time in Ecuador you will notice the different styles of clothing that individual groups traditionally wear. The Otavalo men are characterized by their white, calf-length trousers, rope sandals, grey or blue ponchos, and long single braid of hair. The women wear a colourfully embroidered blouse and a bulky gold-coloured necklace. The Salasaca men wear distinctive broad brimmed white hats, white shirts, and black ponchos. The Indians of the Saquisilí area are most often seen wearing red ponchos and little felt 'pork pie' hats.

Another interesting and attractive feature of Indian life is the fiestas which often celebrate church holidays. One of my favourite fiestas is that of All Souls Day (November 2) when throngs of people visit cemeteries to pay their respects to the dead. Everyone does this, from rich *Quiteños* to poor *campesinos* (peasants), but the cemeteries near the Indian villages are the most colourful. Hundreds of people show up in their best clothes and leave wreaths and flowers on the graves. To ensure that their departed friends and relatives also enjoy the day the people bring food and drink and leave some in remembrance and offering. The majority of the food and drink is, of course, consumed by the Indians themselves and the atmosphere is generally festive rather than sombre.

CLIMATE

Most descriptions of Ecuador's climate agree that its most reliable aspect is its unreliability. Unfortunately, this really seems to be the case, so I can't give you foolproof advice on which months will be best for your visit. However, here are some generalizations.

In common with other tropical countries, Ecuador does not experience the four seasons known in temperate parts of the world. Instead there are wet and dry seasons. Despite its small size, Ecuador has several distinct climatic zones with wet and dry periods varying from area to area.

The coastal areas are influenced by the cold Humboldt current which flows up from the south Pacific, but during December a warm current from the north, seasonably called 'El Niño' (the Christ Child) predominates. This marks the beginning of the coastal rainy season. The northern coast is wet from January to June and dryish for the rest of the year, while further south the coast experiences a shorter wet season and in the dry season, from May to December, it is much drier than in the north. The effects of 'El Niño' are not yet fully understood, and in some years there are devastating floods in the coastal lowlands during the wet season.

Inland, the climate is completely different. It rains most of the time in the Oriente though some months are a little less wet than others, depending on the area. The weather in the mountains varies from east to west. The eastern mountains, especially Antisana, El Altar and Sangay, and to a lesser extent Cayambe and Tungurahua are influenced by air from the Amazonian lowlands. The wettest months are June through August. December and January are when the highest number of successful ascents have been made on the difficult El Altar. Ecuadorian climbers favour February for climbing Antisana and October through January are suggested for Cayambe.

The situation is reversed in the western mountains. Here, the dry season is late June through early September, with a short dry spell in December and early January. The wettest months are February to May with April being the wettest of all. Edward Whymper claims to have spent 78 days in the vicinity of Iliniza during February to April of 1880 "... yet we did not see the whole of the mountain on any single occasion." During the dry season temperatures tend to be very low at night and high winds can be a problem, particularly in August. The weather in October and November tends to be variable. Snow build-up during these months sometimes provides quite good snow conditions for the short December-January season.

The temperature variation is mainly influenced by altitude. From sea level to about 900 m it is hot with an average temperature of 26°-28°C. The warm zone is from 900 m to 2000 m with an average temperature range of 20°-26°C. From 2000 m to 3000 m it is quite cold with an average of 12°-20°C. (Remember average includes warm afternoons and freezing nights.) Above 3000 m is the *páramo* with temperatures averaging from 0-12°C and above the lowest snow line at about 4500 m the mean temperature stays below freezing, although the strong sun sometimes makes it feel much warmer.

There have been noticeable recent changes in the world's climatic patterns and Ecuador has been experiencing a period of relative drought compared with a century ago (although this is difficult to believe when you are caught in a torrential Ecuadorian downpour). This has also contributed to the receding glaciers on Ecuador's mountains. Some people also claim that sun-spot and other solar activity affects the climate in a seven to eleven year cycle. Certainly, a year of greater precipitation is experienced at irregular intervals. Although proper detailed records have been kept only since about the 1960s, it is known that the periods 1965, 1972/3 and 1975/6, and 1982/3 have been particularly wet. This cycle is said to be wet to begin with and drier in later years; the drier years mean a significant reduction or disappearance of glaciers. 1981 was the last year of the most recent cycle and many mountains which have permanent glaciers shown on the IGM maps were completely bare of snow. Examples include Iliniza Norte and Sincholagua. After the wet years 1982/83 more snow and ice were again found on these peaks but the last few years have been considerably drier as evidenced by the glacial recession on most of the peaks.

Not only is there variation in the climate from year to year, but the daily weather is also highly unpredictable. There is a local saying that in the mountains all four seasons can be experienced in one day. As Michaux notes in his *Ecuador: A Travel Journal* (1928)

"Morning summer.
Noon springtime. The sky is beginning to get overcast.
4 p.m. rain. Freshness.
A night cold and luminous like winter.
For this reason clothing is a problem if you must be out for more than a few hours.
You watch the accursed setting forth, armed with straw hat, canvas, furpiece, and umbrella."

It is amazing and confusing that so much variation can be found in such a small area. With windows of good weather and seasonal variations, climbing any given mountain in any given month is feasible. However, as a general rule of thumb, December to January are the best months to be in the Ecuadorian mountains and March to May the worst. If you're there in June through September, avoid the east and climb in the west. In October through February concentrate on the east. Cotopaxi lies in a strange dry micro-climate of its own and can be climbed during most of the year.

MOUNTAINEERING — A HISTORICAL VIEW

Despite some legends there is no evidence, as found in the more southerly countries, of any mountain ascents by the local Indians prior to the arrival of the Spanish *conquistadores* who contented themselves with noting major volcanic activity in their journals, their first records being of the eruptions of Cotopaxi and Tungurahua in 1534. The earliest recorded ascent is that of the Ecuadorian* José Toribio Ortiguera who reached the crater of Pichincha in 1582. There is a disputed record of an ascent of Pichincha by Padre Juan Romero in 1660, the same year that a major eruption buried Quito in 40 cm of volcanic ash, but generally speaking during the first two centuries of Spanish occupation there was little interest in geographical aspects. The windfall of a treasure-laden Inca civilization was something the Spaniards wished to exploit themselves and so all foreign visitors, including natural historians or explorers, were regarded with suspicion. It was not until well into the eighteenth century that a European scientific expedition was first

*Note: I use 'Ecuadorian' for convenience here and later in the chapter although the country was not known by that name until 1830.

permitted to make a serious attempt at mapping and exploring Ecuador and this led to an awakening of interest in the mountains of the country. By the beginning of the eighteenth century it had been established that the world was round, but controversy still raged over the concept of polar flattening. In an attempt to settle the issue, the French Académie des Sciences organized expeditions to the arctic and the equator. At this time Africa was still the 'dark continent', Indonesia was little known, and the Amazon basin was virtually unexplored. Consequently Ecuador, with its capital just 25 km south of the equator, was the obvious venue for such an expedition. This took place from 1736 to 1744 and was led by the Frenchman Charles-Marie de La Condamine, accompanied by two countrymen, two Spaniards, and an Ecuadorian. Surveying was undertaken, and their calculations of the distance from the equator to the North Pole became the basis of the metric system of weights and measures. The flora, fauna, geology, and geography were also studied. The explorers were very interested in the highlands, and during the course of their investigations concluded that Chimborazo (6310 m) was the highest peak in the world — a belief which existed until the 1820s. They made the first serious attempt to scale this mountain, reaching an altitude of about 4750 m. The less important peaks of Pichincha (4794 m) and Corazón (4788 m) were successfully climbed and most of the major peaks were surveyed.

This expedition's surveys and measurements started a series of disputes which have not been resolved to this day. For example Cotopaxi, Ecuador's second highest peak, was measured at 5751 m by La Condamine's expedition. Succeeding expeditions turned in considerably higher measurements: 5753 m by Humboldt in 1802, 5978 in by Whymper in 1880, 5940 m by Martínez in 1906, and the highest of all, 6005 m was published by Arthur Eichler in his *Ecuador — Snow Peaks and Jungles* (1970). His is the only figure of over 6000m and the height most generally accepted today is 5897 m as surveyed by the Instituto Geográfico Militar in 1972. Nevertheless many recent sources are still unable to agree on the correct elevation. The same perplexing situation exists with other peaks (see *Appendix*).

After the departure of the French expedition, the eighteenth century saw no more major exploration of the Ecuadorian mountains. It was not until 1802 that an expedition led by the famous German scientist and explorer Baron Alexander von Humboldt reawakened interest in the Ecuadorian highlands. Humboldt visited and studied various peaks including Cotopaxi, Pichincha, Antisana, and El Altar but it is for his research on and attempted ascent of Chimborazo that his expedition is particularly remembered by mountaineers. Accompanied by the Frenchman Aimé Bonpland and the Ecuadorian Carlos Montúfar he identified many plants including some new species, as well as noting barometric data during his attempted ascent of the southern flanks of the mountain. He made a sectional sketch map of Chimborazo which shows the plant species, various geographical landmarks, the expedition's penetration beyond the snowline and finally, high above the surrounding *páramo* the comment, "Crevasse qui empêcha les voyageurs d'attendre la cime" (crevasse which prevents travellers from reaching the summit). This indicates the point at about 5875 m where Humboldt and his companions, suffering from high altitude sickness, with cracked and bleeding lips and badly sun-burned faces, were forced to turn back. This attempt is particularly noteworthy since despite their failure to gain the summit, they did reach the highest point so far attained by western man. Since Chimborazo was still considered the highest mountain in the world, other attempts on its summit soon followed. The Venezuelan liberator of the Andean countries, Simón Bolívar, climbed to the snowline in 1822 and nine years later Bolívar's colonel, the French agronomist Joseph Boussingault, managed to reach about 6000 m on Chimborazo's southern slopes, again increasing the altitude so far attained by western explorers. Boussingault also made several attempts on other peaks, but without notable success.

President Gabriel García Moreno, a much criticized and despotic ruler, was nevertheless the first Ecuadorian leader to take an active interest in the environment. He enacted several conservationist laws and in 1844 climbed to the crater of Pichincha. In succeeding years several European expeditions arrived. Around 1847 the almost forgotten Italian traveller Gaetano Osculati spent a year in Ecuador, and although he made no attempts to climb any of its peaks he left us with some interesting paintings and drawings of Ecuadorian mountains. 1849 saw the first recorded expedition to the highly active volcano Sangay (5230 m) where the Frenchman Sebastian Wisse counted 267 strong explosions in one hour. During the 1850s and 1860s several expeditions from various nations visited Ecuador but achieved little, and it was not until 1872 that the next major breakthrough in Ecuadorian mountaineering occurred.

In this year the German Wilhelm Reiss, accompanied by the Colombian Angel M. Escobar, succeeded in reaching the 5897 m summit of Cotopaxi by climbing the southeastern flank, rather than the northern route which has since become accepted as the normal route. The following year another German, Alfonso Stübel, accompanied by four Ecuadorians, Eusebio Rodriguez, Melchor Páez, Vicente Ramón, and Rafael Jantui reached the summit via the same route: the first major peak to have been climbed by Ecuadorians. The two Germans then joined forces and in 1873 made the first ascent of the active volcano Tungurahua (5016 m) as well as attempts on other summits.

A disastrous volcanic eruption on June 26 1877 left the slopes of Cotopaxi bare of ice and snow, and several climbers took advantage of this situation and climbed the volcano by the northeast side. Then a remarkable expedition in 1880, led by the renowned English climber Edward Whymper, succeeded in reaching the summit and spending a night by Cotopaxi's crater. Whymper had already established his reputation as a climber by making the first ascent of the Matterhorn, at one time reputed to be impossible. His Ecuadorian expedition must surely rate as one of the most successful mountaineering expeditions ever undertaken. With the Italian cousins Louis and Jean-Antoine Carrel, Whymper proceeded to climb not only Cotopaxi but also made the first ascent of Chimborazo, a climb which raised a storm of disbelief and protest. To quell his critics Whymper repeated the climb later in 1880 accompanied by two Ecuadorians; David Beltrán and Francisco Campaña. Ecuador's third highest peak, Cayambe (5790 m), and Antisana (5704 m), the fourth highest, also fell to the ice axes of Whymper and the Carrels as did Iliniza Sur (5263 m), Carihuairazo (5020 m), Sincholagua (4893 m), Cotacachi (4939 m) and Sara Urco (4676 m). In addition to these eight first ascents several other climbs were made by this expedition including Corazón and Pichincha as well as an unsuccessful attempt on El Altar (5319 m) which is Ecuador's most technical snow peak and which was not climbed until 1963. Edward Whymper is remembered in Ecuador to this day; there is a street named after him in Quito and the country's highest mountaineers' refuge, the new and well equipped hut at 5000 m on Chimborazo's eastern slopes, has been named Refugio Whymper.

After Whymper's memorable exploits no important expeditions occurred until the twentieth century. Whereas the nineteenth century had seen many important European expeditions to the Ecuadorian Andes, the twentieth century saw an awakening of interest in mountaineering by national climbers. The father of Ecuadorian mountaineering is Nicolás Martínez who in the first decades of this century succeeded in making many notable ascents. In 1900 Martínez climbed Tungurahua (5016 m), and in succeeding years climbed this peak several more times. His interest in mountaineering awakened, Martínez made first Ecuadorian ascents of many major peaks: Antisana in 1904, a failed attempt on Cayambe in 1905, and successful climbs of Cotopaxi and Chimborazo in 1906. Succeeding years saw various successes and failures in Martínez's climbing career. A particularly noteworthy ascent was that of Iliniza Norte in 1912; this 5126 m peak is the only one of Ecuador's ten 5000 m peaks which was first climbed by an Ecuadorian.

The first world war and its aftermath left little time or money for new foreign expeditions to Ecuador and it was not until 1929 that a United States expedition, led by Robert T. Moore, achieved the first ascent of Sangay (5230 m). This, the most continuously active volcano in Latin America, was experiencing a rare period of tranquillity at the time. Moore's expedition also made various other notable climbs, including the first US ascent of Chimborazo.

By 1929 all but one of the major Ecuadorian peaks (the ten 5000 m ones) had been conquered. The exception was El Altar (5319 m) Ecuador's fifth highest peak which was not climbed until 1963 when an Italian Alpine Club expedition led by Marino Tremonti succeeded in reaching the summit. In the intervening years many repeat ascents of the major peaks were made by climbers of various nationalities and several minor peaks were conquered for the first time. These included Cerro Hermoso (4571 m) by four Germans in 1941 and Quilindaña (4878 m) by a large party of Ecuadorians, Colombians, French, and Italians in 1952.

The 1960s and 1970s saw a new approach to mountaineering in Ecuador. With Tremonti's first ascent of El Altar in 1963 all the major peaks had been climbed and emphasis was laid on climbing new routes and lower summits of the more important mountains. El Altar's eight other virgin peaks provided great impetus and excitement to Ecuadorian mountaineering as, one by one, they were climbed between 1965 and 1979 by climbers of various nationalities, including three first ascents by Ecuadorian climbers. During these decades Ecuadorian mountaineers were consistently in the forefront of finding new climbs, such as the second and third summits of Antisana, new routes on Cayambe and Iliniza Sur, the Central Summit on Chimborazo, the first ascents of the minor peaks of Achipungo and Ayapungo, and many others too numerous to mention. In connection with these new climbs the names of the Ecuadorians Bernardo Beate, Marco Cruz, Milton Moreno, Ramiro Navarrete, Romulo Pazmiño, the Reinoso brothers, Santiago Rivadeneira, Hugo Torres, Iván Rojas, American James Desrossiers, and Frenchman Joseph Bergé will long be remembered. Many of these and other Ecuadorian climbers have also made notable ascents in different parts of the world. Mention should also be made of Fabián Zurita who, perhaps more than any other Ecuadorian, has brought the mountains of Ecuador closer to its people through his frequent and non-technical articles in the Ecuadorian press.

In the 1960s it was realized that mountaineering in Ecuador was economically important as a tourist asset and refuges were constructed to accommodate visiting foreign as well as national climbers. The first of these was the now badly damaged Fabian Zurita refuge built in 1964 at 4900 m on the northwest slopes of Chimborazo. Since then several more mountain huts have been built; some are extremely basic and others very comfortable.

Today, with its network of climbing huts and their easy accessibility, Ecuador has become an important mountaineering centre. For professionals and experts it still provides the opportunity for good new routes but it is of particular interest to intermediate climbers who wish to experience the excitement of high altitude ascents. It is also very useful as a high altitude training ground for climbers wishing to test and improve their skills before attempting ascents in the difficult mountains of the more southern Andes.

CHAPTER 2

Preparations

A journey is a person in itself; no two are alike. And all plans, safeguards, policies and coercion are fruitless. We find after years of struggle that we do not take a trip; a trip takes us.

John Steinbeck

GETTING THERE

From Europe there are direct flights on major airlines but these are expensive. Discounted tickets are often available. In London try Trailfinders (tel. 071-938 3366) or Journey Latin America (JLA) who are the experts in arranging discount fares for this part of the world and are pleased to answer unusual travel queries from their customers (tel: 081-747 3108). There is also Ecuador Travel (tel. 071-437 7534) who specialise in travel arrangements for this country.

From North America there are no really inexpensive flights. Your best bet is a cheap excursion ticket from Miami. Ecuador is well placed for overland journeys from either Colombia in the north or Peru in the south so look out for cheap flights to those destinations. Bear in mind that there is a 10% tax on air tickets bought in Ecuador and a US$25 departure tax (payable in cash dollars, sucres or travellers cheques) from the airport for international flights.

Finally, passenger and cargo ships call at Guayaquil from all over the world — but voyages are often more expensive than flights.

DOCUMENTS

Everyone needs a passport valid for at least 6 months and a tourist card which is valid for up to 90 days and is available from any port of entry. You are legally required to be able to show evidence of 'sufficient funds' (as much as US$20 per day) and an exit ticket the country — but this is rarely asked for, particularly if travelling overland. An MCO (Miscellaneous Charges Order) from any IATA airline is often adequate. Your tourist card is easily renewed at the Department of Immigration in Quito at Av. Amazonas 3149 and in other major cities, but tourists are allowed a maximum of only 90 days in any one calendar year. Obtaining permission for a longer stay is relatively easy. Tourist visas can be renewed after the maximum 90-day stay has expired for a fee of US$12 per 30-day extension. Normally only 3 extensions (for a total of another 90 days) are granted. Technically the fee is a fine paid in advance to Immigration for overstaying the 'official' 90-day tourist visa. Under no circumstances should you allow your visa to expire while you are in the country. On-the-spot police checks are frequent and a trip to jail possible.

WHAT TO BRING

In the words of Edward Whymper, "It is indeed true that nearly everything may be obtained in Ecuador. It is also true that we often had great difficulty in obtaining anything." Although climbing and backpacking equipment is available for sale and hire it is usually very expensive and often inadequate. If you're large then you'll have difficulty in finding clothing and particularly footwear to fit you since Ecuadorians are generally small. It is best to bring what you need with you. It is easy enough to find storage facilities for your excess gear whilst you are hiking or climbing.

The following checklists reflect the fact that while you may be a mountaineer one day, you'll be just a tourist the next. I've included everything I consider useful but doubtless some people's needs will differ from mine.

BACKPACK   Bear in mind that an external frame pack, while very comfortable, is awkward if hitch-hiking and liable to break during the rough treatment it will receive on planes, buses, and trucks. External frame packs tend to snag on everything from hotel doors to tropical vegetation and to throw the climber off balance; an internal frame or frameless pack hugs the body better. Buy as large a pack as you can carry — when the weather's terrible and your hands are cold it's easier to stuff a sopping wet tent and gear into a large pack than to struggle with a small one which held everything so snugly when you were warm and dry in your hotel.

SLEEPING BAG   It gets cold — but not very cold. Even when mountaineering high above the snowline temperatures below -10°C are not very common, so you don't need the most expensive sleeping bag. A medium weight one is adequate, especially if combined with a bivouac sac (waterproof sleeping bag cover or a down jacket. If you plan on doing a lot of backpacking then you should consider a bag with artificial filling because it will stay fairly warm when wet, whilst a soggy down bag is almost useless. At present artificial fillings are cheaper than down, though heavier and bulkier, but lighter new materials are constantly being developed.

MATTRESS   This is essential. Any closed cell (ensolite type) foam pad will do. I use a cheap light one which works as well as more expensive ones for insulation (which is the most important thing) although for comfort you may want a more elaborate one such as a Thermarest, which is a combination air mattress/foam pad.

TENT   You can manage without a tent if you climb only the major peaks as good mountain refuges are available. If planning extended hikes or climbs, however, you'll need a tent which is waterproof and withstands buffeting by high winds, although some climbers make do with bivouac sacs instead. I used a single-walled Gore-Tex tent for two years and it stayed more or less dry even in all night epic rain storms. Gore-Tex is unique in that it 'breathes' so there is less condensation problem. All tent seams must be carefully waterproofed with seam-sealer before leaving home.

STOVE   Four of Ecuador's climbers' huts have kitchens with stoves but if you plan trips away from the huts you'll need a stove as there is little firewood in the highlands. The best stove for high altitudes is the American MSR G/K which runs on paraffin (kerosene, sold as 'Kerex' in Ecuador), white gas (which is virtually impossible to find in Ecuador), and even car and aviation fuel. The drawback to this excellent stove is its cost and the difficulty of obtaining it in Great Britain. In this country the best alternative is probably the Optimus 96 which burns paraffin. Another very good stove is the Bleuet Gaz 200 which operates on gas cartridges which are obtainable in Ecuador as well as in Europe and the USA. If you use this stove don't litter the mountains with 'dead' cartridges, and remember that you may not carry them on aeroplanes.

COOKING UTENSILS AND CUTLERY   Bring your own or buy them in Ecuador; the locals use cheap, lightweight pans which are available in any town. Aluminium spoons and plastic cups are also easily found.

WATER BOTTLE   I carry one or two light plastic 1 litre water bottles and a 2 gallon water bag (which weighs 4 oz and packs smaller than my fist) for carrying water to campsites.

LIGHT   Being on the equator means you can be sure of one thing: 12 hours of darkness. So you'll be needing light more than in the northern summers. Torches (flashlights) and batteries are usually available throughout Ecuador, as are candles. Slow-burning candles are particularly useful but cannot be bought in Ecuador. For large groups you can bring a lantern to fit Bleuet gaz cartridges.

FOOD   With a little imagination you can find plenty of food suitable for backpacking and climbing in Ecuador's stores. Freeze dried food is virtually unobtainable but you can use noodles, dried soups, chocolate, raisins, nuts, oatmeal, powdered juices, dried milk, cheese, crackers, biscuits, salami, cans of fish, and peanut butter.

FOOTWEAR   You can climb most peaks with heavy hiking boots although double climbing boots are warmer. Medium weight hiking boots are adequate for all the hikes and some of the lesser peaks; you'll need good Vibram soles. EBs and similar rock climbing boots with smooth rubber soles are useless. Ex-army jungle boots are the best footwear for jungle and lowland trips. In Ecuador, knee-high rubber boots (*botas para agua*), (equivalent to the British Wellingtons), are good for jungle excursions which do not require heavy hiking. Venus brand is considered one of the best. Bring a pair of light shoes, sneakers, or sandals, for sitting around camp and walking in cities, and some rubber thongs (flip-flops) for use in dubious hotel bathrooms.

   All footwear stops at English size 9-10 (43 metric) in Ecuador. This includes socks, so large people should bring spares. Heavy woollen socks are best for keeping feet warm, and cotton and nylon liners help prevent blisters.

CLOTHING   Thermal underwear (both top and bottom) can be slept in and keeps you warm at high altitudes. Jeans are useless in the mountains as they bind on your legs when climbing and offer no insulation when wet. They are also too hot to wear in the sun, heavy to carry, hard to wash, and take ages to dry. (Despite this, they're the gringo item most frequently stolen from washing lines.) For climbers, woollen mountaineering trousers are excellent, or a pair of fibrepile trousers combined with rain pants to keep out the wind. One or two pairs of lightweight slacks are good for town and lowland use. Gaiters are useful for mountaineering.

Bring at least one light long sleeved shirt to protect against the intense tropical sun. You can buy thick woollen sweaters (even large sizes) cheaply in the Indian markets, so think twice about carrying sweaters from home. I like fibrepile pullovers or jackets which stay warm when wet, dry quickly, and are lighter than wool. Bring your usual assortment of tee shirts etc., and one warm wool shirt.

Without a doubt, a down jacket (or one with artificial filling) is the single most useful clothing item. Even if you're not planning any high altitude mountaineering it's useful for the hikes which go over 4000 m and are very cold at night.

Raingear is essential as it can rain even during the 'dry' season. Nylon ponchos are better than nothing but are a problem in the wind. A rain jacket and separate trousers are better. Gore-Tex is expensive but it works — this waterproof material allows sweat to evaporate so you don't get wet from perspiration.

A hat is essential for mountaineering and high altitude hikes. Up to 40% of your body heat can escape from your exposed head and neck so it really helps to keep warm if you wear a wool hat or better still a balaclava which also protects your face and neck. A wide brimmed sun hat is good for calm, sunny days and in the lowlands. Two pairs of gloves are needed by mountaineers: a light inner pair and a heavy wool outer mitt. Hikers will get by with one warm pair. Shorts are not worn in the towns but are comfortable for lower hikes in remote regions and for visits to coast, rivers, and hot pools. Also bring swimwear. All trousers should have deep pockets, preferably secured with buttons, zipper, or velcro (see *Security)* and they're handy in shirts (and skirts) as well. You may have to add them yourself.

MOUNTAINEERING EQUIPMENT   Rope, ice axe, climbing harness, and crampons are the basic necessities for snow climbs — often you can get by with nothing else. A second tool (ice hammer) is useful for some mountains (as detailed in the text). Protection may be needed for less experienced climbers, particularly whilst descending and for crevasse rescue. Two long ice screws and two snow stakes (with their respective slings and carabiners) will normally suffice. Make prussiks in case you fall into a crevasse. A helmet is occasionally useful. A bivi sac is worth throwing into your pack just in case.... A mountaineers' headlamp is needed for the predawn departures which are standard features of most snow climbs. Bring one from home as Ecuadorian ones are too heavy. Alkaline batteries are available in most cities, but don't seem to last as long as those you'd bring from home. Buy extra if depending on local batteries. Lithium batteries, which can last for 60 hours of continuous use, are available at a few photo developing shops in Quito.

Glacier cream (not ordinary sun-tan lotion), lip salve, and climbers' goggles are essential — the power of the equatorial sun bouncing off glaciers at 6000 m will astound you. A friend of mine became snow blind while wearing ordinary sunglasses.

Footpaths in Ecuador are not signposted or marked in any way, so a compass is essential for following my directions particularly when hiking cross-country. Bring marker flags or wands (which can be made from sticks and strips of plastic from plastic bags). Gaiters and good climbers' gloves should be packed. Other useful but not essential items are ski poles and an altimeter.

MISCELLANEOUS USEFUL ITEMS   Pocket torch (flashlight) with spare bulbs and batteries; travel alarm clock; Swiss Army style penknife; sewing kit (including large needles and thick thread for heavy repairs); scissors; a few metres of cord (for clotheslines, emergency repairs, spare shoelaces, tent guys, etc.); spare glasses; sunglasses; binoculars; camera; plenty of film. A compass is more than useful, it is essential.

Plastic bags (including large trash bin liners to cover packs at night); flat rubber universal bath plug; soap for clothes and body (in a soap dish); shampoo; tooth brush and paste, and dental floss (great for emergency repairs); towel; toilet paper (rarely found in cheaper hotel and restaurant lavatories); ear plugs for noisy hotels and buses; insect repellant; sun-tan lotion; hand-cream.

Pens and pencils; address book; notebook for journal and letter writing; paperback book (easily exchanged with other travellers when you've finished); pocket Spanish-English dictionary; waterproof matches or cigarette lighter; waterproofing for boots; small padlock (for cheap hotel rooms or locking gear in storage); a large lightweight nylon bag for leaving gear in storage; medicine kit (see *Health* section).

MONEY MATTERS

The Ecuadorian currency is the sucre, divided into a hundred centavos. At May 1991 there were 960 sucres to the US dollar and its value was fluctuating weekly with a slow downward trend.

The pound sterling, the German mark, and the French or Swiss franc can normally be changed in Quito but the US dollar is the most readily accepted currency, especially outside the capital. There is normally little difference in exchange rates between dollar travellers cheques and cash, and converting cheques to cash dollars is easily done. There are slight variations in exchange rates between different banks and *casas de cambio* (exchange houses) so it pays to shop around if exchanging a lot of money. Rodrigo

Paz, a *casa de cambio* which has several branches including the main one at Amazonas 370 in Quito, usually gives a good rate. Exchange facilities are available at the airport seven days a week or try the Hotel Colón. There is a small, but illegal, black market in operation. The exchange rate will not be much better, so stick with the official *cambios*.

Travellers cheques are the most convenient and safe way of carrying large amounts of money. Guard against robbery by dividing your travellers cheques and keeping them in different places, and be conscientious about recording each cheque cashed so that if the worst happens you can get a quick refund. Be careful which travellers cheques you buy. American Express are recommended; in the event of loss or theft refunds can normally be arranged within 48 hours if you report the loss promptly and back up your claim with a police report (easily obtained), the receipts to show you paid for the cheques, and personal identification (passport). Other companies are less efficient. I had about US$400 in travellers cheques stolen over a year ago; half were American Express and were replaced in 3 days, but I am still waiting to receive my money from First National City Bank. So don't use the latter.

If you run out of money it is relatively simple to have more sent from home. Unlike most Latin American countries, Ecuador will pay you all your money in US dollars. All you need to do is pick a Quito bank which will co-operate with your bank at home (e.g. Bank of America, Lloyd's Bank, Banco Holandés) and ask family or bank manager to deposit the money in your name in the Ecuadorian bank you have chosen; if you use the telex your money can arrive in 72 hours if there are no hitches or holidays.

You can also use credit cards to get money. The easiest way is to buy American Express Travellers cheques with your AmEx card. The charge is 1%, and the entire process takes about 10 minutes. (You must have an account at home from which the money can be drawn.) In Quito, the American Express office is at Ecuadorian Tours, Amazonas 339 and Washington. With MasterCard or Visa, you may get a cash advance, but often this is given in sucres. Banco Pacifico is the Mastercard representative, and Filibanco handles Visa credit cards.

BUDGETING   With the continued devaluation of the sucre Ecuador is one of the cheapest countries in Latin America for visitors with hard currency. As long as this situation prevails you could manage on the classic bare bones budget of US$5 per day. Buses running from the Colombian border to the Peruvian border cost the ridiculously low total of about US$10 for the 1000 km journey. Basic hotels charge only about a dollar a night, and there's usually a good selection of more comfortable ones that are still very economical.

If you're broke and desperate (I've been down to my last US$50 in the world a few times in South America), don't give up. You can always sell your climbing and backpacking gear easily. Good quality equipment is difficult to find in Ecuador and imported items are heavily taxed so local climbers like to buy North American or European gear from penniless mountaineers. The same applies to your camera or cassette recorder or whatever. Used but good equipment can often be sold for its original price — even more if you're a shrewd businessman or a smooth hustler, depending on your point of view. A good place to advertise is the well known budget hotel, the Gran Casino (see *Accommodation* in Chapter 3). You can also approach climbers you meet on the mountains or go to climbing clubs. Another way of making money is by teaching English. This will at least leave your weekends free to hike and climb, and you'll still have the gear to do it with. There are several language schools and the turnover is high. You don't need experience, just act schoolteacherish!

INSURANCE

Carrying Amex travellers cheques insures your money but you should get comprehensive travel insurance against theft, accidents, and illness. Most travel agents will advise you of available policies but shop around and read the small print carefully. Often you'll find that certain activities, including mountaineering, aren't covered. In the UK, the British Mountaineering Council can supply a comprehensive and not too expensive climbers' insurance policy. This is available to members only. Write to the BMC Insurance Department, Crawford House, Precinct Centre, Booth St East, Manchester M13 9R2, and ask for Expedition Remote Area forms. The insurance company, after hearing your plans, will offer a policy to suit your needs.

In addition to hospital coverage, you should consider a policy which includes evacuation to your home country if you become seriously ill or injured.

PHOTOGRAPHY

This is worth thinking about before you go. Cameras are expensive in Ecuador so bring everything you'll need. Film prices are reasonable, and certainly less expensive than in most Latin American countries. The choice of film is limited and my personal favourite, Kodachrome 64, is not available in Ecuador. (If you're hoping to publish anything on your return, remember that some magazine editors won't consider anything but Kodachrome.) Slide films which are available are Ektachrome, Fujichrome, and Agfachrome.

High speed Ektachrome 400 is good for the jungle, which is always darker than you'd expect. Kodacolor print film and most black and white film is easily found but always check the expiry date; I've seen professional looking camera stores selling film which is 2 years out of date. Film processing is sometimes shoddy and Kodachrome cannot be developed in Ecuador.

Shadows in the tropics are very dark and come out almost black in photographs. A bright cloudy day is therefore often better for photography than a very sunny one. Taking shots in open shade or using fill-in flash will help. The best time for photography is when the sun is low: the first two hours after dawn and the last two before sunset. At high altitudes a haze can spoil your pictures; using a UV filter will improve them.

The people of Ecuador are both picturesque and varied. From the handsomely uniformed presidential guard to a charmingly grubby smiling Indian child — the possibilities of 'people pictures' are endless. However, most people resent having a camera thrust into their faces without so much as a 'by your leave'. Indians in markets will often proudly turn their backs on pushy photographers. You should ask for permission with a smile or a joke, and if this is refused don't become offended. Some people are fed up at seeing their pictures in magazines or on postcards — they realize that someone must be making money at their expense. Others are still superstitious about bad luck being brought on them by cameras. Carrying a cheap polaroid is one way of gaining people's confidence — you can give them one photo whilst shooting more for yourself with your better camera. Sometimes a 'tip' is asked for. Taking photos from a discreet distance with a telephoto lens is another possibility. Be aware and sensitive of people's feelings; it is never worth upsetting someone for a good photograph.

HEALTH

BEFORE YOU GO   Though not required by law, normal precautions for tropical travel should be taken. Vaccinations against typhoid, tetanus, and poliomyelitis are strongly advised, as is a yellow fever immunisation if you are visiting the Oriente. A cholera inoculation is advised at this time because of the epidemic announced in Peru and Ecuador in 1991. This shot is only about 50% effective and your best defense is to avoid eating uncooked food or unboiled water until the epidemic is over. Cholera is not passed by casual contact, it is contracted by eating or drinking contaminated food or water. The disease can be easily treated, but can kill within 24 hours if not treated. The current epidemic may well be over by the time you read this book. Smallpox has been eradicated worldwide and inoculations are no longer required.

A full course of the necessary inoculations with boosters can take 6 weeks or more so be sure to see your doctor well before departure. Carry, and keep up to date, your international vaccination card.

Another inoculation to consider is gamma globulin which is fairly effective against hepatitis. The only real cure for this debilitating liver disease is a couple of months complete rest in bed. Hepatitis is caused by ingesting contaminated food or water; salads, uncooked or unpeeled fruit, unboiled drinks, and dirty syringes (even in hospitals) are the worst offenders. Infection risks are minimized by using bottled drinks, washing your own salads with purified water, and paying scrupulous attention to your toilet habits. Gamma globulin shots should be repeated every 6 months, although some authorities recommend more frequent shots. Constant research is being carried out to combat this disease and it is expected that more effective prophylaxis will be available within the next few years.

If you're planning a visit to a lowland area anti-malaria pills are recommended since the disease is on the increase in Latin America. If you stay above 2500 m you aren't at risk since malarial mosquitoes don't live this high. Pills must be taken from 2 weeks before you enter a malaria area until 6 weeks after you leave. Check the dose carefully as it varies with the brand. Until recently, Chloroquine (Aralen) was the drug of choice, but chloroquine-resistant strains of malaria are now present in Ecuador. The new drug Mefloquine (Lariam) is now preferred in the US. In the UK phone the Malaria Reference Laboratory (071-636 7921) for the latest tape recorded recommendations. You can also avoid getting bitten by always wearing long sleeved shirts and long trousers, using frequent applications of insect repellant, and sleeping under a mosquito net. If you buy insect repellant remember that the active ingredient is diethyl-metatoluamide (or DEET). Some repellents contain less than 10% of this and others over 90% so check the composition of the repellant before you buy. I find that the rub-on lotions are the most effective, and the pump sprays (use environmentally friendly ones) are useful for your clothes.

Finally, think about your physical condition. If you are planning a short, intensive trip and hope to climb several major peaks you should carry out regular pre-departure exercises such as swimming, running, cycling or whatever you prefer. If planning a longer trip then doing some of the Quito area day hikes will help get you into shape.

IN ECUADOR   The drastic change of diet you will experience during your stay means you'll probably be sick at least once. Stomach upsets are almost unavoidable but this is nothing to worry about. Diarrhoea is the most common ailment; drink plenty of fluids, rest, and fast, and the condition will normally clear up in about 24 hours. Many travellers find that eating yogurt (commercially available and pasteurized) helps the digestive system adapt more quickly to the new bacteria being introduced into the diet. Symptoms and remedies for other travellers' maladies are easily found elsewhere, so I am concentrating on the more specialized area of mountain health. If you get very sick, see a doctor. Many Ecuadorian doctors speak English, have been educated in the US, and are very good. Your embassy or hotel can recommend one.

A useful thing to know is that many prescriptive medicines are available in Ecuadorian pharmacies at a much lower cost than in the US or Europe and these are sold 'over the counter' without a prescription. This includes a variety of antibiotics, cold medicines, pain relievers, etc. Extreme caution is advised against trying to treat yourself without the benefit of a professional medical opinion; however, the availability of certain medications within the country will make it much easier to put together a decent first-aid kit and at a much lower price.

MOUNTAIN HEALTH

Hiking and climbing in the Ecuadorian countryside is more likely to keep you healthy than to make you ill. However conditions can be extreme and perhaps disastrous for the uninitiated. The major medical problems you may be faced with can be classed in four groups: those caused by cold, heat, altitude, and injury. This section is designed to help you recognize and deal with these problems.

HYPOTHERMIA   Often known as 'exposure', this insidious killer occurs when the body loses heat faster than it can produce it. Medically it exists when rectal temperature falls below 35°C or 95°F. Heat loss leading to hypothermia often occurs when the temperature is well above freezing, and is caused primarily by wet clothing and by the removal of body heat by the wind, especially from the head and neck which can lose up to 40% of body heat.

Prevention is better than cure. Put on rain gear as soon as it begins to rain and not after you're soaking wet. Wear several layers of clothing which can be removed to regulate your temperature; one very thick layer may cause you to get wet through perspiration. If you do get wet remember to wear a windproof layer; at least your wet clothes will stay a little warmer. Cotton clothes (e.g. jeans) lose 90% of their insulating properties when wet, whilst wool only loses 50%. Artificial fibrepile is also a good wet insulator and has the added advantage of drying much more quickly than wool. Remember to keep your head and neck warm. Exposed hands should be covered — use spare socks in an emergency.

If you take the above precautions you are unlikely to get hypothermia but lack of judgement or an accident can soon change a normal situation into a dangerous one. The hypothermia victim will begin feeling tired and start shivering uncontrollably. At this stage one can still stop hypothermia by getting out of the wind and rain and wearing more dry clothes (camping, getting into a dry sleeping bag, and eating some warm food). If this is not done, the person affected will begin to lose co-ordination, have difficulty in speaking, and show a lack of judgement. By this stage the victims are in serious trouble as they can't get themselves warm and must be rewarmed by their friends. Climbing into a cold sleeping bag is inadequate as the victim won't have enough body heat to warm the bag. The bag must be warmed. The best way is for someone to share the victim's sleeping bag after first removing wet clothing. If you're alone then try to make a hot water bottle with your canteen and drink small quantities of warm liquids. The final stage of hypothermia is a lapse into irrationality and incoherence, with hallucinations and disorientation, and a slow irregular pulse. The skin becomes blue and cold, and drowsiness and dilation of the pupils follow. Then come unconsciousness and death. The whole process can take *as little as two hours*. The combination of cold, wet, and windy weather is common in the Ecuadorian highlands, so be prepared; even on a day hike carry hat, gloves, wind and rain jacket, and a spare warm sweater.

FROSTBITE   This occurs when any part of the body becomes frozen. Backpackers are less likely to experience it but snow and ice climbers are possible candidates. The usual ways of getting frostbite are by exposing or wetting skin or by cutting off blood circulation to the extremities. These problems can be avoided by always wearing gloves and balaclava helmet in extremely cold conditions. The nose and cheeks are more difficult to protect. A scarf or handkerchief wrapped bandit style around the face will help, as will rewarming your nose with your hand at frequent intervals. (Rubbing snow onto the area, the traditional 'cure', is actually dangerous.) Ensure good blood circulation in your feet by not lacing boots and crampon straps too tightly. Keep your socks dry and unwrinkled. Bear in mind that exposed flesh will freeze more rapidly in windy conditions (the 'wind chill factor').

Some people are more susceptible to frostbite than others. Frostbite is liable to recur in those areas of the body which have been previously frozen. Smokers are more susceptible as are people weakened by hypothermia, exhaustion, drugs, injury, or blood loss.

The first symptom is pain. Warm and protect the area with extra clothing or by putting in a warm place (e.g. warm your face with your hands or put your hands in your groin). Restore circulation to your feet by stamping them and loosening your laces. The pain may often increase in intensity during the first minutes of rewarming but this will soon disappear. If the pain disappears without rewarming and numbness takes its place, then the problem is getting serious. The area becomes whitish and hard. Even at this late stage a small frostbitten area can be rewarmed without damage. If your feet are involved then they could be rewarmed on a friend's belly or armpit.

If a whole finger or toe (or larger area) becomes deeply frostbitten then the situation is grave. This is because rewarming the part will cause it to become extremely delicate and sensitive so it cannot be used at all for several weeks. For this reason a badly frostbitten climber should be taken to hospital to be rewarmed. Once a part has been frostbitten it can remain that way for several days without much more damage and so climbers with severe frostbite should be evacuated under their own steam as soon as possible. This is entirely feasible in Ecuador as most climbing areas are within a couple of days of Quito. Once in hospital, a badly frostbitten area must be gently thawed in water just above blood temperature or damage will result.

HEAT EXHAUSTION   A calm, sunny day in the high Andes can be extremely hot and heat problems are not uncommon, although they are more of a danger on lowland hikes. Lack of liquids aggravates this condition so drink as much as possible before setting off on a hike or climb. If you are unusually tired, thirsty, giddy, suffer from cramps, and are not urinating much, you're probably suffering from heat exhaustion. Rest in the shade and drink as much as you can. Salt pills help (but only with plenty of liquid). Refrain from activity till you recover.

If symptoms of heat exhaustion are ignored, more serious problems such as heat syncope and heat stroke could develop. Therefore these warnings must be taken seriously. Ensure a high fluid intake and wear a wide brimmed sun hat and loose light clothes.

SUNBURN   This is a major problem for climbers on snow or ice because they are unaware of the power of the equatorial sun at 6000 m. The sun will reflect from the glacier and burn in all sorts of surprising places such as behind the ears, under the chin, and in the nostrils. These areas are very sensitive and must be carefully covered with glacier cream or sun block. Lip salve is needed to prevent cracked and bleeding lips. Ordinary sun-tan lotion is helpful but normally doesn't offer enough protection for climbers on a glacier. A sun protection factor of at least 15 should be used. When making a pre-dawn departure remember to stop when the sun rises and put cream on. Reapply frequently. Good glacier cream is readily available in Ecuador, as is the heavier zinc oxide. Don't be fooled by a cloud layer; the ultraviolet rays of the sun will burn you anyway. Wear a wide brimmed hat when possible. Backpackers should also be aware of sunburn and use plenty of sun-tan lotion, especially at the beginning of a trip.

SNOW BLINDNESS   The only cure for this is to have your eyes completely covered for a few days — obviously inconvenient at the top of a mountain! Snow and ice climbers must use the darkest goggles available as ordinary sunglasses are inadequate.

HIGH ALTITUDE SICKNESS   Until the 1960s this unpleasant and often dangerous reaction to high altitude was medically unknown and climbers suffering (and dying) from it were said to be suffering from pneumonia. Recent studies have shown this not to be the case and today high altitude sickness is recognized as a major mountaineering problem and studies are continuing to increase our knowledge of this condition.

It is known that high altitude sickness can be divided into three categories: Acute Mountain Sickness (AMS), Pulmonary Oedema, and Cerebral Oedema. All three are caused not just by the lack of oxygen at high altitude, but by a too rapid ascent to these heights. The best prevention is acclimatization which means not climbing too high too fast. It is unusual for anyone to be seriously affected at elevations around 2850 m (Quito's), so using Quito as a base for acclimatization is recommended. Spending about a week at this altitude is normally adequate acclimatization for climbing high.

Research has shown that an ascent rate of about 300-500m per day is normally slow enough to prevent problems, but it is impractical to spend over a week climbing Chimborazo which at 6310 m is almost 3500 m above Quito. Once acclimatized in Quito, it is quite common for one day ascents to be made with little danger. Remember that high altitude sickness usually takes from 6 to 36 hours to reveal itself and so a quick ascent and descent can normally be made with few ill effects. The old maxim "Climb high and sleep low" is a good one.

Despite these reassurances, one should bear in mind that cases of high altitude sickness can occur even if precautions are taken. Every mountaineer should be able to recognize these symptoms and know how they must be dealt with.

Acute Mountain Sickness *(soroche)* is the most common of the three variations. The symptoms are severe headache, shortness of breath, nausea, vomiting, fatigue, insomnia, loss of appetite, and a rapid pulse. Irregular (Cheyne-Stokes) breathing during sleep affects some people but is relatively harmless, although disturbing to both the sleeper and his companions. The best treatment is rest and deep breathing. Analgesics may alleviate the headache (some doctors recommend non-aspirin based ones) and an adequate fluid intake must be maintained. If a victim doesn't improve then a descent is called for. A climber should never force him or herself to ascend when symptoms of AMS are present as the conditions will probably worsen.

Acetazolamide or Diamox (a mild diuretic) taken for several days before the ascent may help prevent an attack of AMS. Climbers who are short on time to acclimatize should talk with their doctor about the drug. Despite encouraging reports from several recent expeditions, it should be stressed that this drug is still not completely accepted in medical circles. Apart from the annoyance of frequent urination, other possible adverse reactions include increased cold sensitivity, numbness, and tingling in the extremities.

Pulmonary Oedema kills climbers in South America each year. It is a more extreme form of AMS and in addition to the symptoms mentioned the victim suffers from increased shortness of breath when at rest and a dry, rattling cough. As the condition worsens, frothy bloodstained sputum is produced and the victim turns blue. Fluid collects in the lungs, literally drowning the person if the condition is not recognized. Victims must immediately be assisted to a lower altitude (at least 600 m lower) and taken to hospital if necessary.

Cerebral Oedema is less common but equally dangerous. Here the fluid accumulates in the brain instead of the lungs and may cause permanent brain damage or death. Symptoms include an agonizing headache, giddiness, confusion, and hallucinations. Anyone showing these signs must immediately be assisted to lower altitude. Poor judgement is also one of the symptoms so strong persuasion may have to be used to evacuate the victim.

Finally, remember that not everyone is prone to AMS and that youth and fitness make no difference. It is important for the less affected members of a climbing party to keep their eyes on climbers who may be trying to push themselves beyond sensible limits. Climbers are often so determined to reach a summit that they can jeopardize the whole expedition by trying to cover up an attack of AMS. Being affected by high altitude sickness is not a sign of inherent weakness. It often takes more courage to stop, rest, and acclimatize further than it does to keep pushing dangerously close to an attack of pulmonary oedema.

ACCIDENTS   These can vary from a simple twisted ankle on a hiking trail to multiple injuries caused by a major climbing fall. The most important advice here is never to hike or climb alone.

If a person is injured on a trail or route which is frequently travelled then it is best to wait for help or rescue. The partner should stay with the victim and ensure that the injured party is as warm, comfortable, and reassured as possible. If you are climbing an unusual route or hiking cross-country then waiting for help may be pointless. If you go for help make sure that you will be able to find the victim again — leave wands or markers and arrange a whistle or flashlight signal if the victim is conscious. Don't leave injured climbers alone unless it is totally unavoidable.

All climbers should carry a booklet on the principles of first aid, particularly with reference to mountaineering injuries. The value of a course in first aid cannot be over-emphasized.

WATER PURIFICATION   Since many diseases are caught by drinking contaminated water, it is very important to sterilize your drinking supply. The simplest effective method is boiling for 20 minutes but this is both time consuming and uses a great deal of the precious fuel you've carried. Various water purifying tablets are available but they aren't wholly effective against everything: hepatitis, for instance. An effective method is using a saturated iodine solution. Take a small (1 oz) glass bottle and put about 2-3 mm of iodine crystals in it (both iodine crystals and suitable bottles can be obtained from pharmacies, or from the South American Explorers Club in Quito.) Fill the bottle with water and give it a good shake for about a minute, then let the crystals settle to the bottom. The resulting saturated solution is added to a litre of water and left for 15 minutes to produce clean drinking water. The advantage of this method is that the crystals can be used and reused hundreds of times; very little of the crystals actually dissolves and you pour only the iodine liquid into the water and leave the crystals in the 1 oz bottle for reuse. This is more effective than water purifying tablets and doesn't taste as bad. The only danger is for people who have been treated for thyroid problems and for pregnant women (whose ingestion of iodine may cause thyroid problems in their babies). Otherwise this is a safe and recommended method.

MEDICAL KIT   Assuming there is no doctor in your party, the following basic first aid kit is suggested:

Antiseptic cream, aspirin and more powerful analgesics, Lomotil for diarrhoea, ampicillin and tetracycline antibiotics, throat lozenges, ear and eye drops, antacid tablets, travel sickness pills, alcohol swabs, water purifier, vaseline (useful for cracked or chapped skin), lip salve, foot powder.

Thermometer in a case, surgical tape, assorted sticky-plasters (band-aids), moleskin (for blisters), gauze, bandages, butterfly closures, scissors, first-aid booklet.

Sleeping pills are useful at high altitudes where inability to sleep at night is often a problem. Drugs such as Valium should be used with caution, however. Koerner reports a case of a climber sleepwalking into a crevasse after taking Valium.

Remember that some people are allergic to even simple drugs like penicillin.

CHAPTER 3

In Ecuador

*I never travel without my diary. One should always have something sensational
to read on the train.*
— *Oscar Wilde*

ARRIVAL

Most visitors will fly into Quito International Airport. This is about 7 km
from the new city or 10 km from the old section. Taxis into town are cheap
and will charge about US$2. Within the city, taxis are required by law to use
meters, but from the airport fares will have to be negotiated. Those taxis
waiting directly in front of the international area will be harder to bargain
with than the others posted near the national section of the airport. If you
don't have too much to carry, walk left from the international exit about 25
meters and look for a taxi there. It is normal to agree on the price
beforehand. Drivers will accept cash US dollars but the airport bank is
usually open for incoming international flights. If you're really broke, take
a bus southbound (to your left) from outside the airport to town.

ACCOMMODATION

The best first class hotel in town is the **Colón** at Avenida Amazonas and
Patria. A good middle range hotel is the **Residencial Carrión**, Carrión 1250
and Versalles. There are many more listed in *The South American
Handbook, Ecuador & the Galapagos Islands — a travel survival kit*, or other
guide books. Hotels and hostels tend to come in all price ranges. Family run
hotels known as *pensiónes* or *residenciales* are usually good and economical.

One hotel that has become a legend in Quito is the **Grand Casino** (sometimes known as the 'Gran Gringo') at García Moreno 330 and Ambato in the old town. Simple rooms go for just over a dollar (US) per person per night. For years it has been an excellent meeting place for travellers and a source for the latest information on just about everything. There's a message board where people advertise all sorts of gear, look for travel companions, or try to get in touch with someone. Unfortunately, it has gone downhill in the last few years and that area of town has become slightly risky, especially at night. Many travellers opt to pay a little more (about US$2.50 per night) and stay around the corner at the better-kept **Grand Casino International.**

Other inexpensive options in the old town include the **Grand Hotel** at Rocafuerte 1001 and Móntufar and the **Hotel Viena** at Flores and Chile. In between the old and new sections of Quito is the **Residencial Marsella** at Los Ríos and Castro just above Parque Alameda.

If you like the idea of staying in a house with kitchen privileges and washing facilities, a couple of good choices in the new town are **La Casona** at Andalucía and Galavis, and **Casa Feliz Eliza** on Isabel la Católica and Salazar, charging US$4.50 and US$4 respectively. Both are run by friendly folk and have luggage storage available.

Accommodation is cheap all over Ecuador. You can always find a basic hotel for US$1 to US$2 per night, and if you want something a little more luxurious than four walls and a bed you'll find plenty of reasonably priced accommodation in all the major cities.

TRANSPORTATION

Quito has a slow, crowded, but cheap bus service which covers the city thoroughly. If you're in a hurry there are many yellow taxis which are required to use meters. Know the base rate and be sure your taxi driver starts the meter at this figure. At night and for trips outside the city, fares will have to be negotiated. In most other cities, meters are not used so fares must be agreed upon in advance.

A train service runs daily from Quito to Riobamba. In order to continue to Guayaquil on the coast by train, you must catch a bus to Alausí (2 hours), and take the Aluasí-Durán train the following morning. There is also a daily train from Ibarra in the north to San Lorenzo on the Pacific. See Chapter 8 for more details.

The best way to travel in Ecuador is undoubtedly by bus. Quito's central bus terminal, the Cumandá Terminal Terrestre, is located in the old city on Av. Cumandá and scores of buses leave here every day. Buses heading south on the Pan American through 'The Avenue of the Volcanoes' past Latacunga, Ambato, and Riobamba are very frequent. If you can't get a direct bus to a less well known destination, take one to the nearest big town and change; the construction of central bus stations in all major Ecuadorian cities means that if you have to change buses you don't have to go looking for out of the way bus stops — all departures are from the same place.

Using the bus system is easy but here are some suggestions to make your journey more enjoyable. If you go to the offices in the Terminal Terrestre the day before your departure you can nearly always buy a seat in advance; this also means you can choose your seat number, and obviously the front means better views, more leg room, and a more exciting trip. With luck, you can get these front seats as late as an hour before departure; if travelling during long holiday weekends, however, everything may be sold out several days in advance, so book early.

Both small microbuses (holding twenty-two passengers) and large coaches are used. The small buses tend to be faster and more efficient.

The drivers and their assistants usually run around yelling out their destinations and looking for passengers. Often you will be on a bus going your way within a few minutes of arriving at the terminal.

There is also a separate, interprovincial bus area for departures to the small towns around Quito. This is located in the area of Plaza La Marin, and is not really a terminal but is a central location from where buses leave. It is located around the end of Av. Pichincha in the old town only a few blocks from the main bus terminal, Cumandá. Plaza La Marin is also the end of the line for scores of city buses. Look for any bus that has a La Marin sign displayed in the window or as part of its route name. A few other nearby bus destinations, especially for Machachi, leave from Villa Flora, a neighbourhood south of Quito. To get there you can catch any city bus marked 'Villa Flora' along Av. 12 de Octubre south of Patria, or along Av. Colombia above and west of Parque Alameda. It's called the Villa Flora bus terminal, though it is just a street where buses line up and depart for Machachi every 15 minutes.

Air transportation is growing in Ecuador and the main cities of Cuenca and Guayaquil have several inexpensive flights a day from Quito. Lesser cities often have daily flights. The major internal flight companies are TAME and SAN.

Hitch-hiking is also possible and may be the only transportation in more remote areas. Often you will be expected to pay the driver — arrange this beforehand. Free rides are more common on the major roads.

SECURITY

Rip-offs are a fact of life in Latin America, but Ecuador is safe in comparison with the worst offenders, Colombia and Peru. Nevertheless, certain precautions taken before and during the trip will make your stay a happier one.

Thieves look for easy targets. Tourists who carry a wallet or a passport in a hip pocket are asking for trouble. Leave your wallet at home; it's an easy mark for a pickpocket. Carrying a roll of paper money loosely wadded under a handkerchief in your front pocket is as safe a way as any of carrying your daily spending money. The rest should be hidden. Always use an inside pocket or (preferably) a body pouch to protect your valuables. A money belt is good; so is a neck pouch under your shirt or a leg pouch as available from the South American Explorers Club in Quito.

Bag snatching is another problem. Motorcyclists sometimes zoom past unsuspecting pedestrians and grab a shoulder bag or camera. If you put luggage down it can be stolen in seconds whilst your attention is diverted.

Crowded places are the haunts of thieves and pickpockets. A bustling market or an ill-lit bus station are prime venues for robbery so be particularly alert. Razor blades are sometimes used to slash baggage (including a pack on your back) for a grab and run raid. Don't wear expensive watches or jewellery as this also invites snatch theft.

Armed robbery is still rare in Ecuador. The area with the worst reputation is the coast, with Guayaquil being the most dangerous, particularly the south end of town near the waterfront. Assaults along the Atacames beach in Esmeraldas have also been reported.

I've heard recent travellers' reports of an extremely insidious form of robbery. Gringos are offered biscuits or chocolates on a bus by seemingly friendly passengers and they wake up several hours later in an alley with just a tee shirt and a pair of trousers. One person I talked to had been unconscious for two days. Unopened packages are injected with horse tranquillisers using hypodermic syringes. So... don't take sweets from strangers.

When travelling by public transport watch your luggage being loaded to ensure that it's not left behind, and try to keep your eye on it during stops. Don't leave valuables in vulnerable places like the easily opened outside pockets of your pack.

Beware of theft from your hotel room. Many hotels have signs that they are not responsible for theft unless valuables are placed in deposit at reception. If using cheaper hotels, you'll find you can often lock the door with your own padlock. A combination lock is more secure than a normal padlock. Some travellers carry a short length of chain for securing baggage in storage areas or on luggage racks. Camera or bag straps can be reinforced with thin chain or guitar strings to prevent slashing.

Before you leave home make a photocopy of your passport to show embassy officials should yours be stolen. Take out travellers' insurance.

When you're climbing or hiking you'll want to leave your excess luggage in a safe place. Your hotel is usually OK, but beware of other gringos claiming your luggage. Not all travellers are honest! Many hotels will give you a numbered receipt — this way no one else can claim your bag. A small charge sometimes accompanies this service.

In some of the mountain *refugios* you'll be able to lock up your gear in one of the storage compartments provided, or in a spare room. Bring a small padlock for this purpose. When camping, it's best never to leave gear unattended. Some climber friends had everything but their tent stolen from the Italian base camp on El Altar whilst they were scouting Obispo. Always leave someone to guard the camp. If your entire group wants to climb, I suggest you hire a local *mulero* or muleman to look after your gear.

TOURIST INFORMATION AND MAIL

The main tourist office in Quito is at Av. Reina Victoria 514 (the intersection with Roca), and a small kiosk is open daily on Amazonas at the corner of Carrion. They are helpful for standard queries (museums, buses, restaurants, etc.).

The Post Office is on Benalcázar at Chile. They will hold mail for you addressed Lista de Correos, Correos Central, Quito, Ecuador. In the new part of the city, you may receive mail at the main post office located on Av. Eloy Alfaro between 10 de Agosto and 9 de Octubre. Have mail addressed Lista de Correos, Correos Eloy Alfaro, Quito, Ecuador. The American Express office will also accept mail for their clients and for holders of their travellers cheques. Their postal address is Aptdo. 2605, Quito, Ecuador and their street address is Amazonas 339. Members of the South American Explorers Club may have their correspondence sent to the clubhouse, Apartado 21-431, Quito.

The best single general guide book to the country is *Ecuador & the Galápagos Islands — a travel survival kit*, published by Lonely Plant Publications, 3rd edition expected in 1992.

THE SOUTH AMERICAN EXPLORERS CLUB

Founded in 1977 by Don Montague and Linda Rojas in Lima, Peru, this club has now opened a branch in Quito to the joy of many travellers who have made use of its services over the years. It primarily functions as an information network for travellers, adventurers, scientific expeditions, etc. and provides a wealth of advice about travelling anywhere in Latin America, with an emphasis on Ecuador and Peru.

The club is an entirely member-supported, non-profit organization. Annual membership costs US$25 per person (US$35 for a couple), and includes a subscription to their excellent quarterly journal, *The South American Explorer*. In addition, members have full use of the clubhouses and their facilities (in both Quito and Lima) which include an information service and library, paperback book exchange, equipment storage, discounts on books and maps, mail service, equipment sales, and many other benefits. It's a relaxing place to have a cup of tea and chat with other members. Non-members are welcome to come by for a one-time visit, but must come up with the US$25 membership fee to take advantage of the numerous benefits. If you're in Quito, you can stop by the club, Toledo 1254 and Cordero in the La Floresta section, and sign up. Otherwise, you can send your US$25 and any questions you may have direct to the club at Apartado 21-431, Quito, Ecuador. The club is open 9.30 a.m. to 5.00 p.m., Monday through Friday. Tel: 566076.

You can also contact the Lima clubhouse, postal address: Casilla 3714, Lima 100, Peru; street address, Av. Rep. de Portugal 146 (Breña), tel: 31-4480; or get in touch with the US office for a free catalog: P.O. Box 18327, Denver CO 80218; tel: (303)320-0388. Bradt Publications can organise membership in Britain.

MAPS

All maps, ranging from Quito city plans to wall charts of Ecuador, are published by and available from the IGM (Instituto Geográfico Militar). Their offices and map sales department are on top of a hill on Av. T. Paz y Miño, off Av. Colombia, behind the Casa de Cultura.

There are very few buses up this hill but it's not a very hard walk. A taxi will take you. A permit to enter the building is available in exchange for your passport at the main gate; it is open from 8.00 a.m. to 4.00 p.m. (without closing midday), Monday to Friday.

There is a single 1:1,000,000 chart of Ecuador or four sheets making a 1: 500,000 map. Most of the highlands and some of the coast are covered by 1:50,000 topographical maps and some 1:100,000 sheets of the mountains are also available. There are 1:50,000 planometric sheets of some otherwise mapless areas. The Oriente is largely unmapped. All extant maps are displayed in large folders so they can be examined before buying. Topographical sheets are available immediately but you have to wait a day for the planometric ones. A few maps of 'sensitive' areas are sold only with a permit; this is usually obtainable from an IGM officer in the same building. The 1:50,000 topographical maps are those useful for hikers and climbers. A few areas have been mapped to higher scales: 1:25,000 or even 1:10,000.

The maps supplied with this book are made to complement rather than replace the IGM sheets, so details of the sheets needed for each hike or climb are given in the text. Many of these maps are available from Bradt Publications.

RENTING AND BUYING EQUIPMENT

There are many sports stores in Quito that have a variety of gear for hire and for sale. Most of the new equipment for sale is locally made, reasonably priced, but of lower quality than in the US or Europe. Rental items are a mixture of Ecuadorian-made products and imported equipment, most of which is sold to the shops by travellers who are either broke or tired of lugging the stuff around. The quality of rented gear is extremely variable. A friend of mine rented some locally made crampons but the front points bent downwards at his first attempt to climb a small ice wall. Ecuadorian ice axes are somewhat primitive but boots and sleeping bags are OK. For simple climbs you could get by with this rental gear but your own is obviously better.

Most of the sports stores are open Monday through Saturday, from 9.00 a.m. to 1.00 p.m. and from 3.00 p.m. until 6.00 p.m. Renting equipment is relatively inexpensive but a sizable deposit is required (travellers cheques, or sometimes the return portion of your international flight coupon, will do). These outfits are also good sources for information on clubs and meetings, etc.The following is a selection of those shops which have proven to be the most reliable.

Sierra Nevada, Av. 6 de Diciembre 1329 and Roca, tel: 553658, is owned and operated by Freddy Ramirez, an experienced climber who guides trips to the mountains and arranges excursions into the jungle.

Campo Abierto, Av. 6 de Diciembre and Roca, is run by climber Iván Rojas, and along with renting equipment, has a selection of magazines for sale, including their own interesting publication, *Campo Abierto*.

Altamontaña Expediciones, Av. Universitaria 464 and Armero, tel: 520592, offers a guiding service along with equipment rental. They have a good selection of larger-sized boots.

Equipos Cotopaxi, on 6 de Diciembre 929 and Patria, tel: 526725, has a wide variety of gear for sale, mostly Ecuadorian products, and buys and rents used hiking/climbing gear.

Adventure, Juan Leon Mera 404, tel: 322331, buys, sells and rents equipment. Owner Hugo Torres is a long-time climber and guide.

Agama Expediciones, Venezuela 1163 and Manabí, is run by Eduardo Agama, rents and sells equipment and arranges trips into the mountains.

Outside Quito, equipment rental is hard to come by. Gerhard Schutz operates a shop in Ambato at Av. Los Shyris and Luis Cordero, tel: 827349/821353. In addition to renting gear, he also provides accommodation, guides mountain trips, and has begun to manufacture good quality, custom-made backpacks and other specialized equipment.

The sports store at Flores 220 at the corner of Plaza Santo Domingo sells fishing, snorkelling, and camping gear and is useful for visitors to the Galápagos and Oriente.

Don't forget the notice board at the Gran Casino Hotel for buying and selling equipment. The South American Explorers Club handles used equipment on consignment. Stop by, or give them a call at tel: 566076 to see if they have what you're looking for.

CLIMBING CLUBS

The International Andean Mountaineers Club, which for many years assisted gringo climbers was operating in recent years under the name of the International Hiking and Climbing Group. At this time, the club is dormant, but seems to come back to life from time to time. To find out if it's once again functional, you can contact the British Embassy or the American school, Academia Cotopaxi, both of which have a high participation in the club when it is active. The other clubs are all Ecuadorian and don't often organize trips for the general public. There is a certain amount of rivalry and cliquism in these Quito clubs. They are useful as centres of information but don't expect to arrive and be taken climbing the following weekend. Nuevos Horizontes meets on Tuesday and Friday evenings in an upstairs room at Venezuela 659. Sadday has evening meetings on most weekdays at Manabí 621. Most of the major colleges and universities have a mountain club. The best known of these is the Colegio San Gabriel group which meets at the school on Wednesdays at Av. America and Mariana de Jésus, also irregularly publishes *Montaña* magazine. The club at the Universidad La Católica sometimes has climbing films and lectures open to the general public. General meetings are held at 7.30 p.m. every Tuesday at the university. One of the greatest contributors to Ecuadorian climbing over the years is the Polytécnica Climbing Club. The group meets regularly on Wednesdays at 7.00 p.m. on the 6th floor of the Ingeneria Cívil de la Polytécnica Nacional, across the street from the Universidad La Catolica on Av. Isabel de la Católica.

In addition, one of the main climbing organizations in Quito is the Asociacíon de Excursionismo y Andinismo de Pichincha, comprised of amateur climbers who meet irregularly at the Complejo Deportiva de la Vicentina, Calle La Condamine and Manuel Cajías in the Vicentina section of Quito.

There is also the Asociación de Andinismo de Chimborazo at Chile 3321 and Francia, in Riobamba.

GUIDES

This book aims to get you to the top of most mountains without a guide. Many inexperienced climbers, however, will feel more confident with one to start with.

Climbing in Ecuador can be deceptive, especially to the novice mountaineer. A climb of only 8 to 10 hours to a summit nearing 6000 meters may sound like a piece of cake requiring little commitment. This, however, is not necessarily true. The affects of high altitude combined with abruptly changing weather patterns and variable snow/ice conditions can put heavy demands on the most experienced of climbers. In 1990 alone, six people perished on Chimborazo, a technically easy climb. For these reasons, guided climbs on the major peaks may be the best alternative for some.

Choosing a guide is as important as deciding whether or not you need one. 'A little knowledge is a dangerous thing' applies unequivocally to some locals who consider themselves capable climbers on any peak after one or two ascents of minor summits. I ran into one fellow at the Cotopaxi refuge who had been hired as a guide by couple of Americans. In a casual way, he chatted to me about the route up, wanting to know where it went exactly, and what time was I leaving, perhaps he and his 'friends' could tag along? It turned out that he had gone up Tungurahua a few times and decided he could climb anything, not to mention actually guide other people! Fortunately, the weather turned sour, and no one got out of the hut that night. The thing to realize is you get what you pay for. Some so-called guides charge as little as US$30 per person to climb one of the major peaks, while the going rate for an experienced, professional guide is somewhere between 3 to 4 times that amount, depending on group size.

The best way to locate a reliable guide is to contact the climbing/rental shops in Quito. Many of these, as described in the previous section, are owned and operated by experienced climbing guides. You can get recommendations from other travellers or contact the South American Explorers Club which keeps updated information about local guides and guiding services.

One of the best known and most experienced professional guides in Ecuador is Marco Cruz who can be contacted in advance c/o Metropolitan Touring, Amazonas 239, Quito, Ecuador. He is expensive and often booked

up well in advance. Other consistently recommended guides are Freddy
Ramirez at Sierra Nevada and Hugo Torres at Adventure.

NATURAL HISTORY

The great variety of habitats in a country which rises from ocean to snow
peaks and drops back to tropical rainforest ensures an abundance of wildlife.
The best known wildlife reserve is the Galápagos Islands; the plants and
animals found there are fully described in several good guide books. The
mainland, on the other hand, is a relatively unstudied naturalist's paradise.
Since there are no comprehensive field guides to the flora and fauna,
Ecuador offers wonderful opportunities for study for a field researcher but
many frustrations for the ordinary traveller who has difficulty in identifying
this bewildering wildlife.

Although Ecuador lies in the heart of the tropics you wouldn't call the
natural history of the highlands tropical. Indeed, the vegetation here has
been compared to that of the arctic tundra. This is because altitude as well
as latitude has an important influence on the flora and fauna of an area.
Pioneer work on this concept was done in Ecuador in 1802 by the German
scientist Alexander von Humboldt. He related ecology to altitude and
recognized three major ecological zones: lowland (hot), central (temperate),
and highland (cold). This last is said to begin at about 3200 m and continue
to the glaciated mountain tops. It can be sub-divided into the snow region
above about 4700 m, where insects and birds are occasionally seen, and the
area below the permanent snow line which is known as the *páramo*.

The *páramo* is a highly specialized zone unique to tropical America, and
found only from the highlands of Costa Rica at 10°N down to northern Peru
at 10°S. Similarly elevated areas in other parts of the world differ in their
climates and evolutionary history. Most of the hikes and climbs in this book
will pass through the *páramo* and so this section concentrates on highland
ecology rather than giving space to the overwhelmingly diverse flora and
fauna of low lying areas which deserve a book to themselves. (See
Bibliography for suggested further reading on the subject.)

Páramo weather is typically cold and wet, with frequent rain often
replaced by moist mists and clouds. Snow falls occasionally and strong winds
are common. Night time temperatures are below freezing and glaring
sunlight can be a hazard during short spells of fine weather. In short,
conditions are harsh, and comparatively few animals are seen. Plants, on the
other hand, have adapted well to this difficult environment and as a result
the vegetation looks strange and interesting.

The Andean flora has evolved over approximately 60 million years of
uplift of the range. Thus the vegetation has had adequate time slowly to

modify itself. The major adaptations have been the formation of smaller and thicker leaves which are less susceptible to frost; the development of curved leaves with thick waxy skins to reflect or absorb extreme solar radiation during cloudless days; the growth of a fine hairy 'down' as insulation on the plant's surface; the arrangement of leaves into a rosette pattern to prevent them shading one another during photosynthesis and to protect the delicate centre; and the progressive compacting of the plants until they grow close to the ground where the temperature is more constant and there is protection from the wind. Thus many *páramo* plants are characteristically small and compact, some resembling a hard, waxy, green carpet. There are exceptions to this however, including the giant *frailejones* and the *puyas*.

Giant *espeletia*, locally known as *frailejones*, are a weird sight as they float into view in a typical *páramo* mist. They are high enough to resemble human beings, hence the name *frailejones* which means greyfriars. Despite their size they retain certain features of other *páramo* vegetation, such as downy hairs for insulation. *Espeletia* belong to the daisy family, and are an unmistakable feature of the northern *páramo* of Ecuador, particularly in the region of El Angel.

Further south the *páramo* is rather drier and here we often find the *puyas*, members of the bromeliad family which replace the *frailejones* of the wetter north. The *puyas* are some of the least understood of the *páramo* plants, having very few of the normal characteristics of the plants found here. They are very large (reaching a height of over eight metres in Peru) and have no typical downy insulation. Their leaves, though still in a rosette pattern, are not small and compact but long and spiky and grow on top of a short trunk instead of at ground level.

Another attractive plant of the dry southern *páramo* is the *chuquiragua*. In some ways it resembles a tall thistle topped with orange flower heads and with stems densely covered with tough spiky leaves. This plant has medicinal properties and is used locally to soothe coughs, and for liver and kidney problems.

Apart from the flowering plants there is a great variety of other vegetation found in this zone. Everywhere you go you will encounter a spiky, resistant tussock grass (ichu) which grows in clumps and makes walking rather uncomfortable. In the lower *páramo* (below 4000 m) dense thickets of small trees may be seen. These are often of the rose family and a particularly common tree is the *quinua (Polylepsis sp.)*, locally known as *el colorado* (the red one) because its bark is a dull reddish colour. If you push your way into one of these thickets, which are common in the *páramos* of Las Cajas in the south of Ecuador, you will observe a variety of lichens, mosses, epiphytes, and fungi.

Animals have not adapted themselves quite as well as plants to this harsh environment and are never plentiful. You are most likely to see birds, toads,

During Whymper's visit he observed a condor hunt. A horse carcass was used to entice the birds to the ground.

and rabbits.

The most exciting bird species is the Andean condor (*Vultur gryphus*). This is the largest flying bird in the world. With its three metre wing span and effortless flight it is indeed magnificent — particularly from a distance. Close up, its vicious hooked beak and its uncompromisingly hard eye set in a revoltingly bare and wrinkled pink head identify it as a carrion eater. Often it soars hundreds of metres in the air and its huge size is difficult to appreciate unless there is another bird close by for comparison. It is best identified by its flat, gliding flight with 'fingered' wing tips (formed by spread primary feathers), silvery patches on the upper surface of its wings and a white neck ruff. The rest of the body is black. Condors are becoming much rarer now than in the days of Whymper, who wrote after his visit in 1880 "... we commonly saw a dozen on the wing at the same time." Good condor spotting areas include El Altar and Cotopaxi National Park. I even saw a pair flying over Cerro Pasochoa, just 20 km south of the capital.

Smaller birds of prey are also seen in the *páramo*. The black-chested buzzard-eagle (*Geranoaetus melanoleucus*) is quite common especially in the Papallacta area. At 58 cm in length it is one of the largest of the Ecuadorian hawks (though small compared to the 108 cm of the condor). It is identified by a very short, dark, wedge-shaped tail, a white belly finely barred with black, and blackish sides of head and breast. The throat is almost white. The most common hawk is the variable (or puna) hawk (*Buteo poecilochrous*) which is limited to the open *páramo*. 52 cm in length, its most distinctive feature is a white tail with a black band near the end. As its name suggests its plumage varies; it is usually light bellied and brown backed. The fairly small (44 cm) cinereous harrier (*Circus cinereus*) is sometimes seen. It is mostly grey with a white rump and belly barred with brown. Finally, the distinctive carunculated caracara (*Phalcoboenus carunculatus*) with its bright orange-red facial skin and legs, white belly and black above is also sighted here.

One of the most common *páramo* birds is the Andean lapwing (*Vanellus resplendens*). It is unmistakable with its harsh noisy call and its brown/white/black striped wing pattern, particularly noticeable in flight. Of the ducks, the speckled teal (*Anas flavirostris*) with its blue grey bill and brown head is the most common. Lago Limpiopungo in Cotopaxi National Park is a good place for both these species, as well as the yellow-billed pintail (*Anas georgica*), the Andean gull (*Larus serranus*) and the American coot (*Fulica americana*).

If you wake up in your tent during the dark early hours of the morning to hear a weird whizzing sound like a lost UFO, don't be too alarmed. It's probably a cordillera snipe, also known as the Andean snipe (*Chubbia jamesoni*). They often fly at night and produce this strange drumming noise with their outer wing feathers. Another night flier in the *páramo* is the owl.

You may catch sight of the great horned owl *(Bubo virgianus)* or even the well known barn owl *(Tyto alba)*. More frequently seen is the short-eared owl *(Asio flammeus)*, because it hunts during the day.

Of the small birds found in the *páramo,* the most easily identifiable are the hummingbirds, at least 126 species of which have been listed as occurring in Ecuador alone. The Andean hillstar *(Oreotrochilus estella)* is one of the most common found at high altitudes. I've often been amazed to see one come humming past my tent at a snow line camp at 4700 m. This tiny bundle of life survives the intense night-time cold by lowering its metabolism by as much as 95% and entering an almost lifeless state, similar to hibernation. Its body temperature drops dramatically; one researcher measured a decrease from 39.5°C to 14.4°C overnight. The bird passes the night in a protected crevice or overhang and regains its day-time temperature in the morning sun with no ill effects. Hummingbirds are the smallest birds in the world and the most manoeuvrable. The Andean hillstar, at 13 cm. in length, is comparatively big; the short-tailed woodstar *(Myrmia micrura)* which is common on the coast is a mere 7 cm in length and this includes the needle like bill. Hummingbirds' wings beat in a shallow figure of eight instead of the normal up and down; this, combined with a 'humming' 80 beat a second wingspeed enables them to hover and even fly backwards and speeds of up to 110 km per hour have been recorded.

Swallows are frequently sighted in the *páramo;* look particularly for the brown-bellied swallow *(Notiochelidon murina)* and the blue-and-white swallow (N. *cyanoleuca);* both are common. The thrushes are represented in the *páramo* by the great thrush *(Turdus fuscater);* the only pipit found is the páramo pipit *(Anthus bogotensis).* Other small species tend to come under the category of 'small brown birds'; of these the cinclodes are the easiest to recognize with a distinctive white eye stripe. The stout-billed and the bar-winged cinclodes *(C. excelsior* and *C. fuscus)* are among the commonest of all *páramo* birds.

Good places for highland ornithology are the Papallacta area and Cotopaxi National Park. Don't forget that this is a harsh environment so you won't see birds flocking in their hundreds. In the Cotopaxi park station there is a small museum which displays several dozen species of stuffed *páramo* birds; this should help you with identification. (This museum was closed for renovation in 1990 — it is not known when it may reopen.)

Looking groundwards instead of skywards you'll frequently find another animal in the *páramo:* the toad. At this altitude they usually belong to the *Atelopodidae* family and are recognized by their lethargic movements and diurnal activity. They are particularly active after a heavy rain. On one walk in Cotopaxi National Park I saw literally hundreds of *Atelopus ignescens* toads almost falling over one another. They are jet black with bright orange bellies and are locally known as the jambato toad. In the more southerly *páramos* these black toads are less common and are replaced by more ordinary looking green examples of the same genus.

When talking of wildlife, it is the mammals which tend most to arouse the general observer's excitement and curiosity. Interesting and strange species live on the *páramo,* but most, unfortunately, are extremely rare and difficult to observe. The first species you will see will be rabbits *(Sylvilagus spp.)* which need no description. Semi-wild horses and cattle range in the highlands, but llamas, perhaps the animals most closely associated with the Andean mountains and their people, are found only in domestic situations. An experimental herd can be seen in Cotopaxi National Park.

Three species of deer are found in the highlands. The familiar white-tailed deer *(Odocoileus virginianus)* occurs at various altitudes and is seen fairly often in Cotopaxi National Park. Two smaller species are infrequently observed. Between 3000 and 4000 m one may see a small brocket deer *(Mazama rufina rufina).* It is about 50 cm tall and of a rusty brown colour with a blackish face. Its horns are limited to tiny 8 cm long prongs. One of the smallest and rarest deer in the world is the dwarf Andean pudu *(Pudu mephistophiles)* which averages under 35 cm in height. It is light greyish-brown and lives in high scrub over 3000 m, usually in the Eastern Cordillera.

Both felines and canines are represented in the *páramo.* The American lion or puma *(Felis concolor)* has been observed around 4000 m and the erroneously named Andean wolf *(Dusicyon culpaeus),* which is in fact a fox, is also occasionally seen.

The largest Ecuadorian land mammals are the tapirs. The mountain or woolly tapir *(Tapirus pinchaque)* is one of the rarest South American animals, and inhabits the high cloud forests and *páramo* of the Eastern Cordillera from 1500 to 4000 m. It is comparatively common in the Papallacta and Sangay regions, but is extremely difficult to sight because it spends most of its time in thick cover. Its heavy brown body, relatively short legs, large ears and emphatically elongated nose make it unmistakable — if you ever see it! You're more likely to find its tracks, four toes in front and three on the rear foot.

Finally, the smallest bear in the world may be seen in the *páramo* by the extremely lucky and very patient observer. *Tremarctos ornatus,* the Andean spectacled bear, is extremely versatile and has been observed from just above Peru's desert coast to *páramo* at over 4000 m. It is called 'spectacled' because of its irregular light-coloured eye patches on its otherwise almost black hair. In Ecuador it has been sighted on both the outside slopes of the Western and Eastern Cordilleras and, as with the woolly tapir, the Papallacta region is favoured.

MINIMUM IMPACT

One look at the areas around base camps and huts on some of the more popular Ecuadorian volcanoes will show you that not all mountaineers are environmentally aware.

Minimum impact means that a place is unchanged by your visit: no garbage, no fire-scars or other damage, no Indians taught to beg by thoughtless handouts of sweets or money.

Don't litter. All your trash should be burned, carried out with you, or disposed of properly at mountain refuges. If you can bring yourself to clean up after less considerate climbers, so much the better.

When nature calls, go well away from the trail, campsite or river, and dig a hole. Bring a light-weight trowel or use your ice axe for the purpose; burn toilet paper.

Don't build fires in the highlands where wood is scarce and is sometimes the only fuel for inhabitants of remote areas. Bring your stove for cooking.

Ecuador's Indians are proud people with their own culture and beliefs. Gratuitous present-giving tends to impose your culture on theirs, so only give gifts or money in return for their help or work. Indiscriminate photography will often alienate you from mountain dwellers. These people, although living under extremely simple conditions, are as sensitive and intelligent as anyone else and resent being treated with arrogance by foreign visitors.

Conservation in Ecuador is the responsibility of the Departamento de Areas Naturales y Vida Silvestre, under the Ministry of Agriculture. An organisation which helps to protect the flora and fauna of the country is the Fundación Natura. They publish a bimonthly newsletter.

LAST WORDS ABOUT CLIMBING AND HIKING

Keep in mind that the conditions related to climbing and hiking, as detailed in this book, are NOT static. Things change constantly. Climbing routes, particularly on glaciers, will vary from season to season. Sometimes this is a minor variation of our description, but at other times the change is drastic enough to make the described route life-threatening. Since the last edition of this book, every major climb has seen a number of route changes. Be a responsible climber. Go with as much information as you can get and use your experience and judgement to evaluate climbing conditions. Treks will see less variation, but water sources may come and go, again depending on the season. New roads, constantly being constructed in Ecuador, will alter, if not completely ruin, some beautiful hikes. Always carry a compass and topographic maps of the area you're venturing into. It is hoped that this guide will be a valuable tool in getting you into a variety of incredible places and on top of a number of beautiful summits, but no guidebook can replace common sense or be a substitute for experience.

THE TOP TEN

Peaks over 5000 metres in Ecuador

CHIMBORAZO	6310 metres	(20703 feet)
COTOPAXI	5897 metres	(19348 feet)
CAYAMBE	5790 metres	(18997 feet)
ANTISANA	5704 metres	(18715 feet)
EL ALTAR	5319 metres	(17452 feet)
ILINIZA S.	5263 metres	(17268 feet)
SANGAY	5230 metres	(17160 feet)
ILINIZA N.	5126 metres	(16818 feet)
CARIHUAIRAZO	5020 metres	(16471 feet)
TUNGURAHUA	5016 metres	(16457 feet)

See page 201 for a list of mountains over 4000 m.

ECUADOR FACT BOX

Size 283,520 sq km (second smallest republic in South America). 685 km from north to south.

Population 10,400,000 (1990 census).
40% Indian, 40% mestizo, 10% European, 10% others.
48% of the population live on the coastal plain, 47% in the Andean sierra and 5% in the eastern lowlands (the Oriente).
Population growth 2.9% per annum.
Population density 37 per sq km (highest in S. America).

Main Towns Quito. The capital, in the highlands.
Population 1,200,000
Guayaquil. Largest city and main port. Population 1,600,000.
Cuenca. Main town of southern highlands. Population 200,000.

History

1527	First Spanish contact; Pizarro's men land at Esmeraldas, in northern Ecuador.
1535	Incorporated into the viceroyalty of Peru; Ecuador is known as the Audiencia de Quito.
1822	Ecuador gains independence from Spain after the battle of Pichincha, May 24, under the leadership of Mariscal Sucre. Incorporated into Gran Colombia.
1830	Becomes fully independent under first president, Juan Flores.
1942	War with Peru; much of the Ecuadorian Amazon lost to Peru but Ecuador still claims this region.
1979-present	Democratic elections; President Rodrigo Borja Cevallos in from 1988-1992.

Weather Quito rainy season: September-May; average annual rainfall 1270mm. Mean temperature 13°C; average high temperature 22°C, average low temperature 7°C. Guayaquil rainy season: December-May. Average high temperature 32°C, average low temperature 20°C.

Holidays

Jan 1	New Year's Day	July 24	Bolívar's Birthday
Moveable	Epiphany	Aug 10	Quito Indepen-
Moveable	Carnival (Monday		dence Day
	& Tuesday before	Oct 9	Guayaquil
	Lent)		Independence Day
Moveable	Holy Thursday,	Oct 12	Columbus Day
	Good Friday, Holy	Nov 1	All Saints Day
	Saturday, Easter	Nov 2	All Souls Day
	Sunday	Nov 3	Cuenca Indepen-
May 1	Labour Day		dence Day
May 24	Battle of Pichincha	Dec 6	Foundation of Quito

CHAPTER 4

The Central Valley

I live not in myself, but I become
Portion of that around me; and to me
High mountains are a feeling, but the hum
of human cities torture.

Byron

INTRODUCTION

Lying in the middle of Ecuador, the Avenue of the Volcanoes is not only the geographical heart of the country but also contains most of its major cities and almost half of the 10½ million inhabitants.

The most important city of the Central Valley is of course Ecuador's capital, Quito. Its high mountainous setting is marvellously invigorating and with its well-preserved old town full of narrow cobbled streets and red-tiled colonial buildings, it is the most attractive capital in Latin America. Quito is proud of its eighty-six churches, which, with their intricate wood carvings, superb colonial paintings, and lavish use of gold leaf, are amongst the most splendid in the continent. The church of La Compañía and the monastery of San Francisco, both in the old town, are perhaps the most extravagantly gorgeous. There are some fine museums. The Casa de Cultura at Av. Patria and Av. 12 de Octubre has museums of natural history, modern and 19th century art, musical instruments, and a gallery of changing shows. The Museo del Banco Central on Av. 10 de Agosto has museums of gold, archaeology, and colonial art on the 5th and 6th floors. Information on tourist sights and a map of the city are available from the tourist office on the corner of Avenidas Reina Victoria and Roca in the new town.

You'll probably find yourself staying in Quito for some time as it is not only a charming city but is also well located as a departure point for other areas. Despite being only 25 km from the equator, its altitude (about 2850 m) gives Quito a pleasant climate. This is an excellent elevation to begin acclimatizing for high altitude and the following seven easy day hikes near Quito are described with this in mind. These are followed by longer and more difficult hikes and climbs.

Short walks in the Quito area

CERRO PANECILLO (3016 m)

This small hill rises about 160 m above the elevation of Quito and, with the huge statue of the Virgin of Quito at its summit, is a major city landmark.

To climb it go down Calle García Moreno in the old town to where it terminates at Avenida Ambato. From here García Moreno continues as a series of steps and footpaths to the summit — about half an hour of puffing. In recent years, this area has become rather notorious for robbery. Take no valuables with you, if going on foot. It is advisable to go in a group. For added security, you can take a taxi, or a No. 22 El Tejar-Panecillo bus to the top if you don't feel like the exercise. The view is very worthwhile especially early in the morning or in the evening when several volcanoes arc often visible. Robbery is not a problem on the summit itself.

Looking a few degrees east of south one sees the perfect cone of the famous Cotopaxi with the large black rock known as Yanasacha visible below the summit. Directly below are the jagged peaks of Pasochoa and just to the right is Rumiñahui. To the left of Cotopaxi is Sincholagua, a lumpy mountain sometimes covered with a sprinkling of snow. Looking further left, a little east of southeast one sees the snowcapped bulk of Antisana, the 4th highest mountain in Ecuador. Roughly east is the jagged sawtooth crest of Las Puntas; then at east northeast you'll see the snow dome of Cayambe, Ecuador's 3rd highest mountain, and further left is a long ridge behind which Imbabura and Fuya Fuya appear. Somewhat to the east of north we see Cotacachi, a rather jagged peak occasionally covered with a sprinkling of snow. Due west of Quito is Pichincha, the capital's backyard volcano, and to the southwest is the long ridge of the extinct crater of Atacazo. Finally, rather west of south, is the lump of Iliniza Norte, with the snow peak of Iliniza Sur just visible behind and to the left of it.

The Panecillo restaurant, just below the summit, offers medium priced meals with a view of the city. They are usually open for lunch and the food is OK though the service is slow.

Public telephones are rare in Ecuador. Many small stores will let you make a local call for a few sucres. For long distance calls, go to the telecommunications building, IETEL. There's one in every town.

LOMA LUMBISÍ (3045 m)

This is a long flat hill lying just east of the capital. It is easy to get to and makes a pleasant walk. The 1:25,000 IGM Tumbaco map covers this area.

Take the No. 8 bus to La Tola (the end of the line) and walk down the hill to the major clover leaf intersection on the southeast side of Quito known as the Los Chillos Autopista (freeway). From here take a bus marked Las Monjas to where there are toll booths on the freeway (or walk southeast along the freeway for about 3 km). Alternatively you can catch a bus from Universidad Central going direct to Las Monjas, or any of the Chillos valley buses from Plaza La Marin and get off at the toll booth. From the toll booths head east up the hill. There is a dirt road which switchbacks up the hill but I took short cuts on paths crossing fields. The dirt road reaches the top of the hill and runs north northeast along the summit ridge for over a kilometre before dropping down. Allow about an hour from the toll booth to the highest point.

The easiest way back is the way you came, but it is more interesting to follow the dirt road as it becomes a track through corn fields and eucalyptus groves and then go down the far end of the ridge. After about 45 minutes you'll come to a major fork where you go left. Going right takes you to the village of Cumbaya about 3 km to the east from where there are buses to Quito. Heading in this direction you'll cross the old, unused railway line which serves as a footpath for the area. Following this will lengthen the walk into Cumbaya, but it's a nice hike with lovely views. Going left soon leads you to the old Quito-Cumbaya road and about 40 minutes walk along this road is a famous Quito church, the Guápulo. You'll pass two bridges in quick succession over the Río Machángara and the (Quebrada El Batán) before reaching the Guapulo and from here it is about a 30 minute walk uphill to the Hotel Quito, or you can take a No. 21 bus into the city.

UNGÜI (3578m)

This small rounded hill can clearly be seen in a west southwest direction from the Panecillo. The beginning of the walk takes you through Marcopamba which is one of Quito's outlying suburbs and has a rural rather than an urban feel to it. You may even see a couple of llamas wandering by with loads of straw or firewood on their backs. The walk ends with some particularly fine views of the capital.

Start by taking a No. 8 Tola-Pintado bus to its western terminal at Cuartel Mariscal Sucre. Just before the end of the line there is a road at your right called Chilibulo. Follow Chilibulo to the end where it makes a left turn to the southwest, and continue along its zig-zagging route out of town. At any intersection take the major cobbled fork and follow the road through the

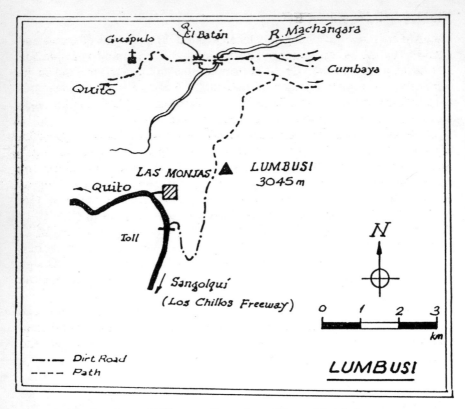

countryside for about 1½ hours of steady walking which brings you to a pass with a statue of the Virgin Mary. The road down from the pass will eventually bring you to Lloa which is a possible starting point for climbing Pichincha. To climb Ungüi, however, you turn right at the pass. A dirt road heads right and goes around the back of the hill, and in the crotch between this and the road you came up on there is a wide grassy lane which follows an aqueduct (marked *acequia* on the IGM map). This runs underground at the beginning but soon comes to the surface. Follow the aqueduct until you reach the point where there is a full view of Quito. Here you'll find rough tracks heading up and down the hill. At the top of the hill is a tiny stone building. Paths which appear to lead to the top before there is a full view of Quito are just water run offs. If you continue following the aqueduct it will, after some 5 km, join with a rough dirt road heading right and back down the hill towards Marcopamba, or you can make shortcuts downhill through fields if you wish. Half a day is perfectly adequate but if you bring a picnic lunch you'll probably enjoy a full day gazing down on Quito.

This route is shown on the IGM 1:50,000 topographical map of Quito.

PULULAGUA CRATER

The extinct crater of Pululagua is located about 20 km north of Quito and is said to be the largest crater in South America. It is about 4 km wide and 300 m deep; its flat and fertile bottom is used for agriculture and in its centre there is a small hill, Loma Pondoña (2975 m). The floor of the crater is at 2500 m elevation. The Ministry of Agriculture (MAG) has set aside part of the area as a protected ecological reserve.

To get there take any Mitad del Mundo bus which runs from Plaza La Marin, through the old town, and north on Av. America. About an hour's ride will bring you to Mitad del Mundo where a huge monument marks the equator — though it should be mentioned that the correct equatorial line as determined by the most recent surveys lies several hundred metres away. Get off the bus at the monument and take the good tarmac road to Calacalí to the right of the monument. Walk, get a ride (expect to pay a few sucres), or catch a bus going to Calacalí to the turn off for Pululagua which is the first tarmac road to the right, some 4 km beyond the monument. There is no sign at present. Less than a kilometre later this road stops at the very edge of the crater.

From here you can walk down a very steep and winding footpath which is the only access to the crater floor, then walk around on several field roads, or climb the Loma Pondoña in the centre. The descent into and ascent out of the crater take only an hour or so.

NONO HIKES

Nono is a sleepy little village located about 15 km as the crow flies northwest of Quito, but vehicles travelling on the beautiful winding mountain road from Quito to Nono cover twice that distance. The village is interestingly situated on the western flanks of the Western Cordillera and from Nono the road continues to the coast, dropping through lush tropical forests as it does so. This road and the surrounding forest are particularly interesting for the number and variety of bird species. A new road serving this area has been completed through Calacalíto the north and little transport uses the old winding road. This, however, makes it an excellent mountain biking road for the so-inclined. Nono itself is the centre of a fine network of jeep tracks and foot trails going into the surrounding hills, all giving good day hikes or longer trips if desired. One day hike will be described, but armed with the IGM 1:50,000 topographical map (predictably named Nono) you will be able to find plenty of other possibilities.

You can reach Nono in a couple of hours from Quito. First take the No. 7 Marin-Cotocollao bus northbound on Av. 10 de Agosto. Get off at the end of the line which is the Cotocollao plaza. Wait at the corner of the plaza by

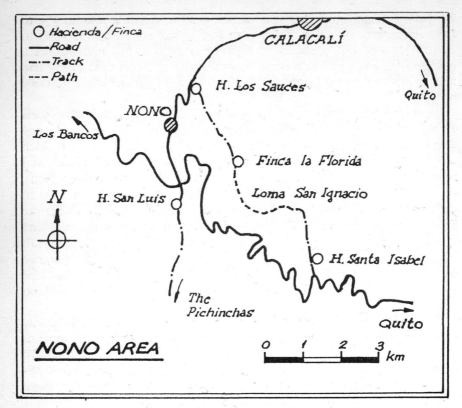

O Hacienda/Finca
——Road
—·—Track
--- Path

CALACALÍ

H. Los Sauces

Quito

NONO

Los Bancos

Finca la Florida

Loma San Ignacio

N

H. San Luis

H. Santa Isabel

The
Pichinchas

Quito

NONO AREA

0   1   2   3
                    km

the taxi stand for a ride to Nono. There are occasional buses, and often
trucks will stop at this corner and pick up passengers for Nono and beyond.
As mentioned, most of the transport will take the new northern route
though a few continue to go along the old road. This ride is very interesting
because after you leave Quito you go past several kilometres of brickworks.
But not brickworks in the sense of the smoke-belching stacks of Britain's
industrial midlands; here you can see *campesinos* mixing, pouring, forming,
drying, firing, and stacking the mud bricks which are so commonly used in
the construction of houses in Andean villages. The mountain road continues
climbing through pine and eucalyptus plantations until it reaches a pass at
nearly 3400 m before dropping down through farmland to Nono at 2700 m.

If arriving via the new route, the ride will be shorter, but the scenery still
beautiful. Very few vehicles actually go into Nono but pass the junction
about a kilometre uphill from the village. From here it's an easy walk into
town.

From Nono there is a jeep track heading south to Hacienda San Luis and
a footpath continuing south to Loma Yanayacu. You could continue south
walking cross-country to Pichincha. There are trails east and west of this

footpath; I understand that one of the eastbound trails goes to Quito although I haven't tried it. Trails also lead to the northwest of Nono to Cerro Chiquilpe and to the north to San Francisco and beyond. Finally a mixture of tracks and trails climb southeast out of Nono over Loma San Ignacio and to the pass on the Quito-Nono road. This is the hike I describe below.

From where the bus or truck drops you off outside Nono walk northwest for about a kilometre into the village, then up the main road until you come to the church plaza at the north end of town. Turn east on a road which twists and hairpins for over a kilometre to the Hacienda Los Sauces, and here take the right hand track (which is still wide enough for a jeep), skirting the *hacienda* and climbing steadily southeastwards for 2 or 3 km to the Finca La Florida (which is wrongly marked on the IGM map). After the finca the track changes into a narrow grassy footpath climbing south and southeast almost to the top of the hill known as Loma San Ignacio. Go through two gates and near the top turn right through a third gate. The trail now widens out again and soon becomes a jeep track which continues for 3 or 4 km past the Hacienda Santa Isabel and onto the main Quito-Nono road.

The whole hike will take about 3 hours of steady walking and is mostly uphill. It could be done in reverse which would be easier. The beginning of the jeep track is marked by a sign for Hacienda Santa Isabel on the right hand side of the Quito-Nono road. The uphill route, however, climbs steadily but gently and is good exercise and acclimatization for those planning more strenuous trips into the mountains.

CERRO ILALÓ (3185 m)

Ilaló is a long extinct and heavily eroded volcano near Tumbaco, a small village located 10 km east of and 400 m lower than Quito. The 1:50,000 IGM Sangolquí map clearly shows both mountain and village. Tumbaco is a delightful place and although essentially Ecuadorian in character it is home to many expatriates working in Quito. Its climate is rather like a warm summer's day in England and its gardens are full of bright tropical flowers, flashing hummingbirds, and lazy butterflies.

To get there take any bus heading north on Av.6 de Diciembre and get off at the 'Partidero a Tumbaco' roundabout. You can take any bus heading down into the valley, as they all go to or through Tumbaco, or you can easily hitchhike. The road passes through the small town of Cumbaya and after another 7 km enters Tumbaco. Get off at the traffic light in Tumbaco (you can't miss it, it's the only one in town) and walk along the main road for a couple of hundred metres until the first right turn, marked by an

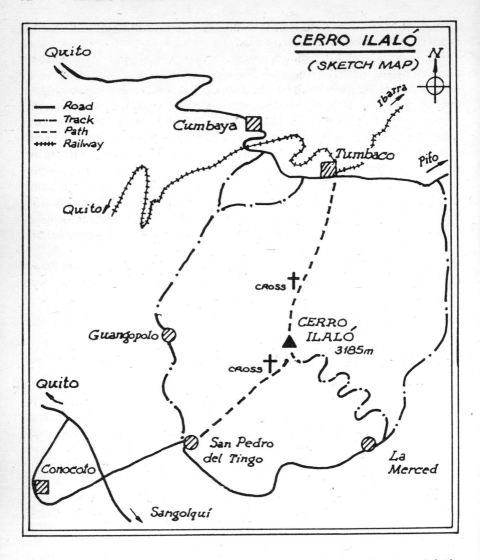

INERHI sign. Walk up this road for over a kilometre until the road forks.
Here take a right fork over a cobbled road marked Centro Comunal
Tumbaco. A few hundred metres further you come to a major junction
where you turn left. Continue up this road as it passes the last houses and
deteriorates into a footpath which you follow until a short distance from the
top of a hill. Here you make a sharp left turn off the main trail about a
hundred metres beyond a small mud brick house next to a lone pine tree.
This trail soon deteriorates into a grassy track zigzagging up the hill and a
few minutes later you reach a huge white stone cross which has been visible

on and off from the beginning of the walk. You should allow almost 2 hours to reach this cross from the main road.

This is a good place to stop and admire the view but you need another hour of hiking to reach the true summit. Continue past the cross on a narrow but well defined trail which leads up a ridge, along a minor saddle, and up another ridge to a white triangulation marker at the summit. Occasionally the trail forks in which case you should always take the upper trail. The trail fades into grass at times but is generally easy to follow. From the top there is an interesting view of Quito to the northwest, nestling in the valley below Pichincha. To the southwest another white stone cross can be seen; a trail leads past this, complete with enchanting tunnels through scrub, and down to San Pedro del Tingo. To the southeast there is a dirt road which zigzags its way down to La Merced. Either of these can be used as alternative descent routes. Both places have hot springs and are rather crowded at weekends.

If you want to do this hike in reverse, buses leave frequently from Plaza La Marin in the old town for Tingo. You can take buses 'La Merced', 'San Pedro', or Transportes San Rafael to get to Tingo.

THE THREE PEAKS OF EL CHAUPI

by John and Christine Myerscough

If you enjoy walking across rough open country and are not particularly interested in altitude records, this walk could be for you. It offers extensive views of snow capped volcanos and provides panoramic vistas of lush and fertile valleys without taking you over 4,000 metres. The three hills are usually free of cloud even when all the surrounding mountains are hidden, making this a useful walk during periods of unsettled weather. The walk can easily be completed from Quito within a day, being only 12 km long with just under 1,000 metres of ascent. It is therefore possible to travel light with only a day pack. However, there is no water along the trail so it must be carried.

Take a Latacunga bound bus from the Terminal Terreste in Quito. They leave every 10-15 minute. Ask to disembark at Minitrack Cotopaxi next to the El Boliche entrance to Cotopaxi National Park. The ride takes about one hour and on the way you will notice three rounded hills ahead and to the right of the road forming a horseshoe. These are the "three peaks" of this walk.

On the opposite side of the road from the entrance to Cotopaxi Park there is a dirt road leading in the direction of the first hill, Loma Santa Cruz Chica, with the smaller mound of Loma Sal Grande in front of it.

Walk down the dirt road passing under electricity cables and by a small conifer plantation. On your left, after about fifteen minutes, you pass underneath another set of pylons and beyond them take the gravel road to the left. This road brings you to the foot of Loma Sal Grande. Heading in a SW direction you should be able to find small paths to take you towards the summit. Keep heading upwards, crossing occasional tracks which skirt around the hill side. Eventually the fields end and you have to continue up through *ichu* grass. Within about one hour of leaving the Pan-Am Highway you should be on the top of Loma Sal Grande.

If you only get this far the view is incredible. Cotopaxi rises majestically to the east, along with the crags of Ruminahui. If you have made an early start you may also see the morning train from Quito wind its way across the miniature landscape below.

From this crest you can view the rest of the walk. Follow the ridge to the south over a shallow col passing the edge of a young conifer plantation, then climb steeply up Loma Santa Cruz Chica keeping to the left high above its craggy western side. It will take about another 45 minutes to reach the trig pillar on the top (3,890 m) from where you may catch a glimpse of Tungarahua and El Altar away to the south if it is still clear.

From here descend a steep, grassy gully on the SW side of the hill to the col between Loma Yuruquira and Loma Santa Cruz. Skirt below the SE face of a small rocky knoll in your way and continue up to the summit of L. Yuruquira, then descend once more westwards crossing a col before beginning the ascent of Loma Santa Cruz, which at 3,945 m is the highest of the three peaks.

Crossing the last col is a small but well used path. If the weather is bad or if you wish to shorten the walk, turn right and follow this path which soon turns into a dirt road. It skirts around the north side of Loma Santa Cruz Chica and eventually brings you back to the Pan-American Highway near the Cotopaxi Park entrance. From here you can get a bus back to Quito.

Going up Loma Santa Cruz you may find a narrow path to take you part way. It fades out about half way up and the remainder of the climb is over tussocky *ichu* grass. From the top of Loma Santa Cruz Chica to the top of Loma Santa Cruz takes about 1½ hours.

From the top of Loma Santa Cruz head northwards following the steep ridge downwards. There is no path but head for the dirt road that passes between this hill and your next peak, Loma Saquigua. On reaching this road turn right and follow it for approximately 400 metres before commencing your final ascent. Loma Saquigua at 3,830 m is the lowest of the three hills and has the gentlest slopes to climb. From the road to its grassy summit will take about an hour. The top gives a spectacular close-up view of the ice-capped volcano Iliniza Sur, and also enables you to look back with satisfaction along the whole length of the walk.

Finally descend to the NW to join a clearly visible track which will take you to the small town of El Chaupi whose church can be seen some 3½ km away to the north. In El Chaupi there is a store which can provide a refreshing and welcome drink.

Small buses leave every 30 minutes to Machachi. The ride takes about half an hour. From Machachi buses leave frequently for Quito. The ride back along the Pan-Am takes about ¾ hour.

MAPS   IGM 1:25,000 Iliniza, 3892-11-SW; 1:25,000 Minitrak Cotopaxi, 3892-11-SE.

ROCK CLIMBING AROUND QUITO

Some folks arrived at the South American Explorers Club in Quito one day, having just arrived from the States. They came in with a ton of gear, plopped it down, plopped themselves down, smiled brightly and said, "Hi, we're here to spend two months rock climbing. Where's the best place?" I smiled brightly back, gave them the best directions to the airport, informed them that the next flight to the States was leaving in a few hours and that, from there, they could go to El Dorado Canyon in Colorado, Joshua Tree or Yosemite in California, maybe try Hueco Tanks in Texas, or, well, just about anywhere — there were a lot of choices. They shook their heads in unison, said, "No, no — we mean, what's the closest place from HERE for good rock climbing?" "Oh," I replied, "from HERE, you mean? Well, head north and when you get to Texas, or Colorado or California."

That more or less sums up the rock climbing situation in Ecuador, though there are a few better-than-nothing areas within the country for the desperate and rock-starved. For the most part, the geology of the region is not conducive to good rock nor has the sport of rock climbing taken hold with Ecuadorian climbers in general. We include rock routes up smaller peaks in various chapters of this guide.

In the Quito area there are a couple of interesting rock climbing possibilities. Most noteworthy is the climbing practice wall found near the Centro Deportivo in the barrio of La Vicentina.

This is a small castle-like structure on the south side of the roundabout at Toledo and Ladrón de Guevara, just a few blocks east of Av. 6 de Diciembre and Patria in the new town. Short routes of varying difficulty are good for an afternoon of muscle-building. On the Tumbaco road, about 1 km down the hill from the Av. 6 de Diciembre turn-off at the Partidero a Tumbaco, are some rock slabs on the left suitable for climbing. You can't miss them because the obvious lines of ascent have been made more obvious with large painted arrows showing the route! Scrambling around in this area will turn up more slabs with more arrows, and hence, more climbs.

Further down the Tumbaco road, all the way past Pifo, is another small area for climbing. It mostly consists of one dihedral with rotten rock. I mention it here only to warn against making the effort, in the event that someone somewhere tries to tell you there's good rock climbing in Pifo (as I was told). However, continuing along this road (which goes to Papallacta and onwards eventually to Baeza) about another 5 km, you'll come to a place where the *páramo* steeply climbs (looking right from the road) to a massive rock outcrop. It's a steep climb up and, though I was assured it's good rock, I can't attest to it personally. It would make a nice day's outing in any case.

Longer climbs

CERRO IMBABURA (4609 m)

This long extinct volcano is located about 60 km northeast of Quito near the town of Otavalo and the pretty lake of San Pablo. It can be climbed in one long day and although technically an easy climb the extremely rotten rock at the top can make the last metres treacherous. Its first ascent is uncertain; it used to be climbed by local Indians who collected ice and delivered it to the town of Ibarra. There are no longer glaciers on Imbabura and so this industry is now discontinued.

Two routes approaching from different sides of the mountain are usually followed. From the San Pablo side, there are several ways to go. One begins from the village of San Pablo del Lago (accessible by frequent buses from Otavalo) and leaves town from the main square on the road to the right of the church. After about 2 km the road turns right (east) and you continue up a track to the north with the mountain some 5 km directly ahead of you. Head for the highest point and find a gully to take you up to the crater at the top. The rock here is extremely loose and rotten. The highest point is to your left at the western edge of the crater. You can also do the same route to the summit by starting from the village of Agato, about 6 km up a dirt road from the main one which circles San Pablo lake. Take any one of the many buses from Otavalo which circumnavigate the San Pablo lake road. Get off at the Agato turn-off, and walk or catch a ride up to the village. Here the route begins from behind the Escuela Agato, and eventually meets up with the track out of San Pablo. Carry on for about 6 hours to the summit more or less cross-country, and allow another 4 for the return.

The alternative route, and the more common approach, is from the village of La Esperanza which lies about 9km northeast of the mountain. Follow the road through town and near the end, take a dirt track which leads off to the right for about 100 m. It connects with a dirt road leading up and left. This can be a little confusing as there are many such dirt tracks. Best to ask for "el camino para Imbabura". This way you'll get on the correct path without a lot of guesswork. Just beyond the village this dirt road divides and both run parallel to, and on either side of a creek bed. Either path will get you to the trailhead about 6km farther up. The left-hand track goes up to a small farm, and then continues on to the left and away from Imbabura. Pick up the trail from the farm leading west across the *páramo*. The summit lies 3 hours away on fairly good trail. Rock scrambling is necessary near the top, but the rock is easily ascended. The right-hand track along the creekbed will take you to an abandoned shepherd's hut. From here you will have to head west cross-country for about a kilometre to the top of the prominent hill. Here you'll meet up with the trail heading northwest to the summit. The round-trip from La Esperanza takes about 8 to 9 hours.

La Esperanza is easy to get to: buses leave frequently from Ibarra (20 km north of Otavalo on the Pan American Highway). There are two very cheap and basic hostels in the rather strung out village.

On the outskirts of San Pablo del Lago is the excellent and friendly Parador Cusín located in a charming old *hacienda* owned by Englishman, Nick Millhouse. Although not for the budget traveller, it is nonetheless extremely good value for money. Horses can be hired for rides in the mountains and the owners are knowledgeable about the area.

IMBABURA CIRCUIT

If going around a volcano rather that up one sounds more appealing then try this circuit of Imbabura. Rather than cross-country *páramo* hiking, this route follows a cobbled path for much of the way and can be completed in one long day. It is an excellent introduction to life in small communities as it wanders through one village after another on its way around the volcano. The IGM 1:50,000 San Pablo del Lago map covers the circuit.

The hike starts in a counter-clockwise direction from the village of La Esperanza described in the Cerro Imbabura climb. For an early start you might decide to stay overnight here; Residencia Aida is basic yet comfortable, and popular with hikers. From La Esperanza the cobbled track heads north to Caranqui and then angles west past Chorlaví to Tahuarin. Here it begins to turn south passing through the important weaving villages of Ilumán, Peguche, and Agato. Beyond Agato you'll connect up with the paved road which circles Lake San Pablo and leads to the village of the same name. In the plaza of San Pablo a road goes up left to Tañahualu Chico where it ends. Above Tañahualu a clear trail ascends toward the pass between Imbabura and Loma Cubiliche offering splendid views of the San Pablo area. Beyond the pass the trail drops down to Las Abras where, just below this village, a left fork takes you down Quebrada Rumihuaycu to the cobbled road leading back (north) to La Esperanza.

This circuit has been a favourite of a group of dedicated Ecuadorian hikers who have turned it into an informal competition. The hike has taken as little as 7 hours and 20 minutes, though the most recent 'best time' can be ascertained at Cafe Maria in La Esperanza.

Loma Cunru and Loma Cubiliche can be climbed from La Esperanza or from San Pablo in a day outing. Take the Zuleta bus and have the driver drop you about a half kilometre south of Aguas Guaraczapa. Here there is a good track which climbs southwest around the south flanks of Loma Cunru. It continues west along the ridge to Loma Cubiliche which has several small lakes in its crater.

LAGUNA MOJANDA

South of Otavalo about halfway to Tabacundo is the high *páramo* lake of Mojanda. A good road with occasional transportation goes all the way up to the lakes from Otavalo and footpaths can be followed across the pass and down to Esperanza (NOT the one at the base of Imbabura) near Tabacundo. There are many hiking possibilities in this area and it's difficult to get tired of the ever-changing, yet always spectacular, views from the high, wide-open páramo. Deciding which route to take is as easy as having a look at the IGM 1:50,000 map of Laguna de Mojanda and taking it from there.

One suggestion for a good day hike would be to leave from Otavalo early, hiring a taxi (US$4) to go the 16 km up to Mojanda. (You could walk but would have to plan to camp at the lake before continuing on the following day. The southern part of the lake is suitable for camping.) From the road at the lake you can look across (south) to a low pass. Climb to the top and you'll see 3 roads heading off in different directions across the *páramo*. Follow the middle road which ascends the western slope of a hill. At the top, as the road begins to drop steeply down the valley, take the vague trail which angles off left (east). It's easy to follow across the open *páramo* as it continues east, first following under a ridge, then across shallow ravines for about an hour. In the distance the twin towers of Esperanza's church will come into sight. The trail eventually begins to drop down along a forested ridge and continues through fields before reaching the village. An option here would be to drop across to the tiny village above Esperanza — Cochasqui — which is interesting for its pre-Columbian pyramids known as the Tolas de Cochasqui. From Laguna Mojanda it's about 5 to 6 hours to Esperanza and buses for the hour return to Otavalo are frequent.

There is a popular annual hike from Quito to Otavalo called Mojanda Arriba which generally coincides with Otavalo's festival at the end of October. A considerable number of hikers gathers at Plaza Cotocollao in north Quito at 6.00 a.m. on the Saturday of the festival and hike all day, camping that night in the village of Malchingui. The next day's hike continues over the pass and down into Otavalo where the town band plays a cacophonous welcome. This hike is not recommended for those solitary spirits wanting to get away from it all!

CERRO PASOCHOA (4200 m)

This mountain is an ancient and heavily eroded volcano which has been inactive since the last ice age. It is located 30 km south of Quito and is easily identified from the Pan American Highway by its huge half blown away crater open to the west. It is an easy ascent and has been climbed many times from all directions except the west face where the crater walls are extremely steep and rotten. I took a bus to Machachi (frequent buses leave from Quito's Villa Flora bus terminal) and from the town square followed the east northeast road heading towards Güitig (pronounced wee-tig) where the famous Ecuadorian mineral water comes from. After two hairpin bends and a bridge you reach Güitig some 3 km from Machachi. Turn left at the main store, then right, and almost immediately take another left (just before the church). If in doubt ask for Güitig Alto. Continue on a cobbled road until just beyond Hacienda Mamijudy where you turn left. At the next major fork head right and keep going uphill until you come to a left turn for Hacienda San Miguel. Go through the cobbled and gated paddocks and continue on a dirt road down to a stream. Just before the stream there is a fork; take the left track which leads to a footbridge. Cross the stream and zigzag up the hill, then traverse northeast and head for a saddle south of the mountain. From here head north passing two smaller peaks to your left before reaching the main summit.

You can descend the same way or continue due north, passing an electric plant after some 4 km and joining a dirt road which takes you another 8 km to the main Tambillo-Sangolquí road from where transportation to Quito can be found. This route is often used by local climbers but it is rather difficult to find the correct track off the main road to get you to the mountain. If you do try this way ask for Cuendina; this is where you turn south off the main road.

On the north side of Cerro Pasochoa a forest preserve/environmental education centre has been established. It was declared a protected area in

1982 by the Ministry of Agriculture and turned over to Fundación Natura, a privately-run conservation organization, for management. This area is unique in that it preserves the last of the original forest and other vegetation that once covered the Quito basin area. Several self-guided loop trails have been set up and the area claims almost a hundred species of birds. There is a park entrance fee of US$5, and US$10 for a camping permit. The crater summit can be climbed from this approach in about 4 to 6 hours.

To get to Pasachoa Forest Preserve, take a bus to Amaguaña (buses leave frequently from Quito's La Marin bus area), about an hour away. Walk along the main road out of Amaguaña for about a kilometre until you get to the Pasachoa park entrance. From here it's about 6 km and 1½ to 2 hours walking to the information centre. Alternatively, trucks can be hired for the trip to the reserve in Amaguaña for about US$4.

Pasochoa is on the IGM 1:50,000 Píntag topographical map but if you start from Machachi you'll need the Machachi and Amaguana maps too. You could manage without any maps in clear weather. The round trip can be done in one long day.

The Inca Road to Ingapirca

INTRODUCTION At the height of its power the Inca Empire extended from northern Ecuador to central Chile. This huge area was linked by a complex system of well made and maintained roads, the longest of which stretched over 5000 km from Quito to Talca, south of Santiago in Chile. This was the greatest communication system the world had known till that time; greater than the roads of the Roman Empire. Although today the road is in a state of disrepair and in many areas the route has been lost or forgotten it is still possible to find and walk along some remnants of this marvellous road system. One such trail can be found in the southern part of Ecuador's Central Valley and leads to Ingapirca, the most important Inca ruin in Ecuador. This 2 to 3 day hike gives a fascinating glimpse of an Andean rural life which has changed little in hundreds of years.

MAPS Three 1:50,000 topographical maps cover the route very well. They are the Alausí, Juncal, and Cañar sheets. When I did the hike the latter two were temporarily out of print, so I bought the 1:100,000 Cañar topographical map which covered the area of both unavailable 1:50,000 maps and was almost as good.

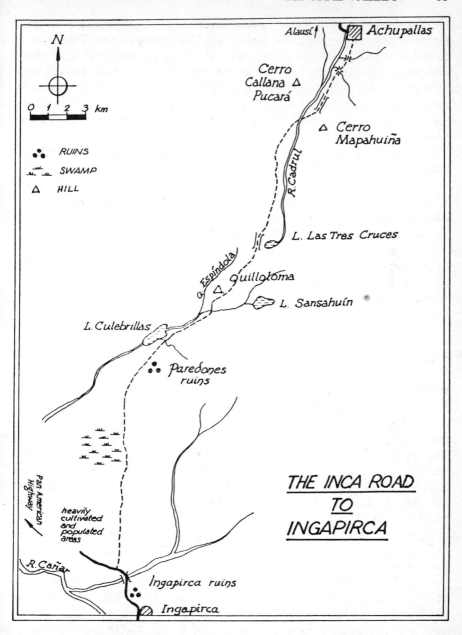

Alausí

Achupallas

Cerro
Callana △
Pucará

N

0 1 2 3 km

RUINS
SWAMP
HILL

△ Cerro
Mapahuiña

R. Cadrul

L. Las Tres Cruces

Q. Espíndola

△ Quillotoma

L. Sansahuín

L. Culebrillas

Paredones
ruins

Pan American
Highway

heavily
cultivated
and
populated
areas

R. Cañar

THE INCA ROAD
TO
INGAPIRCA

Ingapirca ruins

Ingapirca

GETTING THERE   The nearest town to the beginning of the hike is Alausí where there are several cheap hotels. It is situated just off the Pan American Highway 290 km south of the capital. Buses go there from Terminal Terrestre in Quito, but it may be easier first to go to Riobamba and then change to an Alausí bus at Riobamba's Terminal Terrestre. From Alausí there are occasional buses and trucks in the mornings going to Guasuntos, a small town about 10 km further south on the Pan American Highway, or you could hitch-hike. From Guasuntos ask for the trail to La Moya which lies about a ½ km away and 200 m lower; the trail leaves from the far end of town and heads to the right, avoiding the numerous hairpin bends that make the road much longer. (There is no lodging available in Guansuntos, but you can camp in La Moya by the swimming pool with a nearby spring for clean water.) When you reach La Moya stand by the left fork of the road junction to hitch a ride up a steep and spectacular mountain road to the village of Achupallas some 12 km away. There are several trucks a day. You should be able to get from Alausí to Achupallas in a few hours and start walking about midday. A more direct, yet more expensive, alternative is to hire a truck in Alausí straight to Achupallas. This takes about an hour to an hour and a half and drivers charge between US$5 and US$7 per person for the trip.

HIKING DIRECTIONS   In Achupallas head for the arch with a cross at the highest part of the village; take the track left (to the south) of the arch and soon pass the cemetery to your right. The track quickly deteriorates into a stony footpath and crosses a footbridge. At trail junctions continue on the most used trail (usually stony) which follows alongside the river. Some 30 to 40 minutes out of town you recross the river on another footbridge and then follow the left bank of the Río Cadrul (marked the Q. Gadrui on some maps). You are headed for a pass between a pyramidal hill to your left (Cerro Mapahuiña, 4365 m) and a flat-topped hill to your right (Cerro Callana Pucará).

As you get closer to this pass you will see a well-defined notch which you will have to climb. This is interesting as the trail goes up through a hole in the rock: a very tight squeeze. Soon after the notch you should cross the river (it can be jumped) to meet with the trail on the other side. [A user of the first edition writes: "I began to have visions of the man who wrote this book — elongated enough to slither through cracks yet with long spidery legs for leaping across rivers." Yes, the truth will out, you'd recognise Rob R. anywhere. It's also worth noting that the river is only jumpable after a dry spell. Editor.] Within a few hundred metres the trail starts climbing diagonally up the mountain and you reach a height of about 4000 m before the trail contours along the west side of the Río Cadrul valley for several kilometres, reaching the Laguna Los Tres Cruces (by now you are on the

Juncal 1:50,000 map). To this lake is about 6 hours of steady hiking from Achupallas but you can find flat spots on the trail to camp on earlier if you wish.

The following day you follow the trail up beyond the lake and across a pass. Beyond the pass the trail becomes rather indistinct; you'll find it crossing some worn rocks and then it rises up to the top of the left hand ridge. Below you is the valley of the Quebrada Espíndola. Walk along the top of this ridge (marked as the Fila de Huagrarumi on the IGM map) and admire the wonderful views as you follow it to its final peak, Quilloloma. To your left is wild trackless countryside with many lakes, the largest of which is Laguna Sansahuín. This area would doubtless provide several days of excellent off the beaten track camping.

The trail becomes quite distinct again at the top of the ridge and then descends as a rocky path to the left of Quilloloma to the lush and boggy valley bottom beyond. You can quite clearly make out the remains of the old Inca road as a straight line in the grass at the bottom of the valley. At the point where the road crosses the stream you'll find the remains of the foundations of an Inca bridge. This stream has to be crossed; the best place is a little upstream from the bridge where you'll find it narrow enough to jump. There is an obvious trail on the left hand side of the Q. Espíndola which leads you past the southeastern shores of Laguna Culebrillas and to some Inca ruins known as Paredones (ruined walls).

Although it is only an easy half day from Laguna Los Tres Cruces to Paredones this is an excellent place to camp, relax, and enjoy the countryside. Unfortunately the place is a popular stopping point and rubbish has begun to accumulate. If you have extra fuel it can be used to burn the waste, otherwise you can avoid adding to the problem by carrying out your own trash.

The ruin consists of a large main structure whose walls are still more or less standing; there are three main rooms and two smaller ones. The stonework is crude compared to Ingapirca and the famous Peruvian ruins and there is no evidence of typical Inca features such as trapezoidal niches. Around this main structure are the tumbled remains of several smaller buildings. Wildlife is rather limited; I saw caracara hawks and cinclodes. Flowers are prolific however, and you can expect to see gentians, lupins, and daisies among others.

The following day brings you to the ruins of Ingapirca. The walk will take you some 3 to 4 hours and thus leaves you with enough time to explore the ruins and then reach a town to spend the night.

From the Paredones head southwest on the Inca road which is here at its full width of about 7 m. The trail soon swings south and continues straight across the countryside but is extremely boggy. The scenery is rather eerie with huge boulders strewn around like a giant's playthings. Frogs whistle repetitively and brooks bubble up from underground. After 2 or 3 hours the Inca road becomes difficult to follow. There is no specific trail, just walk in a generally south direction, keeping to the right and as high as possible above the river valley, and eventually you should be able to see the ruins of Ingapirca in the distance (also south). The terrain shows increasing signs of cultivation and habitation. You end up walking past fields and houses to a road which leads to the ruins themselves.

INGAPIRCA   This area was occupied by the Cañaris for some 500 years before the construction of the Inca site. In the 1490s the Inca Huayna Capac conquered the area now known as Ecuador and soon after the construction of Ingapirca (in Quechua, Inca walls) began. It has long been known by academicians and the plan drawn by La Condamine in 1739 was accurate enough to be used as a basis for the modern excavations of the ruins which began in the late 1960s.

Ingapirca, with its close fitting, mortarless stonework and typical trapezoidal windows and niches, is the finest example of imperial Inca construction in the country, and evidently built by stone masons trained in Cuzco. The precise functions of the site can only be guessed at, but archaeologists think that the most evident and well preserved structure, an elliptical building known as the temple of the sun, had religious or ceremonial purposes. The less well preserved buildings were probably granaries or store houses and part of the complex was used as a tambo, or stopping place for the runners taking messages along the Inca road from Quito to Tomebamba (present day Cuenca).

Ingapirca is 3160 m above sea level. There is a small visitors' hut and a caretaker, along with an excellent site museum. It is funded by the Banco Central and is well-laid out with many interesting maps and exhibits. A brochure in English is also available for a dollar with decent photos and text. The nearby village of Ingapirca has a few very basic stores but no accommodation. Trucks leave frequently for the Pan American Highway during the day. There are basic hotels in Cañar, about 17 km from Ingapirca and on the Pan American Highway.

They cannot scare me with their empty spaces
Between stars — on stars where no human race is.
I have it in me so much nearer home
To scare myself with my own desert places.
                                    Robert Frost

CHAPTER 5

The Western Cordillera

Never journey without something to eat in your pocket. If only to throw to dogs when attacked by them.

E.S. Bates

INTRODUCTION

The Central Valley described in Chapter 4 is flanked by the Western and the Eastern Cordilleras. (These are often called the Cordillera Occidental and the Cordillera Real.) The western is lower and less massive, although it does contain Ecuador's highest mountain, the extinct volcano Chimborazo, 6310 m. This mountain range is about 360 km long and 30 to 40 km wide and its average height is 3000 to 3500 m above sea level. All the major mountains and some hikes within the Cordillera will be described systematically, beginning with the northernmost mountain.

VOLCÁN CHILES AND THE PÁRAMO DE EL ANGEL

Despite its plural name, Volcán Chiles (4768 m) is a single mountain located on the Colombian border some 24 km west of Tulcán and 130 km northeast of Quito. Although it is extinct, steam vents and sulphur deposits are still found on its slopes and studies of lava flows indicate relatively recent activity. There is a crater which is about 2 km wide and open to the Colombian side. It is an easily and frequently climbed mountain and the ascent can be done in a day. The weather tends to be cloudy and wet with occasional snow so dress accordingly.

There are 2 topographical maps available for the area — IGM Tufiño 1:50,000 and Volcán Chiles 1:25,000. These, however, border with Colombia and may be purchased only with special permission.

Buses take 5 to 6 hours to reach Tulcán from Quito's northern bus terminal, and there is plenty of accommodation in the town. From Tulcán Transportes Norte has a mid-day bus (6 days a week leaving from Calle Sierra) to Chical which runs along the Tufiño-Maldonado road and can let you off at the trailhead for Volcán Chiles. Otherwise, you can get one of the occasional buses and trucks to Tufiño, some 15 km to the west then head west on the road to Maldonado. You may want to hire a pickup truck to take you about 15 km along this road since there is little traffic. You'll see the mountain to the north (to your right) and the Tufiño-Maldonado road passes within 3 km of the peak. Near this point you'll see on the left side of the road a group of *frailejones* more or less in line with the Chiles summit. On the other side is a visible trail heading towards the western ridge of the mountain. You climb up this ridge negotiating small rocky cliffs and a lava flow to the main crater from where the summit is easily reached. No rope is required.

The mountain is in the northern part of the Páramo de El Angel which is interesting because it is the only area in Ecuador where the giant *frailejon* plant is common. (See *Natural History* in Chapter 3). A walk on the *páramo* here will soon enable you to see these strange plants. One possible walk (which I haven't done) would be some 20 km due south of Volcán Chiles which takes you over the *páramo* to El Angel, a village on a main road.

PIÑAN LAKES TREK

The Piñan lakes is an area northwest of Ibarra, a bit off the beaten track, yet worth a visit for its beautiful setting on the high *páramo* below the twin peaks of Yanaurco de Piñan (4535 m). The IGM 1:50,000 Imantag map covers the hike, but the 1:25,000 map Cerro Yanaurco provides a bit more detail of the lakes area, and the 1:50,000 Ibarra map shows the road to the trailhead at Irunguichu.

The 3 to 4 day trek begins from the small settlement of Irunguichu, northwest of Ibarra. Transport direct to the village leaves Ibarra several times a day or you can take a bus to the larger village of Urcuquí and get a ride to Irunguichu from there.

From Irunguichu a trail leads out of the village northwest toward a prominent hill called Cerro El Churo (marked Cerro Churoloma on the 1:50,000 Imantag map). The steep ascent goes through small farming areas and *Polylepsis* forest and eventually skirts around the northeast side of El Churo. The trail then flattens for a short while as it picks up and follows

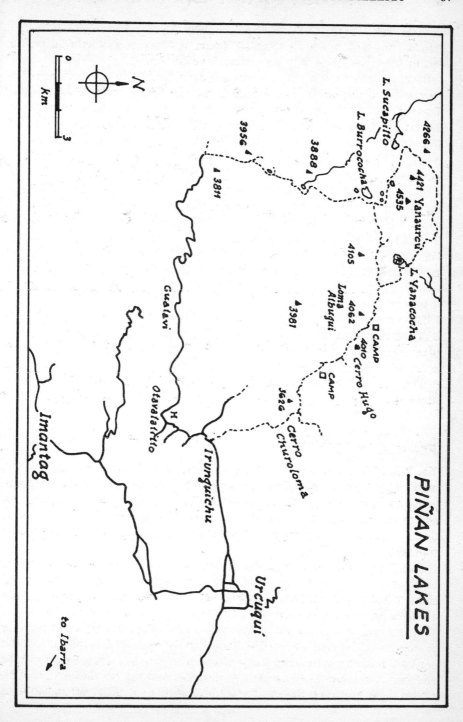

west/northwest alongside a small stream for about 2 km. There is good camping here or you can continue along for another 2 to 3 hours to a small lake/stream junction. Beyond the flat area, the trail leaves the stream and angles north for another steep ascent toward a low pass between Cerro Hugo and Cerro Albugui. Past here the terrain flattens somewhat and you can find an area suitable for camping.

The next day head northwest up to Laguna Yanacocha or across to Laguna Burracocha to the west. Both of these lakes are good basecamps for short hikes in the area. It can be a little boggy around the lakes, but you can find a dry place to pitch a tent. The area has much to offer — herds of wild horses, lots of lakes, spectacular páramo vegetation, trout fishing in the streams, etc. With an extra day, a circuit of the Yanaurco volcano can be hiked in about 6 to 7 hours. Traversing below the mountain in a clockwise direction will bring you to a low pass beneath the west peak. The trail begins as a wide cattle track and narrows to a footpath as it reaches the backside of the volcano. Several trails meander in and out but the route is straightforward. The circuit is a rolling affair — up and down the entire way around Yanaurcu — littered with a variety of wild flowers and there's a good chance of seeing wildlife such as white-tailed deer and condors.

A climb to the summit will take about 5 to 6 hours depending on your starting point and the views from the top are some of the best in Ecuador. With clear weather the whole of the Ibarra/San Pablo valley is visible along with more than 40 lakes scattered across the páramo below. There's not much of a trail but the route up to the summit is not difficult. Head northwest across a relatively flat area of páramo keeping left (northeast) of a small hill. On the IGM 1:25,000 Cerro Yanaurco map this is left of the area marked Tatacho. Ascend the scree along the southeast ridge of the volcano. As usual, the rocks near the top are unstable, watch your footing.

The route out goes south from Laguna Burrococha, descending along the ridge. Keep left (east) along the flanks of a páramo hill (marked Loma Chimborazo on the 1:25,000 map) angling southwest. You'll eventually come to a stream crossing and shortly afterwards pick up a clear trail heading south to the Hacienda El Hospital. This ought to take about 3 to 4 hours of steady hiking. From the hacienda there may be transportation all the way to Ibarra, or you can hike 3 km back to Irunguichu.

The next edition
Our readers are a valuable source of new hikes and climbs, as well as informing us of changes and/or (perish the thought) inaccuracies. This book will be regularly updated so please write to the publishers with your comments.

CERRO COTACACHI AND LAGUNA DE CUICOCHA

In no other part of Ecuador is there anything equalling this extraordinary assemblage of fissures, intersecting one another irregularly and forming a perfect maze of impassable clefts. The general appearance of the country between the villages of Cotacachi and Otavalo is not very unlike that of a biscuit which has been smashed by a blow of the fist. The cracks are all V shaped, and though seldom of great breadth are often very profound, and by general consent they are all earthquake quebradas.

Edward Whymper, 1892

Cerro Cotacachi (4939 m) and Laguna de Cuicocha are located 65 km and 58 km respectively north northeast of Quito. A road leads to the crater called Laguna de Cuicocha which averages 3 km in diameter and is very deep. To get there take any bus from Quito's northern terminal's to Otavalo from where frequent buses go to the village of Cotacachi, famous for its leather work. From here a road leads west about 12 km through the village of Quiroga to the lake. Buses occasionally pass by the lake on their way to Plaza Gutiérrez but it's easier and faster to hire a camioneta from the market in Cotacachi (at the far end of town) for about US$2. Hitch-hiking is also a possibility, but not dependable.

Once at the lake you'll find a restaurant and amenities such as boat rides around the islands. This caldera lake and the area around it has been declared a national park and a path circles the rim, giving marvellous views of the deep blue lake with the snowy peaks of Cayambe and Cotopaxi in the distance. Among the many flowers growing by the path are several species of orchid and puyo with bright green flowers. Giant hummingbirds visit the lupins and condors are sometimes seen.

LAGUNA DE CUICOCHA CIRCUIT

The path begins at the national park check point (where a nominal fee must be paid) and runs counter-clockwise round the lake; allow 5 to 6 hours. The trail is easy to follow initially, keeping to the highest point of the rim, but later veers away from the overlook, running behind some bluffs. Since many hikers have tried to keep the lake in view, there are many false trails. Remember that the trail is always well-worn and clear — if you are on a faint, difficult path you have gone wrong!

After about 1½ hours you'll pass through a gate and then a grassy meadow. The path soon divides: take the lower one which drops down to the river and climbs steeply up the other side (the upper trail is a well-worn mistake which leads you to a lookout point and then a very steep and dangerous descent to rejoin the correct path.) Head for a ruined building and look for the clear path above it (many people go wrong at this point so there are lots of false trails — again!) and follow this to a gate at the top of a steep incline. Do not follow the path through the gate but take the lower less-used trail which leads to a clump of trees at the skyline. Follow the path across a meadow to a national park sign and the road. This will bring you to the hotel and lunch (assuming you started early enough) in about 20 minutes. Resist the temptation to drop down to the lake shore; the paths that look so easy to follow are not — they were made by horses and amazingly nimble horses at that. You will end up thoroughly scratched and bad-tempered.

CLIMBING CERRO COTACACHI   Cerro Cotacachi rises impressively above the northern shore of Cuicocha but the weather is often misty thus obscuring visibility. Whymper and the Carrels claimed the first ascent in 1880. To climb Cotacachi continue up the road to the park entrance and take a sharp right (north) up the cobbled road which quickly deteriorates to loose gravel. This road goes all the way up to a radio tower; you can see the antennae from the road. By hired transport, it's about 1½ to 2 hours to this high point from Otavalo. To do this trip in one day, you'll have to leave Otavalo by 4.00 or 5.00 a.m., or start from the town of Cotacachi at 5.30 or 6.00 a.m. On foot it takes 2 to 3 hours to the station from the main road turn-off. Camping is possible in a flat area on the páramo ridge, with excellent views of Imbabura and Cayambe, but there is no water.

A couple of hundred metres before you reach the tower, the road crosses a ridge and turns sharply south to the tower. At this sharp turn you'll find a distinct trail that heads directly up the ridge to below the base of Cotacachi. As the trail becomes fainter you'll head left across to the top of a steep grassy slope. Here stone cairns mark the way to the base of the summit slope. This section of climbing up and across the slope is particularly dangerous because of rock and ice fall from above. A helmet would add safety. The route ascends to the left (west), circling around and up to the northwest side. A gully of pale yellow sand leads up to the summit ridge. If carrying a daypack, you might consider leaving it here as a little further ahead there is a vertical, 10 m rock face to be negotiated. At the top of this, it's a ten-minute stroll to the summit along a knife-edged ridge of rotten rock with 200 m drops on either side.

LAGUNA CUICOCHA TO LAGUNA MOJANDA

Armed with the IGM 1:50,000 maps of Otavalo and Mojanda, this 2-day hike will take you past several villages, through forested areas and across páramo from one crater lake to another. I've yet to do this hike myself, but it is quite straightforward and interesting for the changing vegetation zones which range from bromeliads to tree ferns to wild orchids along the way. The trek more or less heads due south from Laguna Cuicocha through the village of Ugshapungu. Continue on a variety of footpaths toward Cerro El Quinde where the trail will cross a main road and angle southeast toward Cerro Blanco. Camping near the stream on the east side of the road would be a good stopping place. Heading southeast keeping Cerro Blanco on the left (east) there will be stunning views of the whole area. The route continues southeast until you finally reach Laguna Mojanda. Getting transport down the road to Otavalo should present no problem.

LA DELICIA TO APUELA

This day's outing northwest from Otavalo combines forested valleys with páramo ridges in an area superb for birdwatching.

The trails can often be muddy and suitable waterproof boots may be desirable. The two IGM maps which cover the area are the 1:50,000 series Imantag and Apuela.

The hike starts from the small village of La Delicia (also known as Las Delicias) which consists of a school, a tiny store and some four houses, about 2 hours from Otavalo. There is no direct transport but buses and trucks bound for the villages of Apuela and García Moreno pass through the settlement. Departing from Otavalo at the corner of 31 Octubre and Colón, the earliest truck leaves at 7.15 a.m. except Tuesdays and several daily buses (Transportes Otavalo or Transportes Cotacachi) go until mid-afternoon.

From the store in La Delicia (where you'll be dropped) walk 200 m back up the hill and around the bend to the last house. Here you'll find the beginning of the trail to the community of Azabí which is visible down the valley.

The descent begins through *Polylepsis* forest which is a good area for birdwatching. Once in the valley of Quebrada Agua Azul, the trail follows the river to Azabí. Here, just past the school, the track divides. Keep right for a short yet steep climb up the side of the valley where a good wide trail leads to Plaza Gutiérrez. As it descends the ridge to this hillside village there are some impressive views of the neighbouring valleys. In Plaza Gutiérrez there is a wonderful panorama of the entire area from the old church which is situated on a large (likely pre-Columbian) terrace.

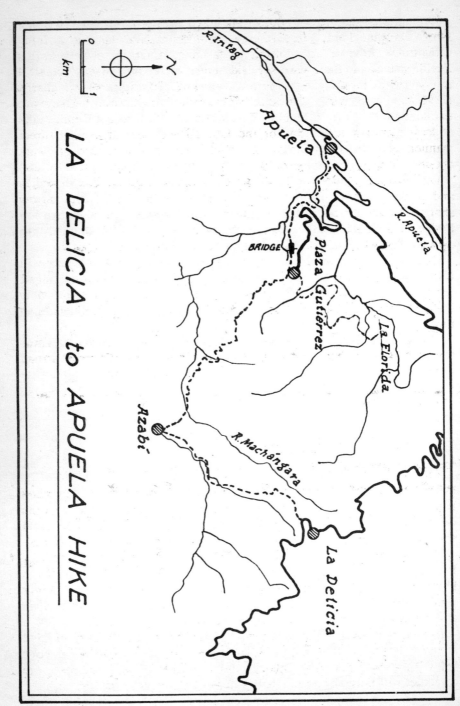

(An optional side trip an hour's walk upstream, north through Quebrada Flores, is the cloud forest reserve La Florida, also known as Intag Cloudforest Reserve. In addition to farming, American owners Carlos Zorilla and Sandy Statz have set aside much of the area as an ecological reserve with lovely guest houses available for visitors. They charge US$25/day with meals. Advance reservations are necessary; they are frequently full. Write to Familia Zorilla, Casilla 18, Otavalo. Replies take at least a month to Europe or the US. To get there in a more direct manner, take a bus from Otavalo to Apuela. Get off at Santa Rosa and walk about an hour along a sometimes muddy footpath to Hacienda La Florida.)

Leaving Plaza Gutiérrez a good jeep track winds west down into the valley and crosses the river. Halfway down to the valley there is a steep, narrow shortcut which eliminates half a kilometre and crosses a rustic suspension bridge. It then rejoins the main track following the Río Toabunchi into Apuela. From La Delicia this hike takes about 5 to 6 hours.

Occasional transport from Apuela makes the return trip to Otavalo in about 3 hours. There are two hostals in town if you decide to stay overnight. Hostal Veritas, rather basic, is on the plaza and Hostal Don Luis (probably better) is 200 m up the hill. Don Luis faces one of the two eating places in town.

This area is full of lovely walks. To the southwest is the village of Vacas Galindo where several trails lead up into the hills. To the northeast a road winds up to Peñaherrera and on through Cuellaje to the Cordillera de Toisan.

THE PICHINCHAS

INTRODUCTION The Pichinchas are two volcanoes known as Guagua and Rucu located some 10 km due west of Quito and so easily visible from the capital. They are normally snow free but an occasional high altitude storm will cover them with a brilliant white layer — a pretty sight from the capital.

The two volcanoes are very distinct. Guagua Pichincha, which means baby Pichincha, is the highest and is presently active. Rucu (old) Pichincha is lower, closer to Quito, and inactive. I have read half a dozen different versions of their elevations; the most recent IGM measurements put Guagua at 4794 m and Rucu at an unspecified but slightly lower elevation.

In 1983 a hut was built on Guagua Pichincha by the Ministry of Civil Defense. It is above the village of Lloa on the south side about half an hour below the crater rim. Although the hut is mainly used by scientists, the caretaker will normally allow small groups of climbers to stay the night.

Because of their close position to Quito and Guagua's activity, the Pichinchas have played a great part in both the factual and fictional history of Ecuador's mountains. They are mentioned by the first *conquistadores* and activity is recorded as far back as 1533. The greatest eruption was in 1660 when ash fell up to 500 km from Quito and the capital itself was covered with 40 cm of ash and pumice. The sky was filled with incandescent clouds and the sun was blotted out for 4 days — it must have been a terrifying time for the inhabitants of Quito and the surrounding highlands. Two centuries of inactivity followed. Minor eruptions occurred in 1868, 1869, and 1881. Recent activity in 1981 has precipitated a scientific interest and the area is now actively monitored. Volcanologists claim that the volcano continues to be potentially dangerous although Quito is unlikely to be affected by anything more serious than an ash fall; the topography of the area would cause lava flows and lahars (avalanches of heated snow, earth, and mud) to be diverted to the relatively uninhabited areas to the north, west and south of the volcano.

The climbing history of the volcano goes back further than other Ecuadorian mountains, with 1582 seeing the first recorded ascent by a group of locals led by José Ortiguera. All the famous scientific expeditions of the seventeenth and eighteenth centuries made successful ascents; first La Condamine and Bouguer of the French Geodesic Expedition in 1742, then Humboldt in 1802, and Ecuadorian President Gabriel García Moreno in 1844. The American photographer C. Fardad spent a week taking photographs in the crater in 1867, Reiss and Stübel (the conquerors of Cotopaxi) spent several days there in 1870, and of course Whymper and the Carrels made an almost obligatory ascent in 1880. There were several other ascents during this period. Climbing in the twentieth century has been dominated by Sr. Pedro Esparza, who began climbing in 1926 and has made well over a hundred ascents of the mountain, often alone, thus earning for himself the nickname, 'the solitary of Pichincha'. In 1959 Ecuador's first mountain refuge was built on Pichincha by Fabian Zurita at 4300 m on the northeast side of the mountain. Unfortunately vandals destroyed this soon afterwards and today the shelter is mainly for scientists, but the well-worn footpaths from Quito make this an easy and popular climb.

Various legends have been told about the mountain. One goes back to early colonial days when the inhabitants of Quito didn't dare to climb the volcano because of frequent explosions and eruptions. At last three adventurous Franciscan friars decided to explore but high on the volcano's slopes became lost in a thick fog. Cold and frightened, the three found a cave to shelter in and the bravest went out to investigate the area and look for the way down. A long terrifying storm followed and the friar became hopelessly lost. The storm ended and his two companions left the cave in search of their lost brother, shouting and yelling but with no result.

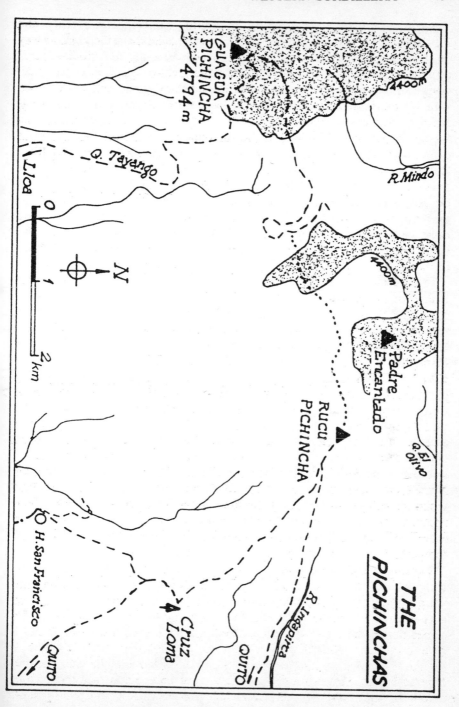

Despondently, they returned to the cave to spend the night. The next morning they went looking for him once again and were overjoyed to see him kneeling in prayer on a high summit. Happily they rushed up to embrace their friend, but their joy turned to terror when they discovered that he'd been turned to stone. They fled back down the mountain and reported to their superiors that the brother had become a rock pillar, praying eternally to God on a peak close to heaven. To this day, Pichincha's third highest peak, lying about halfway in between and a little north of Guagua and Rucu, is named El Padre Encantado (the bewitched priest).

CLIMBING RUCU PICHINCHA

Rucu Pichincha is close enough to Quito that it can be climbed in one long day. An easier hike is a climb up Cruz Loma, the green hill topped by a radio and TV antenna about halfway up Rucu Pichincha, or the hill to the right of Cruz Loma which is known as Loma de las Antenas (Antenna Hill) because it is covered with a veritable forest of TV and radio antennas.

In a modern and expanding city such as Quito the roads and buildings on the outskirts are constantly being changed and improved, hence it is impossible to give absolutely clear cut directions for Rucu Pichincha. Several roads lead from the city into the foothills and any one of the following will eventually lead to paths up the mountains: Av. 24 de Mayo (not recommended), Av. La Gasca, Calle Alvarez de Cuella (the end of the No. 14 bus route), or Calle Mañosca. This last is my favourite route.

Take one of several buses northbound on Av. América to Calle Mañosca. Walk up this street for about 15 minutes until it crosses the Via Occidental expressway. Directly opposite Mañosca is a signed road leading to a fertilizer factory; ignore this and take the unsigned road some 50 m to the right (north). Follow this road and take your first left up the hill and then continue taking the uphill fork whenever the road divides. Four wheel drive vehicles and good pick-ups can negotiate this road as far as the hacienda about halfway up. The road actually continues up to the antennas, but the hacienda owner has closed the access road to private vehicles. Walkers will have no problem.

To reach Rucu Pichincha you take a distinct path which goes to the left of the motorcyclists' hill behind the car park. This path is easily followed for about 2 hours until it meets with another coming up from Cruz Loma. At this point you have two choices; either head right on a path along the bottom of the rocks to a sandy slope which leads to the summit (the easiest way) or head straight up the rocks which are marked with paint splashes or white arrows. This latter route is more direct although perhaps a little hair-raising for beginners. The summit will take a further 1½ hours from the trail junction. There is some rock climbing to be had on Rucu's summit pyramid if you are so inclined — experienced rock climbers will find their own route.

To make the return trip more interesting use another route. If you climbed up the rocks try descending down the sandy slope and follow the trail at the bottom of the rocks to the trail intersection; here take the wide and clear trail back to Cruz Loma. Soon you'll pass a white survey marker and about 1½ hours after leaving the summit you'll reach Cruz Loma. Occasional vehicles will visit it at weekends and you may be able to hitch a ride back to Quito, coming out at the south end of the city after a long and zigzagging ride. If you are walking however, the quickest route is straight down the hill to the city, following a faint path underneath the electric pylons from the TV and radio antenna. This will bring you out in the La Gasca area. There are other paths as well if you feel in an exploratory mood.

If you just want to visit Cruz Loma you must climb from La Gasca or from Av. 24 de Mayo — the latter is the less steep way but is not recommended. From La Gasca, continue up to the Occidental Highway heading south until you come to Las Tuneles, a network of tunnels and roads. Just past the tunnels look for a trail leading up into a eucalyptus forest. Carry a stick for a possible encounter with aggressive dogs on this lower section. Further up as you approach Cruz Loma the trail may disappear from time to time. Just continue heading up but keep left and out of the quebrada with dense vegetation. If you have access to a car, you can drive up to Cruz Loma by following the Occidental Highway through the tunnels to Av. Libertadores. Go right and continue up to near the end of this road where there is a military museum, Cima de La Libertad. About 100 m before the museum there's a dirt road turn-off that leads to Cruz Loma. From the museum it will take about 45 minutes by car to the top. There is no easy way to reach Cruz Loma from the Antenna hill except by going to the rocky foot of Rucu Pichincha as described.

NOTE: Hikers going up Rucu Pichincha have encountered a variety of problems over the last few years. Aggressive dogs in the inhabited areas at the base of the mountain below Cruz Loma have been responsible for numerous bites. Assaults along Av. 24 de Mayo have happened all too frequently, and a series of ongoing attacks (and in some cases, rape) in the area around Loma de las Antenas (Antenna Hill) are causes for concern. Be wary of dogs, avoid altogether the walk up Av. 24 de Mayo, and enquire as to the safety of climbing up to the antennas before you decide to go. Contact the South American Explorers Club for the latest information.

CLIMBING GUAGUA PICHINCHA

This is a 2 day trip so come prepared to camp out. Carry water as it is not available higher up. The usual route to Guagua is via Rucu Pichincha. From behind the summit continue on a distinct path marked with paint splashes. This becomes less distinct after a while but Guagua is the only big mountain a little south of west so you can't miss it. If you don't want to follow those white arrows painted on rocks, the summit via the easier sandy slopes takes about 1½ hours to reach from the trail junction. The rock route is more direct although perhaps a little hair-raising for beginners. The rock is solid because this is a popular route and gets many day ascents from Quito, so all the loose rock gets tossed off. The first few metres onto the rocky ridge are the most difficult. Once you're on the ridge you'll find that the rock has been worn a lighter colour along the main ascent route. Almost an hour into the climb there's a narrow section which you have to climb down to. It's only a metre wide and rather exposed so beginners may want a short rope here, though experienced climbers won't have any difficulty. From here it's about 20 minutes to the top.

An alternative and shorter route to Guagua, avoiding Rucu completely, is via the village of Lloa. Take a No. 8 Tola-Pintado bus along Av. Vencedores de Pichincha (formerly Av. Bahia de Caraquez) to the end of the line at Cuartel Mariscal Sucre. Just before the end of the line take a road to the right up the hill on Av. Chilibulo and follow this as it winds through the suburb of Marcopamba, past pine plantations to a pass 6 km away, which is marked by a statue of the Virgin. From the pass a winding road drops into the valley and after 4 km reaches the agricultural village of Lloa. You can walk this route or take one of the occasional buses from Av. Chilibulo in Quito or hitch-hike. From the village follow the road until you come to the end of the cultivated fields on your left, about 1½ to 2 hours walking. Here you'll see a house on the left and a Guagua Refuge sign on the road, and an obvious dirt trail heading left. Follow this as it meanders up through the *páramo*, eventually reaching the refuge just 15 minutes below the crater rim. The facilities are minimal but it has bunks and foam mattresses, and you can use the stove if the caretaker is there. If staying overnight, bring a sleeping bag and a stove, just in case. From Lloa, it's about 5 to 6 hours to the refugio on foot. By car, you can get up to just below the refugio, but there are many rough sections along the road, and a four wheel drive vehicle is essential in all but the driest of seasons. The dirt track turns into a mud wallow after a bit of rain. If you have any doubts about the strength of your car engine, I suggest you burn high octane (92) for the trip up to the refuge. It can really make a difference in the power output — and you'll need all you can get! From the refuge, follow the trail up to the crater rim and then follow the rim path right to the summit. The return trip from Lloa can be done in one very long day.

More interesting, however, than climbing to the summit of Guagua, is the descent to the crater floor. If you have your own transportation to the refuge, this trip can be done in one day. Otherwise, you'll need to bring camping gear for a stay at the refuge, or even better, camping in the crater.

Follow the path up to the rim from the refuge and pick up the trail that begins to drop on the other side. The path is very steep in places and you'll want sturdy hiking boots for traction in the loose volcanic sand and manoeuvring over the rough lava rocks. The descent is often shrouded in mist, but rock cairns and wands mark the well-worn path. The smell of sulphur grows stronger as you descend, but you'll eventually get accustomed to it. For both the descent and ascent, follow the path carefully. An occasional false trail could likely end you up at one of the many precipitous cliff edges.

The trail winds down and angles to the right. After about 2 hours it flattens out as it reaches the crater floor and crosses a rock-strewn gully with a small fresh-water stream running through it. This is the only fresh water source in this part of the crater but it often dries up in June through August. A small camping area is found among clumps of *ichu* grass just to the right of this rock gully. There is also camping possible about 5 minutes farther down on the trail near some small fumaroles. Friends claim that dinner can be cooked using these natural 'stoves' but we didn't give it a try.

The crater is an immense area, about 1½ km in diameter and 700 m deep, resembling a strange looking valley. From the campsite you can see and hear a huge geyser spouting steam halfway across the crater floor. Following the trail down toward the centre, you'll see on the right the huge central cone, 400 m high, which produces the greatest amount of volcanic activity. Hills of lava scree and volcanic rock at its base are ripe for lots of exploring in what feels like the moon.

For the highlight of the entire excursion, head cross-country for the prominent central cone and pick up the trail that follows around its base to the left. This trail descends out of the crater floor and winds through dense tropical vegetation caused by the heat of the thermal water stream running along on the left. At the bottom of the trail, about 45 minutes later, you'll discover natural thermal pools that provide a steaming hot bath for the weary hiker. A little exploring will reward you with several 'hot tub'-like pools, blocked off with rocks by former visitors. The return to camp takes about an hour, and then it's another 2 hours back up to the crater rim.

There is also an approach to the summit of Guagua from the north, although I haven't met anyone who has done it. Head to the village of Nono (see *Nono Hikes* in Chapter 4) and then head south on a jeep track to

Hacienda San Luis and continue south on paths and then cross-country to the Pichinchas.

From the refuge you could return to Quito via Rucu Pichincha in one long day. It's a beautiful hike because the west side of Rucu has a large variety of flowering plants. From the hut traverse north then east. Follow the ridge past Padre Encantado and then climb up a basin that looks steep and long with a lot of loose rock. It's much easier than it looks and takes about half an hour to climb. Rucu is just beyond. If you look carefully you'll be able to follow a faint path for most of the way.

For rock-starved climbers, the area behind the refuge is loaded with possibilities. A huge slab at the base of a rock face has several lines of solid climbing that can be top-roped, and the face itself may have potential though I haven't tried it out.

Whymper's second camp on Pichincha.

CERRO ATACAZO (4457 m)

Atacazo is an ancient and eroded volcano located about 20 km southwest of Quito. With a four wheel drive vehicle you can drive to within an hour of the summit; if relying on public transport this is a two day trip. It is not a difficult climb and, unusual in Ecuador, the rocky summit is not composed of rotten and dangerous rocks but is quite solid. Because transport is somewhat of a hassle, this area is rarely visited, but worth the effort to get there. The summit views are spectacular — of Quito and the Pichinchas to the northeast, and the countryside dropping down to the lowlands to the west. The IGM 1:50,000 Amaguaña map covers this area.

Begin by taking a bus to Chillogallo from Plaza La Marin in Quito's old town, and walking 3 km west on the old Santo Domingo road (it's the only westbound highway) to the village plaza in La Libertad. Alternatively the more expensive and faster microbus will take you from Plaza La Marin all the way to La Libertad. From here you will find occasional trucks (or you can walk or hitch-hike) as far as San Juan, a tiny village about 10 km to the west. A beautiful mountain road climbs and hairpins steeply from La Libertad at 3000 m to San Juan, at about 3450 m. Continuing westward from San Juan the old highway now drops down giving fascinating opportunities to observe the ecological changes from 3450 m to sea level and providing excellent birding. To climb Atacazo, however, you leave San Juan on a southbound jeep road heading towards some TV and radio antennas. Anyone in the village will point out the road; it reaches the antennas in 10 to 12 km, but there is almost no traffic. If you need drinking water you'll pass near the last streams about 2 to 3 km before the end of the road.

From the antennas head south up gently sloping, grassy *páramo* (the "bit of shaved lawn" of Michaux's poem) to an obvious notch in the crater rim. It is an easy walk which will take a little over an hour. From here the highest point is to your left: a gentle scramble over grass and rocks. Below you is the delicately coloured crater, wide open to the west, and filled with pastel shades of sand and lava and brighter splashes of vegetation. It is not difficult to scramble down and explore "These dwarf plant Japanese gardens".

The descent can be made in different ways. The shortest is to head almost due east across the *páramo* for about 7 km until you reach the Estación Experimental Santa Catalina which lies roughly a kilometre west of the Pan American Highway. (This is also a common ascent route.) A more interesting descent is to head south on the crater rim for about a kilometre beyond the highest point, then head southeast along an obvious ridge to a small hill (4166 m) about a kilometre away; from here head south southwest along another ridge to a long flattish hill (Cerro El Pilcacho, 4082 m) almost 2 km away. A short distance before you reach the top of El Pilcacho

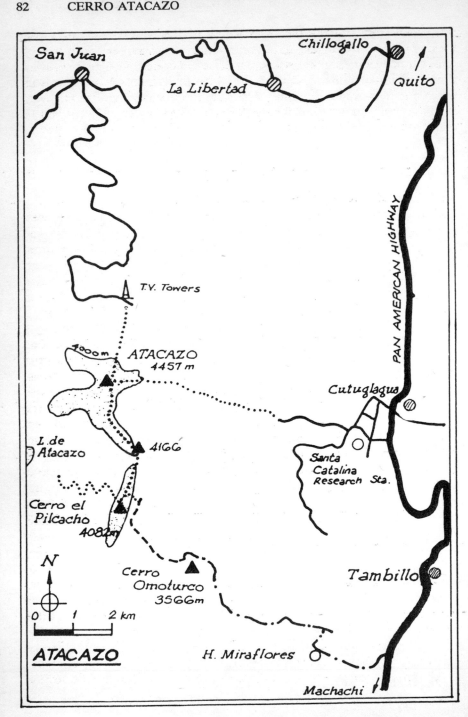

San Juan

Chillogallo

La Libertad

Quito

PAN AMERICAN HIGHWAY

T.V. Towers

4000m

ATACAZO
4457 m

Cutuglagua

L. de
Atacazo

4166

Santa
Catalina
Research Sta.

Cerro el
Pilcacho
4082m

N

Cerro
Omoturco
3566m

Tambillo

0   1   2 km

ATACAZO

H. Miraflores

Machachi

you'll find a trail crossing the ridge. Westward, it winds through interesting looking *páramo* to Laguna de Atacazo some 3 km away; eastward it soon joins a trail heading southeast towards Cerro Omoturco, 3566 m, 2 km away. From Omoturco a dirt road winds 7 to 8 km to Hacienda Miraflores from which a road continues a further 2 to 3 km to the Pan American Highway. If you go north along the Highway for about 3 km to Tambillo, it will be easier to catch buses to Quito.

EL CORAZÓN (4788 m)

Corazón is an ancient, eroded, and extinct volcano about 40 km southwest of Quito. The first recorded ascent was in 1738 by La Condamine and Bouguer and this easy peak has been climbed many times since. Preconquest ruins have been reported on the northeast slopes, but they are very overgrown and have yet to be investigated. The name Corazón means 'heart' and is said to refer to two gullies on the northwest slopes which, when seen from a distance, appear to join together roughly in the shape of a heart.

To get there take a bus from Villa Flora in Quito to Machachi, then walk south on the Pan American Highway for 2 km until you see a signed road on the right hand side leading to Aloasí, or take a Latacunga bus from kQuito's Terminal Terrestre and have the driver drop you at the Aloasí entrance. Go through Aloasí on a good cobbled road as far as the railway station, 3 km from the Pan American Highway. About 100 m past the station, take the dirt road going left. If travelling by car, this road will get you within 2 hours of the summit. It winds its way through *páramo*, passing directly beneath a neatly squared forest of pine trees. Whether driving or hiking, this forest is an excellent landmark. A four wheel drive vehicle is unnecessary unless the track is muddy. On foot, you'll have to keep pretty much to the road until past the pine forest. Fenced off, cultivated fields make heading cross-country fairly difficult lower down. Look for trails leading west up across the páramo, otherwise it's probably easier to keep to the switchbacking road as tramping through the dense *ichu* grass is tiring and time-consuming. Near the end of the road, beneath the foothills of Corazón, you will come across various irrigation canals running in several directions. There is one which runs near the road, leading just off to the right and well below the rocky summit. Follow alongside this canal until it runs out, then angle up bearing slightly left for the summit approach. The route goes fairly straight ahead to a rocky area at the saddle just below the summit. Aim left (south) scrambling up through a rock band and continue to the top. An occasional rock cairn and a few rocks painted with arrows mark the way, but these are not obvious. Allow about 5 to 7 hours of steady hiking to reach the summit.

There is another route from the north. About 5 km before Machachi there is a right turn onto a major road leading to Santo Domingo and the coast. Follow this road about 3 km to Alóag and at the railway station just beyond Alóag take a left fork down an old dirt road. Between 11 and 12 km down this road you'll find the Hacienda La Granja where it is possible to hire mules. From here head south across the *páramo* about 6 km to the peak, reaching the saddle on the north side as described in the first route. *Note: the Corazon map is on page 86.*

Machachi and Corazón.

The Ilinizas

INTRODUCTION   These are two peaks located about 55 km south southwest of Quito. Iliniza Sur (5263 m) has the distinction of being the sixth highest mountain in the country whilst Iliniza Norte (5126 m) is the eighth highest. Prehistorically they were one volcano but today the two peaks are separated by a saddle and are about 1 km away from one another. Jean and Louis Carrel of Whymper's expedition logged the first ascent of Iliniza Sur in May 1880, but Whymper himself never reached the summit despite two attempts in February and June of the same year. The first ascent of Iliniza Norte was interesting in that it was one of the few first ascents made by Ecuadorian climbers and the only Ecuadorian 'first' of one of the country's ten peaks of over 5000 m. Ecuador's Nicolás Martinéz accompanied by Alejandro Villavicencio reached the summit in March 1912.

There is a simple refuge known as Refugio Nuevos Horizontes at 4650 m just east of and below the saddle linking the two mountains. It can accommodate about two dozen persons but has no facilities. Water is obtained from the stream running a few metres away from the hut. The area is covered by the IGM 1:50,000 Machachi topographical map.

The twin peaks of the Ilinizas offer some of the more enjoyable climbing in Ecuador. For the hiker, Norte is a truly fun climb with some heart-stopping scrambles thrown in. For the experienced climber, Sur provides several interesting and demanding routes that serve to remind one just what climbing is all about.

ACCESS   About 40 km south of Quito and 8 km south of Machachi on the Pan American Highway there is an unsigned right turn for the small community of El Chaupi. The turn off is at a place known locally as Tarqui about 100 m before a bridge (not after the bridge as indicated on the IGM map). Buses bound for Latacunga pass this turn off, or you can take a bus to Machachi and walk or hitchhike. From the Pan American Highway to El Chaupi is about 7 km of cobbled road; there are occasional trucks acting as buses and a few private vehicles.

At El Chaupi turn right onto the road behind the church. The surface changes from cobbles to dirt. Walk or drive up this dirt road for about 3 km until you come to a white cement shrine which houses a white cross on the right — turn about 50 m beyond this cross, just before the main road begins a sharp left curve. This turn-off goes through fields, then crosses an avenue of pine trees where it forks (keep right), about 2 km from the main road. It then passes the Hacienda El Refugio, and after 3 km begins twisting and climbing past the Lomo Pilango. About 3 km of climbing brings one to a shrine. This point, approximately 16 km from the Pan American Highway, is a parking area and the drop-off point for hired transport. With a four wheel drive vehicle you can continue up the very badly gullied road for another 2½ km. The road then deteriorates into a footpath leading to a sandy ridge. A trodden path heads left up this ridge and a short way from the top veers right to the refuge. You cannot see the refuge until you are almost there. From the parking area, it's 3 to 4 hours to the refuge on foot and 2 to 3 hours from the higher, final drivable point; from El Chaupi to the refuge takes more than half a day.

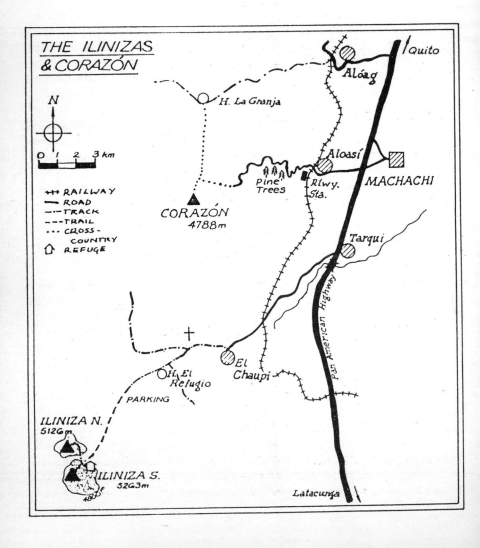

CLIMBING ILINIZA NORTE (5126 m)

Despite the glacier marked on IGM maps, Iliniza Norte is a rocky mountain with no permanent snow. It can easily be climbed in 2 hours from the refuge. Technical equipment is unnecessary.

From the refuge walk across the saddle between the two mountains and climb up the sandy slopes on the left flank of the southeast ridge of Norte. The ridge narrows about halfway up and crosses the 'Paso de Muerte' (Death Pass) which is far easier to cross than its name implies. The summit is a near vertical wall which is best avoided by skirting it to the right for 200 to 300 m and then climbing left to the top. The climb is easy except for the last few metres which are the usual rotten rock.

CLIMBING ILINIZA SUR (5263 m)

This relatively steep and crevassed mountain is one of the more difficult climbs in the country, and is not for beginners. There are two frequently-climbed routes to the summit. What was for years considered the normal route has become even more difficult, especially when there's a lack of snowfall. Some of the steeper sections can approach 80 degrees in certain seasons so front pointing is necessary. This is a tiring technique, particularly at over 5000 m, and should be learnt and practised at lower elevations if possible (in the Alps or the Rockies for example). Protection such as ice screws or snow stakes will be required by all except extremely experienced and highly confident climbers. Rockfall can be a hazard and a helmet is suggested. Avalanches occur often enough to pose a danger and a detailed route description is difficult due to constantly changing conditions.

THE DIRECT ROUTE The difficult direct route is via the north face and begins from the Nuevos Horizontes hut then heads west into the saddle between the north and south mountains. From the saddle ascend the steep moraine northwest to get onto the glacier, and then climb up a gently sloping rock-strewn snow-field. After gaining the main glacier, you will be almost exactly below the direct route which begins as an increasingly steep snow gully between two large rock outcrops. Several crevasses may have to be negotiated (often you can climb around them) until you reach the east ridge. Here you go up and left heading for the top, bypassing a rocky outcrop known as 'el hongo' (the mushroom) before reaching the summit of Iliniza Sur. The descent is via the easier alternate route described below. In good conditions the round trip can be done in 6 hours, but a full day is not uncommon. You should plan a pre-dawn departure to minimize rockfall and avalanche danger caused by the melting of the snow in the midday sun.

ALTERNATE ROUTES This is an easier route to the summit, but still requires climbing experience and technical safety equipment. Follow the same route as the direct up to below the steep north face. Here, continue to traverse the glacier west (right) to the next snow ramp just beyond a low rock band. Take some caution here as rockfall is frequent. Ascend the slope as it winds northwest then more or less west, traversing the mountain. This area is quite heavily crevassed, making the route extremely interesting and calling for caution at the same time. After ascending and traversing for a while, you'll come to a flat area where the logical route seems to be straight ahead and up. This is the wrong route and leads to a huge crevasse which is very difficult to cross. Instead head up the steep snow ramp to the left (north) with a prominent rock face at the top left. Here go right and away from the rock up another small snow ramp which brings you into an open bowl area on the upper glacier. Traverse the side of the bowl to a short steep ice wall and climb up to flat area above. Here is where the Direct Route comes in from the right, both routes joining to traverse under 'el hongo'. One last steep ice wall is negotiated before following the summit ridge to the top. From the hut, it's about 4 to 5 hours to the summit.

A more difficult route is known as the east ridge or Celso Zuquillo route (after one of its first climbers). From the hut go left around the mountain for a few hundred metres and then climb up what is in fact the northeast ridge which has heavy rime build up. The most difficult route of all was done by the French and Ecuadorian climbers, Joseph Bergé and Marco Cruz, in October 1973 and goes up the south ridge. A bivouac and highly technical ice climbing are required. The route was repeated by Martin Slater, Travis White and Peter Hall in March 1974 and again by George Gibson and Allan Miller in June 1977.

A new route on the southwest face was climbed by Tom Hunt and Jorge and Delia Montpoli in September 1982. This route is approached from the 3600 m Loma de Huinza pass on the Sigchos road, south of the mountain. Head for the base of the westernmost glacier located just north of the prominent, crumbling rock towers that divide the south and west sides of the mountain (8 hours). Camp here. Climb the left side of the heavily crevassed glacier to a 40 degree snow ramp which bears further left and above the first rock walls. Ascend a steep couloir to the right (75 degrees, 50 m) and at the top angle right along a mild ridge to a 5 m ice wall. Ascend the final 100 m to the summit via the southwest knife ridge. Total climbing time from camp was 5 hours for 900 m of ascent.

SIGCHOS TO LA UNIÓN DE TOACHI

INTRODUCTION   This 4 to 5 day, sierra to lowlands hike traverses a number of vegetation zones as it descends 1800 m through the Toachi River valley. Small pools and streams offer numerous opportunities for swimming and an incredible variety of orchids and birdlife are present in this area. Rain is always possible and the trail is sure to be muddy in parts. An established trail begins in Sigchos and follows the valley through small settlements and logging operations to La Unión de Toachi. The IGM 1:50,000 maps which cover this trek are Sigchos, San Roque, Manuel Cornejo Astorga and Alluriquín.

ACCESS   The easiest way to get to Sigchos is to take a bus from Quito to Latacunga and then catch a Transportes Reina de Sigchos bus leaving for Sigchos at least once a day. From Quito there is only one direct bus which departs Sunday mornings. Sigchos is not far from Latacunga, but it's a long ride. This is not entirely disagreeable since the scenery along the way is beautiful. Once in Sigchos, there is one small residencia if you decide to stay overnight and get an early start the next morning.

HIKING DIRECTIONS   The hike begins from the north of town following the dirt road that runs along the east side of the church. As the last of the straggling village is left behind, the road turns left (west) alongside a deep wooded valley. Stay on the dirt road as it crosses the river valley and climbs out to the northwest. At the pass where the track levels a wide open pasture lies ahead and the road bears off to the left. Take the foot trail which angles left through the pasture and continues straight down the ridge. The trail is clear for a couple of hours until it comes down into a flat area where you'll see a farmhouse. Just before the house a small trail leads off to the right. Follow this down as it crosses several pastures. Along the way you'll pass a small deserted wooden house which could be used for shelter. The trail weaves back and forth as it continues down the slope passing a few small farms and several pleasant springs. The final part of the descent, as the track passes two thatched adobe houses, is a little difficult. The trail heads to the right and leaves you with an extremely steep (100 m) descent through a pasture, ending up at a junction with another trail coming from Cunuyacu to the east.

At the trail junction are two waterfalls known as Dos Chorros and from here it's about a half hour walk to the valley floor. After the trail crosses the first of many log bridges it begins to follow alongside the west bank of the Toachi River. Shortly you'll come to a field on the right which is good for camping and a house nearby has a water source. From Sigchos to the campsite it can take about 6 or 7 hours if you don't spend too much time

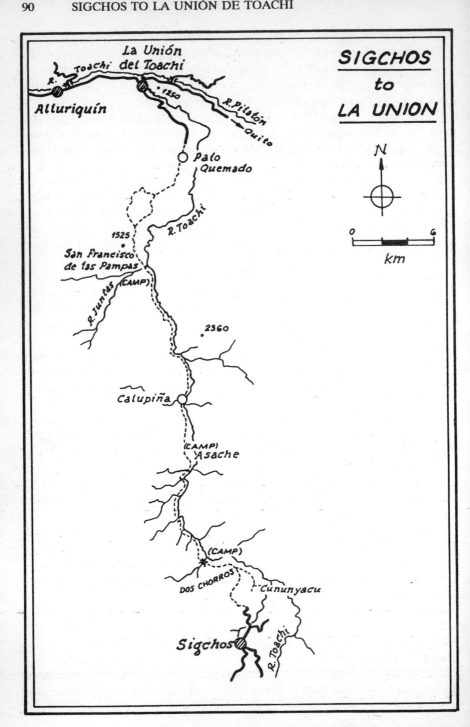

marvelling at the wonderful variety of orchids and the fantastic views.

The second day's walk is along a scenic trail following the Toachi river. You'll cross several small tributaries excellent for bathing. The birdlife is abundant. The village of Asache, 5 to 6 hours down the trail, is a delightful place to stop for the night. The people are friendly and the place has a nice feel to it. It may be possible to sleep in the community house. Across the river are the Montes de Santo Cristo, an area of steep forested mountains. A new logging road is being put in from the east and the villagers expect to have electricity soon.

The third day continues alongside the river, crossing numerous tributaries with many small cascades and waterfalls. Stopping for a swim may be hard to resist. Occasionally you'll see a single wire cable stretched above the wide Toachi. Believe it or not, this is what the locals use to get across to the other side. Tying a simple sling around the cable, they then slip their upper bodies through the loop and cross hand over hand to the other side. This technique is not recommended for the uninitiated!

There are several good places to camp along the way and, unless you're really moving fast, it's not feasible to hike all the way to Las Pampas in one day. You'll occasionally pass deserted buildings that can be used instead of setting up a tent.

About 1 to 2 hours before reaching the village of Las Pampas the trail crosses the river junction of the Toachi and the Juntas. Nearby an old stone bridge spans the river. You'll probably want to set up camp before crossing the junction.

On the other side of the stone bridge the trail makes a steep, short climb and then drops down into a small valley before beginning the real (and steep) ascent up to Las Pampas. It's a tough trail especially in the rainy season when it becomes pure mud.

Las Pampas has one basic residencia on the plaza and several places to eat. There is a road head, but the only regular transport is a 7.00 a.m. milk truck to La Unión de Toachi which takes about 2 hours.

On foot, it's about 6 hours of easy walking to La Unión along a dirt road. The road leaves the north side of town, passes through the ridgetop village of Galápagos and continues on to Palo Quemado, an old mining town. Though the gold mine is now shut down, the village maintains its huge church and the look of prosperity.

From Palo Quemado the road continues north past several tiny settlements and eventually drops back down into the Toachi valley. It's unlikely that you'll see any vehicles until the last few kilometres before La Unión. Once in the town of La Unión de Toachi frequent eastbound buses are easily flagged down for the return to Quito. If you'd like to soothe away the weariness you can take a bus to the town of Alluriquín, about 5 km west, and stay overnight at Hotel Florida has a sauna and turkish bath.

Hiking and climbing in the Chimborazo-Carihuairazo area

"Señor, we understand perfectly, that in an affair like yours, it is necessary to dissemble — a little; and you, doubtless, do quite right to say you intend to ascend Chimborazo — a thing that everyone knows is perfectly impossible. We know very well what is your object! You wish to discover the TREASURES which are buried in Chimborazo... "

Edward Whymper, 1892.

INTRODUCTION   Chimborazo is located 150 km south southwest of Quito. Some 10 km northeast of it lies its sister volcano Carihuairazo. Both are ancient and extinct volcanoes. Carihuairazo's rather jagged shape indicates a younger mountain whilst the rounded bulk of Chimborazo testifies to its great age. It is an extremely massive mountain which volcanologists claim is composed of the remnants of two volcanoes.

Chimborazo is, at 6310 m, the highest mountain in the country and for many years was thought to be the highest in the world. It still retains the distinction of being the point on the earth's surface which is farthest from its centre; this is due to the earth's equatorial bulge. It is higher than any mountain in the Americas north of it: McKinley is about 75 m lower. Chimborazo's reputation as such a high mountain led to many attempts on the summit during the seventeenth and eighteenth centuries before it was climbed by Whymper and the Carrels in 1880. Carihuairazo is also an impressively high peak; at 5020 m it ranks ninth in height in Ecuador and was conquered, also in 1880, by the Whymper expedition with the Ecuadorians David Beltrán and Francisco Campaña.

Both mountains are snow capped and snow and ice climbing equipment and technique are required for their ascents. The normal routes are relatively straightforward. For the non-climber, an excellent hike is from the Pan American Highway to the Ambato-Guaranda road. This crosses the pass between the two mountains with beautiful views of these and other major peaks. For the mountaineer, combining the hike with ascents of both peaks provides an exceptional experience.

MAPS   Two 1:50,000 topographical maps from the IGM cover the area: the Quero and Chimborazo sheets. The glaciers on the mountains are inaccurately represented; they have greatly receded in recent years and on Carihuairazo occupy barely half of the area assigned to them on the maps. Thus part of the hike appears to cross glaciers but this is not so. Most of

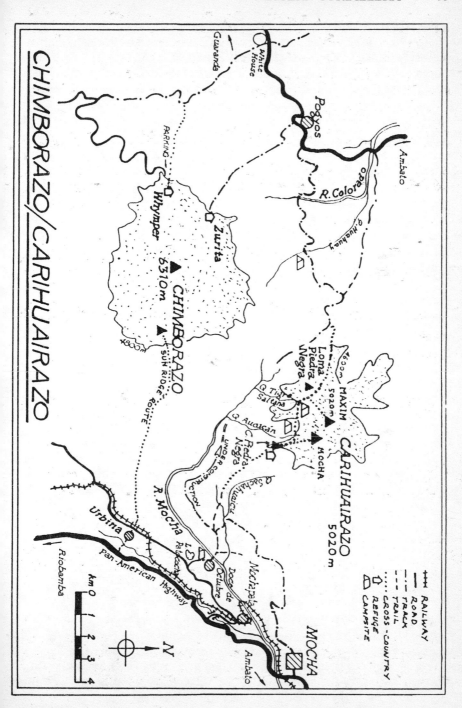

DIRECTIONS FOR HIKERS   From Quito's Terminal Terrestre take a Riobamba bus along the Pan American Highway. About half-way between Ambato and Riobamba you will see a sign on your right for Mocha. Stay on the bus for a further 5 to 6 km as the road climbs steeply until a turn off to Mochapata. There is no sign; the right hand turn off is a steeply descending cobbled road which soon crosses the Quebrada Yanayacu via a stone bridge which is plainly visible from the highway. Allow about 3 hours on the bus from Quito.

Walk down the cobbled road, cross the stone bridge, and look for trails climbing the small hill in front of you. Take one of these over the hill (avoiding a detour through Mochapata), cross a railway track, and you will soon come to a rough road where you turn left. In clear weather Chimborazo's steep and rugged southeastern flanks are visible to the west; this side provides the most difficult ascent routes and the view is splendid. Carihuairazo is seen to the northwest but from this angle the major glaciers are not properly appreciated.

Walk about 3 km along the road until you come to a right hand turn onto a dirt road passing the swampy Laguna Patococha and continuing about a kilometre to the unsigned settlement of Doce de Octubre at about 3560 m and not marked on the IGM map. You may be allowed to sleep in the village hall (four bare walls, no facilities). Alternatively continue about a kilometre along the steeply descending dirt road to the banks of the Río Mocha where you can camp. If you have a heavy load of gear, you can rent mules in Doce de Octubre (though this may take 2 or 3 days to arrange) to take you to the hut at the base of Carihuairazo. A four wheel drive vehicle will reach the settlement after which you must rely on mules or backpacking.

From the village to the refuge on Carihuairazo (at about 4300 m) takes 5 to 8 hours with a pack. Cross the Río Mocha and follow the deteriorating track up towards a flat area known as Mauca Corral. Turn left off the track and head north and then west around the northwest end of Loma Tulutuz which is the large flat-topped hill in front of you after you have crossed the river. After about a kilometre of cross-country hiking you will run into a footpath around the back of Loma Tulutuz. Follow this for another kilometre until you can see two sharp ridges heading northwest towards Carihuairazo. They are separated by a small river, the Quebrada Sachahuaicu. Cross a stream and climb the left hand ridge (Filo de Sachahuaicu) and follow cow paths along the gently rising ridge top which heads west and then curves northwest toward Cerro Piedra Negra (c. 4480 m) which is a southern spur of Carihuairazo and about 4 km away. Keep your eyes peeled for the small hut about ½ km to the east of Cerro Piedra Negra and by the right flank of a small conical hill. When you seem to be heading away from the hut, leave the ridge and go north cross-country towards it. There are no facilities; it is a dilapidated wooden structure which could sleep eight people at a squeeze. There are a few pools of brown water nearby which is all right to drink after boiling or sterilizing.

The hut is used as a base to climb the Mocha peak of Carihuairazo (see *Climbing Carihuairazo*). From the hut it is an easy scramble to the top of Cerro Piedra Negra from which there are views of Ambato as well as four major peaks: Carihuairazo to the north, Chimborazo to the southwest, Tungurahua to the east, and El Altar to the south-east. Accurate information on this hut is hard to come by. Several local climbers told me that it didn't exist and others said that they had looked for it but couldn't find it. Don't be put off by such reports — it's there!

From the hut the hiker continues roughly westwards along the south flanks of Carihuairazo. First climb onto the ridge joining Cerro Piedra Negra with Carihuairazo and continue north along it for about a kilometre until you are near the head of the Aucacán river valley on your left. Then drop down from the ridge, cross the Quebrada Aucacán high up by the central glacier of Carihuairazo, and scramble up the opposite side of the Aucacán valley to the top of the ridge. It's easier than it looks, especially if you follow the diagonal slash of vegetation which is clearly visible on the far side. At the top are flat camping areas with melt water running off nearby. Other good campsites are found near lakes at the head of the Quebrada Tigre Saltana valley, about ½ an hour roughly west from the ridge. Both sites are often used as base camps for the ascent of Carihuairazo's main (Maxim) peak (see *Climbing Carihuairazo*). Allow a half day to reach this area from the hut. This is such a pretty area that it is worth camping early and exploring. A good side trip is to the western flanks of Carihuairazo where many interesting high Andean lakes, streams, and bogs can be investigated.

The hike continues roughly north over a pass between Carihuairazo and Loma Piedra Negra (not to be confused with Cerro Piedra Negra), a pyramidal peak west of Carihuairazo. There is a trail around the eastern and northern flanks of Loma Piedra Negra. It is rather indistinct in places but frequent cairns are an aid. Once you have rounded Loma Piedra Negra the trail fades and you strike west down a gently sloping plain for about 3 km until you come to a road. This is quite accurately marked on the IGM map, but not marked is the new Ambato-Guaranda road which crosses this track after about 6 km at a small community called Yacupatrina. Here you can flag down a bus to take you into Ambato (turn right) or Guaranda (turn left). For ascents of Chimborazo it is about 6 km to the turn off for the Whymper refuge in the direction of Guaranda.

CLIMBING CARIHUAIRAZO

There are two main peaks, Maxim in the centre and Mocha in the southeast. The former is the highest at 5020 m (IGM figures) although some authorities put Maxim at 5116 m and Mocha at 5030 m. Whatever the correct altitude, both peaks are snow covered and require snow and ice climbing experience, though not of a particularly high technical standard.

The hut at 4300 m (described earlier) on the southeastern slopes of the mountain is used by climbers of the Mocha peak. The Maxim peak requires a tented base camp (the best area is the lakes at the head of Quebrada Tigre Saltana) and for a shorter approach than the one described in the hiking directions start from the Ambato-Guaranda road. About an hour out of Ambato you'll see a large sign on the left side of the road which says Río Blanco. A short ways down the road there are a group of buildings and a school 'Colegio Manuela Cañzares' on the right. Have the driver let you off here. Follow the road going left from the community and this will take you up toward Laguna Negra (about 3 to 4 hours) and beyond to Quebrada Tigre Saltana. A drawback is that this route passes through a vicuña reserve and technically you should have permission from the MAG office in Cuenca. Some groups get stopped, others go through without seeing anyone. What seems to be the easiest solution is to 'pay' (about US$1) on the spot for permission to enter if you're stopped.

Camping near Laguna Negra is quite beautiful but you can't leave your belongings unattended. Too many locals happen by to see what's available. Higher up, the lakes camp in Quebrada Tigre Saltana is more secure and reduces climbing time by about 2 hours, yet it's risky leaving anything out and unattended anywhere in the area. It's easy enough to hide your things in the brush near the lakes while you climb.

Maxim Peak is most easily climbed by the Direct Route. From the lakes campsite go right onto a ridge and follow this up and then left around a huge rocky outcrop. Drop down from the ridge left and follow the trail leading up to the glacier. Once on the snow an obvious line leads to the right for the summit ridge. Heading up and left along the ridge will bring you to the summit shortly. There are very few crevasses. The top few metres are rocky and there is some danger from rockfall. Allow 2 to 3 hours for the ascent.

The Variant of the Direct Route can be climbed by heading straight up the slope in front of of the base camp and passing to one's right the huge rock outcrop mentioned in the Direct Route description. The North Cornice Route begins below the rock outcrop and heads left over a ridge towards the left hand horizon, then climbs over a rock band and heads for the summit.

The Mocha Glacier route is steeper and provides an interesting route-finding problem; it can be climbed directly from the Carihuairazo hut in 4 to 6 hours. A pleasant alternative is to place a high camp on the upper slopes below the glacier.

From the hut climb up onto the ridge joining Cerro Piedra Negra with Cariñuairazo and follow the ridge for about a kilometre. Flat spaces are found at the end of the ridge for a high camp. There is no standard route because the glacier is constantly changing. I climbed up scree along the left hand side of the the lower slope, then climbed onto the glacier above the serac field at its tongue and skirted the large ice fall in the centre of the glacier (but beware of rock fall from the cliffs bordering the ice). I then picked my way through, around, and over several crevasses until I reached the top of the glacier. The summit is to the right and is composed of rather rotten rock. The glacier is small and not especially difficult, but a lot of fun is had finding your way.

CLIMBING CHIMBORAZO

There are five summits: the Whymper (or Ecuador) summit at 6310 m, the Veintimilla summit at 6267 m, the North summit at about 6200 m, the Central (or Polytechnic) summit around 6000 m, and the Eastern (or Nicolás Martinéz) summit of approximately 5500 m. The last, although the lowest, is the most difficult. The routes to the highest summit will be discussed more thoroughly.

ACCESS The best way to reach the mountain is by bus from Ambato to Guaranda. Sit on the left hand side of the bus for the best views. About 56 km from Ambato you will come to a dirt road on your left leading to the Whymper refuge. This road is marked by a deserted white house (often painted with colourful political slogans) of cement blocks on the left hand side, immediately beyond the junction. It is the only house on the left hand side for many kilometres. From the junction walk southeast on the dirt road for 3 to 4 km until you come to a hairpin bend. Here you can turn left up a small gully and climb due east for a further 3 to 4 km until you see the parking area and lower refuge below the larger Whymper refuge. (The lower refuge has some facilities, but most parties stay at the Whymper refuge some 200 m above and a half an hour away.) Allow 3 to 6 hours from the junction to the car park at the lower refuge (the high altitude slows you down). If you don't want to go cross-country you can follow the road around to the parking area but this is 10 to 12 km. If you'd rather hire transport, a taxi can be hired in Ambato at the terminal terrestre for about US$15-20 or the equivalent in sucres. Better still is to go by taxi from Riobamba, especially if you plan to stay overnight before going to the refuge the following day. You ought to be able to get a taxi for US$15 or less, and the road up to the refuge via the village of San Juan is straightforward. Riobamba has a better variety of accommodation and restaurants, and a lovely market on Saturdays.

At the parking area and lower refuge, a narrow trail takes off from left of the refuge for the half hour climb up to the Whymper hut. The refuge is well appointed with bunk beds and foam mattresses for about four dozen mountaineers (use your own sleeping bag), toilets, cold water, a kitchen with utensils and a propane gas stove (though this has been known to run out of gas during and after a busy weekend), a small supply of basic foods for sale, a fireplace, and a huge visitor's book with which to while away high altitude storms. There is a hut guardian who will keep an eye on your belongings when you climb; he will also charge you a fee of US$6 per day to use the hut.

THE WHYMPER ROUTE   Head right from the refuge up scree slopes to the prominent rock spires known as Whymper's Needle. Follow the obvious ridge up from the needle to a rock band about 30 m high. Several snow/ice gullies offer access through the rock band. The easiest route will vary from year to year, so it's best to check with the refuge guardian for the latest information. The angle of steepness will vary widely depending on the amount of recent snowfall (or lack of it). It can range from 40 degrees of solid snow to 70 degrees of bad ice. Front pointing is almost always necessary in some parts. Above the rock is a fairly steep snow-field which is best climbed by zigzagging. Towards the top of this snow-field there is another large rock band to your right, but the route traverses under seracs to the left hand horizon. The top of the snow-field and the traverse are usually marked with flags and footprints. There is objective danger from ice fall from the seracs above the traverse. In addition, the traverse itself can be somewhat hazardous, especially during the descent when climbing parties are tired. (By mid-morning the ice/snow gets slick and balls up under crampons and an unprotected fall would be most likely fatal. Stay roped up for the descent.) At the end of the traverse the route heads directly up toward the summit, again usually marked by flags and footprints. There are several small crevasses here. You reach the Veintimilla peak from where it is nearly a kilometre east over a gentle snow basin to the main summit. Late in the day this snow basin is filled with notoriously soft snow and at this altitude it takes great energy to wade through thigh deep snow.

Therefore it is advisable to start as early as possible (midnight) so that the final slog to the summit is easier. Some climbers have spent the night near Veintimilla summit and finished the climb the next day — this is an adventure for experienced, acclimatized, and well equipped climbers. 8 to 10 hours are normally needed for the ascent (although I know of one party which took 20 hours!). Allow 3 to 4 hours for the descent. An alternative route up to the summit climbs the steep snow/ice-field that ascends directly up from the start of the serac-hanging traverse. This, however, is for the experienced only, requiring the use of two ice tools on a slope which often has bad ice that approaches 70 degrees.

Many climbers choose to descend via the Direct Route, as this is faster and avoids the danger of the slippery traverse and falling seracs. The problem lies in descending an unknown route. If visibility is minimal, it could be easy to loose the way.

Experienced climbers can reach the top with just ice axe, crampons, and rope. Less experienced climbers may want the security of a second tool (ice hammer) for the steeper sections (the icy gully through the first rock band) and some ice screws, snow stakes, and deadmen for protection.

THE DIRECT ROUTE   This route is being used more frequently as the normal ascent to the summit. Its steepness is more continuous than the Whymper route, but offers a more direct line to the summit and avoids the serac danger. From the hut, follow the path which leads to the prominent scree slope to the left of the Thielmann glacier. Climb up the scree to the huge horizontal snow ramp just below a prominent rock outcrop. Follow this ramp right up to the main glacier then angle left up a steep snow-field. This lower area tends to be heavily crevassed. As you ascend you'll eventually begin to head northwest (right) toward the Veintimilla summit. Below this lower summit the route joins up with the Whymper route as it passes to the left of the traverse area. Up to here, it's about a 6 to 8 hour climb, with another 2 hours to the main summit. The descent takes another 3 to 4 hours. The route should be indicated with wands during the ascent, and it's not a bad idea to mark the path up the scree to the snow ramp in advance during daylight hours. It's surprisingly difficult to find the track up through the scree in the middle of the night.

THE OLD ROUTE   The old route begins at the village of Pogyos (also spelt Poggios or Pogyo) which is a tiny group of buildings on a bend of the road about 50 km south of Ambato on the old road to Guaranda. About 1 and 4 km before Pogyos are two roads to the left which may help you find it; the bus driver sometimes knows it.

Pogyos is the last place on the route where you can find water, but you'll probably want to sterilize it. Mules can be hired inexpensively to carry water and your gear up to the remains of the Fabián Zurita refuge at 4900 m — about 900 m above Pogyos. To get to the refuge cross the Ambato-Guaranda road and follow a dirt track that leaves the road a few hundred metres west of Pogyos and heads southeast across the sandy *páramo* to the hut which is 3 or 4 hours' walk away.

The hut was built in 1964 and is the oldest still in use in Ecuador. The orange octagonal shelter is now in a very dilapidated condition with a door that doesn't close properly, a leaky roof, and plenty of trash scattered around. Nevertheless it provides basic shelter for about ten people.

The climb from the hut to the summit is becoming more demanding as the glacier recedes. The route goes up the loose scree above the hut to the snowline and then continues on the snow to the base of a large, red, rock band known as the 'murallas rojas' (red walls). At the base of the red walls traverse to your right and continue upwards on snow along or a little beyond the right edge of the walls. Once beyond the walls head towards the peak above you, watching for crevasses which will be predominantly to your right. As you get high on the peak start heading left and to the side of it — this peak is the second or Veintimilla peak. The rounded summit is about a kilometre east of Veintimilla. The climb takes from 8 to 12 hours. A midnight departure is recommended as the summit snow plateau becomes very soft and slushy and avalanche danger on the slopes increases after midday.

When I tried this route I found that the glacier had receded so much that the scree slog up from the hut took several hours. A huge bergschrund had formed between the scree and the glacier and it was difficult to find an easy way onto the snow. Although this climb proved a failure, I found the new Whymper route fairly straightforward. With the good new Whymper hut now available I would suggest the new route as being the best — unless you actually like slogging up loose scree at 5000 m!

PIEDRA NEGRA AND SUN RIDGE ROUTES

These two routes on the eastern side of Chimborazo involve rock climbing and mixed rock/ice climbing, respectively. This area is rarely visited but is located in a spectacular setting formed by a natural amphitheatre of rock and snow. Even if the climbing proves to be too challenging, the area is excellent for exploring and hiking.

ACCESS Transport along the Ambato-Riobamba road will pass the turn-off for the old URBINA train station about halfway between the two cities. From the main highway get off at the "entrada a Urbina" (there's no sign at this time but all drivers know it) and walk 3 km up the dirt road to a refuge which has been set up in the old train station. It has bunks and foam mattresses, gas stove, and a small store. A fee of US$6 per night is charged, but several local climbing clubs are trying to get the price lowered.

From the refuge, a trail leads directly up the *páramo* and begins a steep ascent to the terminal moraine at the foot of Chimborazo. At the top of the moraine, there is a small lake with a flat area for camping, about 4 to 5 hours from the refuge. This is a good base for climbing both Piedra Negra and/or the Sun Ridge route. Another option for camping, particularly if you're not planning to climb, is to continue along the moraine to the right for another 1½ hours where there are magnificent views of Carihuairazo and the surrounding area and plenty of water from streams.

CLIMBING PIEDRA NEGRA   This enjoyable climb is not to be confused with either Cerro Piedra Negra or Loma Piedra Negra, both of which are located across the valley on Carihuairazo. This route was first climbed in 1984 by the Polytechnic Climbing Club but has not been repeated with much frequency. An assortment of technical rock gear is necessary. From the moraine camp you will see the entire east side of Chimborazo clearly — an impressive view. To the northeast (right) is a large rock formation, Piedra Negra, with a long moraine leading directly up to its base, about 1 to 2 hours from camp. At the base, traverse right (northeast) to the obvious ridge and climb to the summit. The difficulty is rated about 5.5 based on the Yosemite decimal system and takes a maximum of 2 hours from the start of the traverse.

A more difficult option, again requiring technical rock gear and experience, is the route up the east wall of Piedra Negra.

This climb, first ascended by Hugo Torres and Francisco Espinosa, begins on the east face just past the obvious overhanging junction of the east and southeast faces. A few meters to the right is a smaller overhang (good to belay below this) with the climb starting in a crack next to it. The crack runs out quickly, and you'll continue up, face climbing between 2 large rocks to a small belay ledge. Because of the rarely-climbed condition of the route, pitons may be more useful for securing belay stances than chocks or nuts, but several well-placed small nuts may do.

The second pitch continues up the face to another, larger ledge. Just below this belay the rock turns a little ugly with downward-sloping holds. From this belay, the third pitch climbs a chimney to the ridge, about one rope length. At the ridge, the route goes left, in 4th class scrambling up and across some big loose rocks. The top is about a half hour to an hour away. There is no easy downclimb; you'll have to descend to the ridge and then rappel/abseil the rest of the way.

Above the second pitch, at the wide ledge, there are several alternatives for reaching the top. One is to go left at the chimney rather than climbing in it, and you'll find easy rock leading to the ridge.

SUN RIDGE ROUTE   This climb ascends to the Nicolás Martínez summit of Chimborazo and is considered by many climbers to be one of the most beautiful mixed rock/ice routes in all of Ecuador. It requires both rock and snow experience and equipment, along with regular camping gear. Carry an assortment of ice screws, stakes, and various sizes of rock protection. A bivouac will more than likely be necessary below the summit, so you'll need to come prepared for that as well. From the moraine camp, follow the same route up to Piedra Negra. Traverse left under the rock and head for the main snow ridge. Once on the glacier, traverse across the snow-field toward the immense rock face of the Chimborazo summits. Camp is set up on the glacier well below and in line with the start of the rock face. Allow about 3 to 5 hours of hiking from the moraine camp.

From the glacier camp, you will see a wide snow ramp to the left on the rock face which leads up into a couloir. Ascend about halfway to a logical point where you can begin a traverse left across the rocks. Be careful of loose rock in this section. The traverse continues across to an area of huge rock slabs/boulders stacked on top of each other. In spite of appearing ready to give way at any minute, this area is quite stable. Climb these slabs up and left to just below a ridgeline. Here the route begins another traverse across a mixture of steep snow and rock up and down across small ridges. (The feasibility of crossing this section depends on the season. If there has been little snow, you'll have to continue up to the main ridge to make the traverse, but this is more difficult.) The traverse continues left and flattens out at the top of a wide snow ramp. It should take about 5 to 7 hours from the camp to reach this point. Here you can make a choice. If the going has been difficult, or the group is moving too slowly, this ramp is an excellent escape route and easy descent back to the lower glacier and camp.

If continuing, traverse for a bit further to a snow-field which is the beginning of the upper glacier. Head left up the snow-field to a section of huge snow 'mushrooms' which begin the final approach to the summit. A bivouac is normally made just after gaining this part of the glacier. The snow and ice is steep, of poor quality, and some route finding is necessary to make your way up toward the summit. From the top of this snow-field you can look up left to pinpoint the final approach to the summit. It should take about 3 to 5 hours of climbing from the bivouac to reach the summit. The descent backtracks to the easy exit snow ramp for the fastest return to the lower glacier.

An easier alternative to this mixed route is to traverse from the snow camp below the rock face to the snow gully used for the descent in the above climb. Climb this to meet up with the other route, and continue up to the summit following the above description. From camp, this could take about 7 hours to the summit and another 3 for the descent.

OTHER ROUTES   Many new routes remain to be climbed on a mountain of this size. There are also routes which have had only one or two ascents. Among these are the following: the eastern summit via the Moreno glacier in the southeast, the main summit from the north, and the central peak via the Humboldt glacier in the south.

These routes are suggestions for highly advanced climbers only. Otherwise stay on the standard routes; if you need a guide see the appropriate section in Chapter 3.

Chimborazo can be and is climbed year round but June and July are considered the best months. August tends to be windy and September is not too bad, but October and November have long spells of bad weather. Late December and early January are good, but the rest of the year has predominantly bad weather, with April the worst month. A tent is only needed by hikers doing the full hiking route described.

Las Cajas National Recreation Area

At the southern end of the Western Cordillera is found an enchantingly beautiful area of *páramo* and cloud forest. This region of rolling hills and sparkling lakes is rarely visited — a fact that adds to its charm. For the naturalist the principal attraction is the variety of plants and a careful ornithologist will see a good number of bird species. The hiker is faced with a profusion of lakes of all shapes, sizes, and colours; the area boasts 275 named lakes and countless minor ponds and tarns. This is the Las Cajas National Recreation Area, a reserve of almost 29,000 hectares set aside for preservation in 1977.

The preserve lies about 29 km west of Cuenca. This charming city, the nation's third largest, is worth a few days' exploration. Getting a bus for the 10 hour trip to Cuenca from Quito's Terminal Terrestre is straightforward or you can take one of the several daily flights. Once in Cuenca you should visit the tourist information office which is on Hermano Miguel between Jaramillo and Cordova. Here you can obtain city maps and brochures about the area. A permit, costing less than two dollars, is required to pass the night in Las Cajas and is issued by the MAG office, along with a marginal map of the area. Their office in Cuenca is on Simón Bolívar between Borrero and Hermano Miguel. You can bypass the MAG procedure and go directly to the park to pay the fees, but no maps are available there. This is actually not much of a loss, since it's best to get the topo maps from the IGM in Quito. The 1:50,000 topographical maps which cover this area are Chaucha, Cuenca, San Felipe de Molleturo and Chiquintad.

There is at least one bus a day which leaves at 6.30 a.m. from the San Francisco market on Pres. Cordova between Torres and Aguirre. This bus has also left from Plaza San Sebastián at the corners of Bolívar and Talvot, so check locally. The bus (marked Sayausi-Miguir) takes about 2 hours to reach the park information centre and ranger station by Laguna Toreadora in the northern part of the park. It makes the return trip to Cuenca at 3.00

p.m. There is a refuge with a few bunks and a kitchen (a small fee charged) but it's better to bring your own tent as the guardian is not always there. Camping is permitted throughout the park and is free. Another route into the park is on the bus to Angas, on the southwestern border of Las Cajas. Buses leave from Av. Loja by the river on Tuesday, Wednesday, Friday, and Saturday at 6.30 a.m.

Once you get away from the immediate environs of the park station you will find that an effort has been made to mark some of the frequently used trails. Still, those which wander some distance from the main area usually peter out fairly quickly and so hiking here is largely a cross-country affair. I walked from the ranger station more or less southwest across the park, passing many lakes to the little settlement of Angas. There are four buses a week to Cuenca via Soldados, so don't rely too heavily on transport out. Your best bet is to bring enough food for a week and just amble around gently; you'll see very few people and the scenery is really marvellous.

The major part of the land area is *páramo* and many typical *páramo* species may be seen. Most exciting of all is perhaps the condor which is still occasionally sighted. You will hear as well as see the Andean snipe. High-

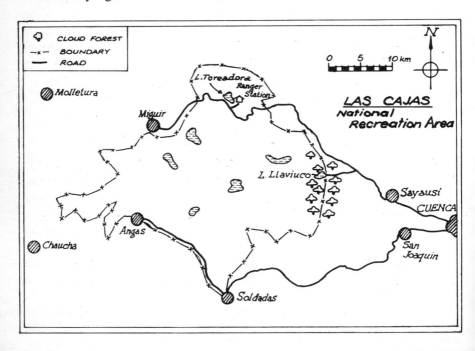

land thickets of the dwarf quinua tree dot the landscape and are filled with a fascinating variety of primitive plant life: the trees and ground are covered with mosses, lichens, fungi, mushrooms, and toadstools. One of the most colourful and common flowers is a small, bulbous, yellow and red flower known locally as *sarazhima*. You'll see rabbits and, with luck, a white-tailed deer or fox. The lakes are filled with trout and sport fishing is permitted. Towards and beyond the park's western boundaries are almost impenetrable cloud forests. There is one area of the park, however, which is known for its accessible cloud forest: the eastern part near Laguna Llaviuco. This is one of the very few areas of cloud forest on the eastern slopes of the Western Cordillera. It is reached by a short signposted dirt track leading from the main park entrance road about a third of the way between the village of Sayausi and the park station. Many more bird species are found here including the grey-breasted mountain toucan *(Andigena hypoglauca)*, the multi-coloured masked trogon *(Trogon personatus)*, and various tropical woodpeckers. Another park station is being planned for this vicinity.

The altitude of the park averages around 4000 m with no areas rising above 4500 m, hence there is no snow yet it can get rather chilly at night and in the early morning. The weather varies so much that it's best to be prepared for all temperatures. Mornings are usually clear with lots of sun — good T-shirt hiking, but by late afternoon clouds often roll in and rain is always a possibility. Visits can be made year round although April to June are said to be the wettest months and August and September the driest.

RÍO MAZÁN TO LAGUNA TOREADORA

This 3-day hike is said to be especially stunning for its changing scenery and vegetation, and the many bird species found in the area. It's a great opportunity to see mountain toucans, highland parrots, masked trogons, woodpeckers and the great Andean condor. Not having had the opportunity to get out and do it myself, I can only offer the following route description. However, in conjunction with the IGM maps of the area (mentioned earlier) there should be no problem in getting from one end to the other.

The hike begins near the park boundary of Las Cajas in a ecological area called Mazán Forest Reserve. This cloud forest reserve is protected by a local conservation group, Amigos de Mazán. (For additional information about walks and guided visits in the reserve, as well as use of the new refuge, the group can be contacted in Cuenca at Gran Colombia 5-20; tel: 824621, or by writing Amigos de Mazán, Casilla 1891, Cuenca, Ecuador.)

From Cuenca take the Las Cajas road to the Mazán reserve entrance. Get off the bus at Hacienda Gulag which is about 8 km out of Cuenca and 5 minutes past the village of Sayausi. Follow the hacienda road left into the valley and then turn right at the gated bridge. An hour's walk will bring you to the Mazán reserve. A trail heads southwest through the reserve following the Río Mazán in beautiful cloud forest. Continue southwest to Laguna Totoracocha where you'll find good camping beside the lake.

The next day the route angles northwest passing to the east side of Laguna Tintacocha. Trails throughout the area will often come and go, but finding your way with map and compass should be easy enough. Past Tintacocha the track heads in a northerly direction, passing Laguna Lagartococha and on to Laguna Osohuaycu (staying on the east side of both) where camp is set up the second night. From here you should be able to pick up a clear trail heading north directly to the ranger station and park entrance of Las Cajas at Laguna Toreadora. This should take about 5 to 6 hours of *páramo* hiking. An option would be to continue northwest from the north point of Laguna Osohuaycu to Laguna Luspa along an old Inca trail. From here you can hike out to the village of Miguir, but finding transport from this little village back to Cuenca may be problematic.

ROCK CLIMBING

LAS CAJAS   From the refuge at Laguna Toreadora, you can look across the road and see a prominent rock block some 300 m away. About 20 minutes of uphill walking will get you to its base. In the centre of the face is a large (35 m) flake with three established routes and several other possibilities. The overhanging face on the main block can also be climbed but bolting is necessary. A top rope can be set up on the flake.

Godzilla is a 5.10b climb first achieved by Juan Rodriguez and Juan Currasco. It begins near the centre of the flake at the base of a tree. Look for a finger crack leading up to a roof. Past this roof the thin crack continues up to a second and runs out to the right while the route angles left, up the face to a ledge. The descent is a matter of downclimbing a chimney (5.6) on the right side of the flake. Another chimney (5.7) on the left side can also be climbed,but both are somewhat dirty.

200 m east (left) of Godzilla is another rock formation (25 m) with an off-width crack starting in its centre which gradually narrows to a fist, then finger crack, called *Salsipuedes*; 5.9.

In addition, there are many huge rocks scattered in this general area which would serve well for an afternoon of bouldering.

CUENCA AREA   In search for good rock a few stalwart Ecuadorian climbers have pioneered many routes and opened up several areas suitable for climbing. Of these climbers, Juan Currasco and Juan Rodriguez seem to have been the most active, claiming many first ascents. While the majority of rock routes described here are not particularly noteworthy by American or European standards, at least for now they offer a sampling of the best available in the country. As mentioned previously, Ecuador is not a rock climbing destination but if you're already here and longing for the feel of rock, the following suggestions and descriptions may be useful.

If you happen to be staying in Cuenca for a few days, you can get in a little climbing practice by 'buildering', or in this case, 'bridgering' (?) near the Tomebamba river. Follow Av. 3 de Noviembre southeast as it runs parallel to the river and crosses under a broken bridge (puente roto) just past Vargas Machuca. The three centre pillars on the west face of the bridge range from 5.7 to 5.8 and a top rope can be set up on the bridge railings.

About 6 to 8 km outside of Cuenca just before the village of Sayausi (buses leave from Plaza San Francisco) is a popular restaurant called Las Cabañas that serves the best trout (trucha) around.

After lunching here, continue along the road toward Sayausi until you come to a dirt road heading left. Follow this road down to a covered wooden bridge about a 100 m away, cross over and backtrack along the river on the other side to just opposite the restaurant. Here you'll come to an eight-meter high boulder called *Piedra de las Truchas* (trout rock) with two climbable faces and lots of routes.

The east face has several established climbs — *Vía Murcielago*, 5.8, starts as an off-width crack leading off of a flake near the centre of the face. It narrows to a finger crack near the top.

To the left of this climb is *Cebiche de Trucha*, a 5.11 face climb which starts from a low rock ramp; it's overhanging and fun. *Encebollado* follows up the northeast arête, not difficult at 5.8. Top roping is possible on the south side and there are other climbs and more possibilities on both the south and north faces.

Another nearby area is located outside the village of Cojitambo. Here you'll find a dome-shaped rock formation, spanning 800 m with a 200 m rock wall, overlooking the village. To get there, take a bus from Cuenca to Azogues (40 min) and get off at the end of the line. The bus for Cojitambo (25 min) passes nearby, at the hospital road junction. You'll have to ask where to wait. Once in the village you'll see the huge east face — about a 20 minute walk from town.

Dead centre in the wall is *Ruta de la Gruta*, a 5.7 crack, dirty with vegetation; the second pitch is better. On the far left is *Viuda Alegre*, a nicer, wide, 5.10 hand crack leading up to a roof. At the roof you can go left (dirty) or traverse right (nice) to a walk-off. Above this area, closer to the ridge and higher up is a rose-coloured wall with two good cracks of about 30 m running up to the south ridge. From here you can hike to the top and walk off via the easy west slope.

More climbing can be found to the south of Cuenca in a beautiful area near the village of San Fernando. To get there you first have to take a bus from Cuenca to the town of Girón on the road to Machala. Here take another bus to San Fernando which is situated at the foot of massive Mount Pablo. The area is loaded with climbing possibilities and is good for camping, hiking and birdwatching. Sometimes groups come up here for hang-gliding practice. From the village hike up to Laguna Buza, 15 minutes away, where you'll find good camping. The approach to the base of San Pablo is somewhat difficult, requiring a steep bushwhack through dense vegetation and forest to reach the rock walls towering as high as 300 m. This could take as long as 3 to 4 hours but the area is beautiful and worth exploring.

Another suggestion that may not offer world-class climbing but promises to get you off the beaten path is the gorge of Río Ridcay, about an hour down the Cuenca-Machala road near the village of Lentag. In Cuenca hop a bus from the main bus terminal going to Santa Isabel and ask to be let off at Lentag. From here find the dirt road that takes off left down to the river. After about a half hour's walk you'll come to a bridge. The rock walls of the gorge will be visible to the right. Cross the bridge and head down into the gorge. Climb on.

CHAPTER 6

The Eastern Cordillera

The journey not the arrival matters.
                    T.S. Eliot

INTRODUCTION

This is perhaps the most interesting region for the adventurous outdoor traveller. The Eastern Cordillera is, on average, higher and more massive than its western counterpart and counts amongst its mountains the famous volcanoes of Cotopaxi, Cayambe, Antisana, El Altar, and Sangay, which rank respectively second, third, fourth, fifth, and seventh highest in the country. The last named is considered to be the most continuously active volcano in South America, if not the world.

The high eastern slopes of these mountains are bordered by a relatively thin strip of *páramo* which changes abruptly to almost impenetrable high mountain cloud forest on the lower slopes before merging into what is commonly called 'jungle' but is in fact the tropical rain forest of the lowlands. Hot air masses rise up the eastern flanks of the mountains depositing enough rainfall to make the high mountain cloud forest the wettest part of Ecuador; indeed, with some areas averaging over 5000 mm of rain per year, it is one of the wettest regions on earth. It is also extremely thickly vegetated and so the middle and lower slopes have been little disturbed by man. The story is often told of the *hacienda* owner who, upon being asked how extensive his land was, replied, "I don't really know — as far as you can go to the east". Even today the eastern slopes are so little explored that *haciendas* with ill defined limits to the east still exist. These are the haunts of the rarely seen mountain tapir and the Andean spectacled bear, the two largest land mammals in Ecuador and considered endangered species. Their rarity is due not only to hunting and land encroachment but also to the almost impenetrable nature of their environment — no one really knows how many of these elusive animals are left.

The mountains themselves tend to be covered with more snow than those of the Western Cordillera because of the higher precipitation on the eastern slopes. The peaks are normally climbed from the western side, partly because the heavily populated Central Valley lies on this side and partly because the eastern side is difficult to get to, often clouded in, and the summits are more heavily corniced. Adventurous climbers seeking new routes could look for eastern approaches to these mountains.

As with the Western Cordillera, the mountains of this range will be dealt with systematically from north to south; descriptions of both climbing and hiking routes will be given and walks into the rarely visited eastern slopes are also described.

CAYAMBE (5790m)

INTRODUCTION Cayambe, a massive extinct volcano, is located about 65 km northeast of Quito and is both Ecuador's third highest peak and the third highest peak in the Americas north of the equator. It also enjoys the distinction of being the highest point on the earth's surface through which the equator directly passes (at about 4600 m on the south side). It was first climbed in 1880 by, you guessed it, Whymper and the Carrel cousins. Although technically not very difficult it is rather dangerous due to crevasses and avalanches. In 1974 such an avalanche killed three well known Ecuadorian climbers: Joseph Bergé, Carlos Oleas, and César Ruales. A refuge with no facilities and an occasional guardian is located on the southwest flanks of the mountain at 4600 m and named after the three climbers.

The IGM have two 1:50,000 topographical maps available, Cayambe and Nevado Cayambe. The Cayambe map shows the old approach used in the days before the hut was built. The area is part of the Cayambe — Coca Ecological Reserve but there is no evidence of development.

DIRECTIONS To get to the hut one first takes a bus to Cayambe which leaves Quito from the Terminal Terrestre. On the southern outskirts of Cayambe there is a turn off to the right from the Pan American Highway. There is no sign at present but many locals know that the road goes to Hacienda Piemonte and then on to the refuge. The 25 km to the refuge can normally be driven all the way if you use a four wheel drive vehicle or one which has a strong engine. There are no buses and hitchhiking is difficult. A truck can be hired in the central square of Cayambe for a lift up toward the refuge. If the road has seen recent repair (this does happen from time to time) some vehicles can get within a kilometre of the refuge and will charge about US$25. Regardless of the road condition, you can always get a ride to H. Piemonte Bajo (6 km), and often up to H. Piemonte Alto at 14 km. The road has been newly cobbled up to this point. (Figure on paying a little less than a dollar per kilometre.) At the *hacienda* turn left (right leads to Sara Urco) and continue until a junction at about km 14 where there is a sign 'Reserva Natural Cayambe-Coca' and the H. Piemonte Alto where you turn left. So far the road has been cobbled all the way but a few kilometres further the cobbles stop though work is continuing slowly. There is so little traffic that midweek you'll have to walk most of the way which makes a good hiking trip even if you don't intend to climb the mountain. There are broad views of the ancient lava flows of this now extinct volcano as well as of the Glaciar Hermoso (the beautiful glacier) near to the refuge.

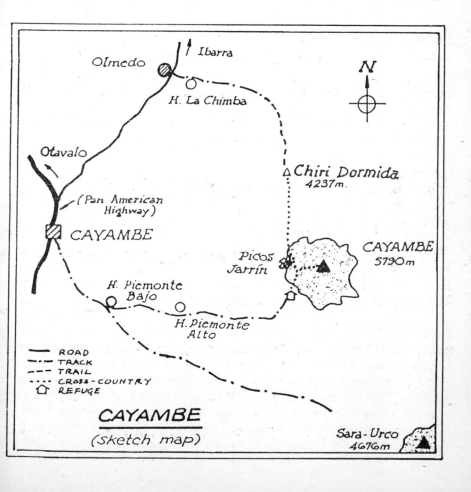

CAYAMBE
(sketch map)

To climb Cayambe, get as early a start as possible to take advantage of the frozen snow; an 11.00 p.m. departure is not unreasonable. It's essential to be back on the lower glacier by 10.00 a.m.; later in the day the softened snow often avalanches. Head directly over the rocky hill behind the hut and climb onto the glacier from the lake on the other side; this will take about an hour. Climb more or less north up the glacier and be alert for crevasses. Some rocky outcrops, the Picos Jarrín, will be seen ahead and will be reached in another 1½ hours. From this area continue north toward a massive rock cliff which is left of the summit. Through this section you may find yourself walking parallel to several crevasses. As you approach the rock cliff you will come to a large bowl. Drop into it, keeping along the left edge as you work your way east (right) toward the summit. Route finding around the gaping *bergschrund* may be necessary. From the bowl the final approach up to the summit may appear improbable due to the steep snow flutes that must be negotiated. However, as you get nearer you'll see that there's an easy route through them. Don't be tempted to ascend the easier-looking, steep snow field running up alongside the rock cliff. It's much longer than it looks and is highly avalanche-prone. It was here that Bergé, Ruales, and Oleas were killed. Expect to take about 9 to 10 hours to the summit and another 3 back to the refuge. During good weather, Cayambe is frequently climbed despite its dangerous reputation so you can sometimes follow footprints and wands from previous parties.

The old route avoids the refuge completely. You head for the village of Olmedo about 10 km northeast of Cayambe town. Mules and guides may be hired from Hacienda La Chimba, in Olmedo's western outskirts. It takes 5 to 8 hours to reach Chiri Dormida where water is available. Camp here. From Chiri Dormida a further 2 to 3 hours are needed to reach Picos Jarrín from where the route continues as on the new normal route. Since the construction of the refuge this route is rarely used.

Cayambe is one of the less explored of Ecuador's major peaks and new routes could be attempted by highly experienced climbers. The mountain has rarely been climbed other than by the Picos Jarrín route described.

Snow storms and high winds are more frequent on Cayambe than on many other peaks. It can be climbed year round although October through January is said to be the best period.

SARA URCO (4676 m)

With turned out toes we went cautiously along the crisp arete, sharp as a roof-top, and at 1.30 p.m. stood on the true summit of Sara-Urco; a shattered ridge of gneiss — wonder of wonders, blue sky above — strewn with fragments of quartz and micaschist... without a hint of vegetation.

Edward Whymper, 1892

Sara Urco is one of Ecuador's few non-volcanic peaks and lies about 15 km southeast of Cayambe peak. Despite its low altitude it is normally snow capped and so many sources and climbers believe it to be higher than the given IGM elevation. It is surrounded by jumbled up *páramo* which is either boggy or brushy and difficult to move through; hence this is not a frequently climbed mountain. It is technically straightforward and was first climbed in 1880 by

Whymper and the Carrels, who seem to have got everywhere. December and January are the best climbing months; the rest of the year is wet.

Although I haven't climbed this peak I obtained the following description from various climbers in Ecuador.

Access is the same as for Cayambe as far as the Hacienda Piemonte after which you turn right (left leads to Cayambe). About 3 km beyond the *hacienda* the road peters out. Somewhere around here lives Señor Juan Farinango who is the local guide and can arrange mule hire. On the first day the guides take you in a generally southeasterly direction past an area known as La Dormida; several small rivers must be forded.

The *páramo* here is known locally as *pantano* which means marsh or swamp. In realistic hiking terms this means you can expect lots of mud and huge clumps of *ichu* grass. It takes a day to reach the Río Bolteado where camp is set up.

The following day you continue in a southeasterly direction to the foot of the southwest ridge which is easy to ascend to the summit. You'll probably need to camp high on the mountain and make the summit on the third day. A small summit glacier will have to be negotiated.

Due to the inhospitable nature of the surroundings it is advisable to hire mules and a guide. The two IGM 1:50,000 topographical maps for this area are Cangahua and Cerro Saraurco.

LAS PUNTAS (4452 m) AND THE OYACACHI AREA

The name of this mountain means 'the points' and indeed Las Puntas is more like a long serrated ridge than a mountain. Some authorities have reported as many as fifty separate small peaks on the ridge which lies 30 km east of Quito.

South and east of Las Puntas is a very wet lake district which eventually leads to the lowland forests. This area could well be explored by those hoping to catch a glimpse of spectacled bear or mountain tapir — but don't be too hopeful.

To get there from Quito take any Av. 6 de Diciembre bus going north and get off at the Partidero a Tumbaco. Catch an El Quinche bus at the eastern exit on the road which heads into the Oriente. The bus goes through the villages of Cumbaya, Tumbaco, Puembo, Yaruquí, Checa, and El Quinche. Get off at Checa some 1½ to 2 hours out of Quito, cross a railway line just beyond the village, and just as the main road curves hard to the right (east) toward Las Puntas, take the obvious cobbled road on the right. About 50 m up this cobbled road, a dirt road goes off to the right. Take it, even though continuing straight seems to be the right way, (it's not). The dirt road passes through Hacienda Santa Teresita and you'll be crossing cattle fields and barbed-wire gates for a while. Continue on the main path and it will take you all the way to the northern base of Las Puntas, the obvious horseshoe shaped ridge in front of you to the east. The western inside of the mountain is steep and difficult to climb; head around the north side and approach via the gentler eastern slopes. It's a day's walk from Checa to the mountain so bring your camping gear. The IGM map 1:50,000 El Quinche shows the approach from Checa and the 1:25,000 Cerro Puntas is somewhat helpful for the climb.

This area can be used as a jumping off point for the adventurous traveller well-equipped with rain gear and food. South of Las Puntas is a large boggy area of dozens of lakes. You will eventually come out on the Quito-Lago Agrio road about 20 km away. A more ambitious hike would be to head to the Laguna Oyacachi a few kilometres away; it is the largest lake to the east of Las Puntas. From here follow the Río Oyacachi which drains out of the south corner of the lake and then flows eastwards towards the tiny village of Oyacachi which is about 13 crow-flying kilometres away; probably twice that on foot. The IGM 1:50,000 Oyacachi topographical map shows a trail on the north side of the river beginning about two-thirds of the way between the lake and the village and continuing into the village. From Oyacachi the trail continues eastwards down the Río Oyacachi valley, crossing the river and then heading southeast to the settlement of El Chaco on the Quito-Lago Agrio road; some 35 km as the crow flies.

I have never done this hike, nor met anyone who has, so you go at your own risk. A few general pointers — Las Puntas is over 4000 m high and El Chaco is at barely 1000 m so trying the hike in reverse would be tough, to say the least. Remember crow-flying kilometres are usually doubled in reality. The trail from Oyacachi to El Chaco will probably be in fairly good shape and your biggest problem will be finding Oyacachi. Expect rain, mud, and more rain. To see any wildlife will require determination and patience. If you want to have something to practice on, try *The Andes to the jungle* hike on page 158.

Need a map?

Bradt Publications imports and sells topographical maps for Ecuador. Send for a catalogue.
Bradt Publications, 41 Nortoft Road, Chalfont St Peter, Bucks SL9 0LA, England

Antisana.

The Antisana Area

INTRODUCTION   Volcán Antisana (5704 m) is the fourth highest mountain in Ecuador, but is seldom seen by tourists because of its position some 55 km southeast of Quito well away from any main road. The broad summit contains four separate peaks which are, in descending order, the central, eastern, northeastern, and southern summits. Their elevations are widely disagreed upon. These four summits represent the highest points of a crater rim; the crater itself is totally filled with glacial ice and doesn't appear to be active. For this reason Antisana is popularly supposed to be extinct, but volcanologists claim that its comparatively recent major eruptions indicate that the volcano is, in fact, still active. The 10 km long lava flow near the Hacienda Pinantura, to the west of the mountain, is attributed to an eruption around 1760 and the 6 km long flow by Laguna Papallacta, to the north of the mountain, dates from 1773. Both these flows originated from fissures in the sides of the volcano, thus a cone is absent. Some fumarolic activity still exists near the highest summit.

The climbing history of this mountain is predictable: another first ascent by Whymper and the Carrels in 1880. Whymper wrote that he could smell sulphurous fumes during the ascent. The lower peaks however, are more of a challenge and did not see conquests until the 1970s by various Ecuadorian climbers.

The access town of Píntag, with its cobbled streets and tiled roofs, is unusually attractive and the surrounding farmland green and beautiful. The *páramo* near Antisana is more varied than usual. Flowering *puya* plants are plentiful, providing nectar for the many hummingbirds, and there are even some rather subdued looking *frailejones*. The further east or 'around the back' of the mountain you go, the more likely you are to see animals such as the white-tailed deer, mountain tapir, puma, and spectacled bear. Lava fields are a fascinating feature of this area. Antisana itself is a splendid sight with its four peaks covered with blue glaciers; to the west is Cotopaxi showing its best profile.

A jeep road runs to the foot of Antisana. Very little traffic uses this track which is in poor condition and ideal for hiking. Many people will choose to return by the same route, but it is possible to hike cross-country to Papallacta on the Quito-Lago Agrio road, or cross the *páramo* to Cotopaxi via Sincholagua.

ACCESS   Buses leave from Plaza La Marin in Quito several times a day for the hour long journey to Píntag through lovely scenery and pretty villages. In Píntag, you may decide to hire transport (US$20-30) to go the 25 km of bad road up to Hacienda El Hato. A jeep track continues a considerable distance past the hacienda, but permission for private vehicles to pass through the locked gate at El Hato is hard to come by. The owner, Sr. José Delgado, generally refuses. On foot from Píntag head south on a cobbled road to Hacienda Pinantura some 7 to 8 km away. Take the uphill road whenever you come to a fork. At one point you have a choice of three roads: take the middle one.

At the *hacienda* the locked gate will pose no problem for hikers but aggressive bulls may. Keep your distance if crossing any grazing areas. Before reaching the *hacienda* look out for the lava field to your left which is over 200 years old and covered with moss and shrubs. You have the choice of following a path across the lava for a while, or continuing to the *hacienda* and picking up the jeep track; a longer but easier route. If you decide to cross the lava, look for a track going up what looks like piles of rubble. This track soon dwindles to a path. There are beautiful little rock gardens between the chunks of lava, and all sorts of flowers can be admired. It's worth going out of your way to find a flowering *puya* with its apple-green flowers. After about an hour of lava-leaping you will want to join the jeep track. Look out for an easy access place on your right where the lava cliff is low and no scrambling is involved. Once on the jeep track you simply keep walking past a string of beautiful lakes dammed by the lava flows, through various gates, and over several bridges. The cobbles have long since finished and if you're driving, four wheel drive will probably be necessary by now. Continue up the road as it twists and turns through broad fields and *páramo* and look out for short cuts if you're on foot.

About 25 km by road after Hacienda Pinantura you'll pass the Hacienda El Hato (also known as Hacienda Antisana). 3 to 4 km due south is Laguna Micacocha which is famous for trout fishing. To reach the mountain turn left, or northwest, on a rapidly deteriorating track. The area is flat pastureland and looks very eerie in low evening sunlight with dozens of cattle skulls dotting the landscape. The track is driveable for about 8 km and peters out high in the *páramo* west of the mountain. From here head east for another 2 km and make your base camp as close to the snowline as possible.

For the following climbs and hikes you'll need a compass and topographical maps. The IGM 1:100,000 Píntag map gives a good overview of the area and is probably all you need for climbing, but the smaller scale 1:50,000 maps of Píntag, Papallacta, Sincholagua and Cotopaxi will be useful for hiking.

The weather is generally wet and cold. If your tent and raingear aren't waterproof you'll probably be miserable. And if you think they are waterproof you'll know for sure by the end of your hike. With Oriente weather conditions prevailing, the driest months are November through February; the wettest months are June through August.

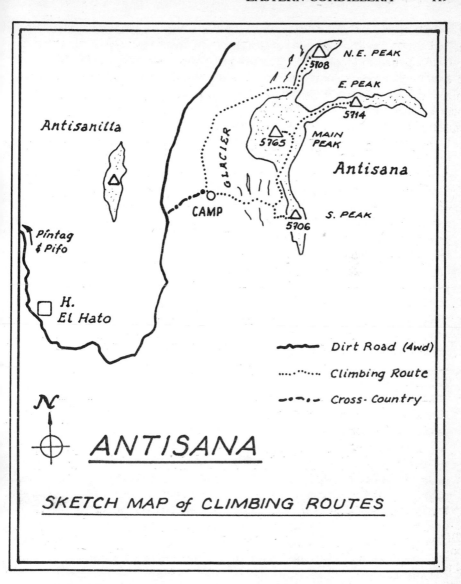

Antisanilla

N.E. PEAK
5708

E. PEAK
5714

GLACIER

CAMP

5765

MAIN
PEAK

Antisana

S. PEAK
5906

Pintag
& Pifo

H.
El Hato

⏤⏤⏤ Dirt Road (4wd)

·····⸱····· Climbing Route

⏤·⏤·⏤ Cross-Country

N

ANTISANA

SKETCH MAP of CLIMBING ROUTES

CLIMBING ANTISANA

Antisana is one of the more difficult peaks in Ecuador to climb and is dangerous because of the many crevasses and bad weather. It is not for the inexperienced. The lengthy access and lack of a mountain refuge compound your problems; this is the highest peak in Ecuador with no hut, and you have to carry complete wet weather camping gear and food for several days.

THE MAIN SUMMIT   From the base camp climb up to the glacier about a half hour away. Looking left you'll see the main summit of Antisana, the south peak to the right and a centre ridge separating the two. Head across and up the glacier aiming for the lowest point on this centre ridge. Because of constantly changing snow conditions there's no 'best way' to get there. You'll have to do a bit of route-finding through the snow-fields (and crevasses) for the best route up to the ridge. This area especially should be wanded. Just before reaching the low point on the ridge, a glacier to the left leads to the main summit, ascending just below the ridge. Approaching the summit, stay east (right) of the ice walls on the southeast face. Keep nearer and parallel to the ridgeline continuing up in a northeast direction as you traverse below the summit. Just as the northeast and east peaks come into view, head left (northwest) up to the main summit. The climb takes about 7 to 8 hours in good conditions and without too many route-finding problems.

THE SOUTH PEAK   This mixed rock/ice route was first climbed by an American team in the '60s. It's a more difficult climb than the main summit and requires technical equipment, not to mention experience. To climb the south peak follow the route for the main summit to below the same low point on the centre ridge. From here you can see the rocky summit of the south peak to the right. Climb the snow-field which ascends right and leads to a high ridge below the summit. Set up camp at the top of the glacier just below the ridge. It's about a 4 to 6 hour climb from the base camp.

The following day climb to the top of the ridge and follow it up to the rocky base of the summit. At the base, traverse right to a steep snow couloir and ascend it, angling up left to an obvious ramp of volcanic sand. Follow the ramp as it angles up and left. Caution is advised here as no belay is possible and a fall would be disastrous. Continue up the ramp to a rock chimney of 50 m, where various sizes of rock protection will be needed for the ascent. Above the chimney there's another 30 m of easy climbing to the top of the rock section. Here you'll come to the upper snow-field for the final traverse (right) to the summit. Allow about 6 to 7 hours to reach the summit and another 3 hours back to the snow camp. The following day will get you down to the base camp and breathing easy.

THE EAST PEAK   This is probably the most difficult of the Antisana summits, first climbed by Hugo Torres and Miguel Andrade in 1973. You'll need the full regalia of ice gear, including screws, stakes, and even jumars would be helpful. Follow the same route up toward the main peak and set up camp about 50 m below the summit. Here you'll find a flat area on the east slope just past the ice walls. A little farther up the snowfield is the ridge which connects the east summit with the main peak. On the second day follow the ridge toward the east summit to a high point called Pico Colgante (hanging peak) about an hour from camp. Here you'll see that 'hanging peak' gets its name from an extremely deep crevasse which cuts off the approach to the summit. Crossing it involves a rappel down and pendulum across to the lower summit ridge. Set up a fixed rope for the jumar/prussik exercise awaiting you on the return. After all that, begin the ascent of the summit ridge which drastically narrows, provides dramatic views of huge drops on either side, and forces you to sit and scoot along. To wrap up the trip to the summit, climb the 20 m ice wall at the end of the ridge — about 60 to 70 degrees.

THE NORTHEAST PEAK   This route was first climbed in 1972 by Santiago Rivadeneira, Leonardo Menses and Hugo Torres. It's not a particularly difficult climb, but some route-finding problems and steep snow/ice make it challenging. From the lower base camp head left along the moraine until you're in line with the main summit. An alternative camp can be set up here as there's plenty of water available. The climb begins by ascending the glacier seen to the left of the main peak. Find the best route up to the ridge which separates the main summit from the northeast peak. Climb this ridge and follow it to the summit. A steep section of snow/ice, about 50 to 60 degrees, will have to be negotiated just below the summit. Allow about 6 to 8 hours to the top.

HIKING TO PAPALLACTA

Hikers wishing to continue northwards to Papallacta will have to go cross-country. This is not easy as there are no paths, the countryside is rough, and the vegetation can be extremely dense, especially in the valley bottoms. From the climbers' base camp one heads roughly north, following the Río Tumiguina valley to a lake by the lava flow some 10 km away. From the right (eastern) shores of the lake you'll find the continuation of the Río Tumiguina and a faint path following it. This soon turns away from the river valley and then crosses the lava flow reaching Laguna Papallacta and the Quito-Lago Agrio road after 3 or 4 km. This is a a rough trail and can be quite muddy. If you wanted to do the hike in reverse, from Papallacta to Antisana, your main problem would be to find the beginning of the rough trail across the lava flow. It begins just beyond (to the east) of Laguna Papallacta but is not very easy to find. Once on it, it is straightforward to follow it to the lake where you head south to the mountain. A longer but perhaps more straightforward route would be to follow in reverse the first day's walk described in the Antisana to Cotopaxi hike. These are both challenging and interesting routes and require maps, compass, and

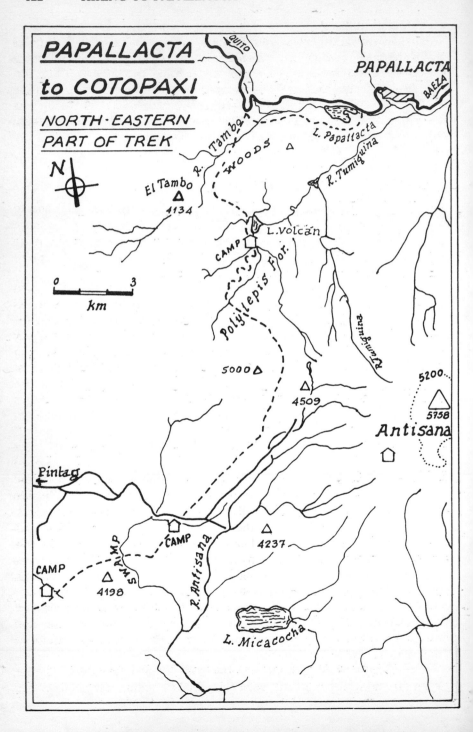

route-finding ability.

Papallacta, some 3 km beyond the lake to the east, has a small, basic hotel and restaurants. Just before the village there is a sign to the left which indicates the kilometre long road to the thermal hot springs. There are several pools and changing rooms and the area only sees crowds on weekends — you may well have it to yourselves midweek. They are the best hot springs I've found in Ecuador. You could probably camp next to them (slip the caretaker a few sucres). The views can be superb.

ANTISANA TO COTOPAXI HIKE

More than a few seasoned trekkers claim that the walk from Antisana to Cotopaxi is one of the best in Ecuador. It certainly is one of the more challenging, being physically demanding and requiring some route-finding ability. It can also test one's capacity for inclement weather and mud-slogging, depending on the season.

This 4 to 5 day trip southeast towards Volcáns Sincholagua and Cotopaxi begins from the Quito-Lago Agrio road to Antisana. Leave Quito on a bus to Baeza or Lagro Agrio in the lowlands — you'll have to pay full fare for the right to a seat. The last village before Papallacta is Pifo; about halfway between the two the tarmac road changes to gravel. After some 24 km you cross a 4100 m pass where there is a shrine to the Virgin and the first impressive views of Antisana. About 6 km after the pass and 8 km before Papallacta you reach a sharp left hairpin bend followed by two small bridges next to one another. There are good views of Laguna Papallacta about 3 km to the east and a wide expanse of green plain stretching out below. Get off the bus here. To your right is the Río Tambo valley and a new road under construction which will eventually be used as the regular approach to Papallacta. Follow this new road for about a kilometre until it crosses the Río Tambo. Here you'll pick up a faint trail which leads up on the right side of the river. After a short way it will cross and continue up the left side.

You'll be heading southwest up the Tambo river valley for 4 to 5 km until you reach the long flat-topped hill called El Tambo (4134 m). By now you should be on the opposite (eastern) bank of the river. Here the trail turns southeast away from the river and heads across *páramo* and through *Polylepsis* forest. Continuing along the trail in a southeasterly direction over boggy countryside for a couple of kilometres will bring you within sight of Laguna Volcán. The trail comes in above and to the right of the lake and drops down to some flat camping areas. From the main road it's about 4 to 5 hours to reach Laguna Volcán.

Camping early by the lake will give you enough time to make the 1½ hour circuit around it, if you're still keen for a bit of walking. Stay high as you

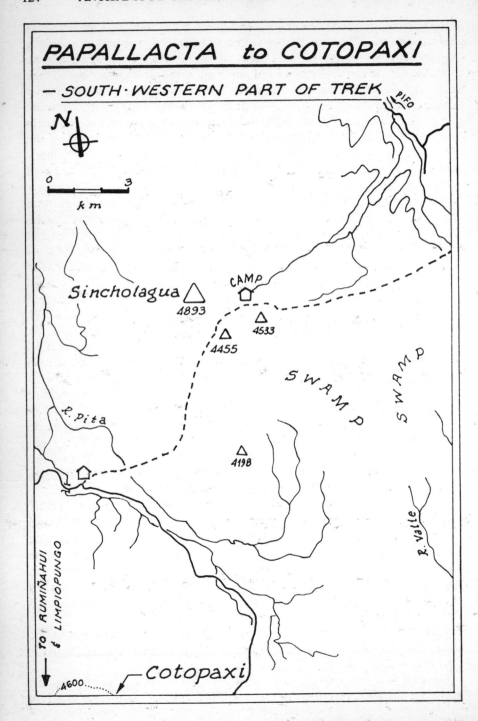

make the round-trip. Below the far end of the lake there is a lava field that you can explore. This area offers a variety of interesting vegetation including orchids near the bottom. To the right you'll see a small hill which can be scaled for some impressive views of Antisana if the weather is clear. There is no trail across the lava and the rocks can be quite rough, so wear sturdy hiking boots and be prepared for a little scrambling. In order to continue the circuit of the lake, you'll have to backtrack across the lava to the main trail. Attempting to continue across the lava and pick up the trail on the other end promises difficult scrambling through high grass and forging many small streams and waterfalls. Add about 3 hours and a high level of frustration if you decide to try it.

On the second day the trail ascends from Laguna Volcán steeply (and boggily) through *páramo* and *Polylepsis* trees for some 3 to 4 hours. As the terrain flattens, you'll cross a small stream. The trail starts to peter out but just head cross-country (a bit boggy) more or less in the direction of Antisana. There are herds of semi-wild horses in this area along with a number of lapwings and perhaps a condor or two. Below the flanks of Antisana you'll once again pick up a trail which ascends an easy uphill section to a plateau. It leads up from here through a low pass on a hill, between Antisana and the small rocky peaks of Antisanilla on the right. As the trail descends it meets a dirt track (the one that passes Hacienda El Hato as described in *Climbing Antisana*). Follow this track to the stream where camp can be set up. Allow about 7 to 8 hours for the day's hike. If time allows, backtrack from camp and scramble up Antisanilla for excellent sunset views. You'll need about an 1½ hours to get there.

The next day's hike of about 6 to 8 hours goes from below Antisana heading across *páramo* toward the volcano of Sincholagua. The going will be mostly cross-country without the benefit of an established trail. Because of this, the route described here may not be exactly what you find but you can't go wrong by heading straight for the high peak of Sincholagua.

From camp, looking right, you'll see a desert-like hill across the stream, which has been overgrazed by a great number of sheep. Climb this hill and continue across the *páramo* where you'll eventually cross another stream and see another overgrazed area to the left. Here and further along there'll be a series of small *páramo* hills on your right and a prominent hill on the left. Skirt the base of the large hill, keeping to the right, and you'll enter a valley of *almohadones* — tussock-like mounds of spongy vegetation — marshy, and awkward for walking.

Cross the valley (as best you can) keeping Sincholagua ahead and to the right. Just beyond there will be two streams to cross in succession. Look for a good camping place between the two.

The following day, cross the second stream and follow the trail leading up a hill, all the time heading directly for Sincholagua. There may be a few cattle tracks in this area but don't follow anything unless it leads in the direction of the volcano. As you near the base of Sincholagua, you'll see another small clump of *Polylepsis* trees and an area of huge rocks looking like ships. The trail meanders between the two, and leads into a wet, marshy valley of more tussock. Crossing the valley, you'll have the base of Sincholagua on the right and high *páramo* hills on the left. Aim for the low point between the two (it's about 1½ to 2 hours from the trees to this low pass) and look for the best place to set up camp as soon as you're out of the marshy valley. It ought to take about 5 to 7 hours from camp to camp. Water is quite variable here. If you can't find any, you may have to continue on another 2 to 4 hours.

From the camp near the base of Sincholagua the trail continues to skirt along the slopes for about 1 to 2 hours to an obvious pass marked by a few cairns. From this high point, you'll see Cotopaxi straight ahead and Rumiñahui off to the right. Descend the slope from the pass, keeping left and making a direct line with Cotopaxi for the easiest way down. It's about 2 to 4 hours down to a river and jeep track where you can camp.

From the jeep track there are several possibilities to finish the trek. If you follow the road going right it's a half day's walk to Laguna Limpiopungo. Heading cross-country will get you to the Cotopaxi refuge in about 3 to 4 hours, or you can pick up the trail to Mulaló which is described in the Cotopaxi circuit hike.

Cotopaxi National Park and Surroundings

Cotopaxi's shape is the most beautiful and regular of all the colossal peaks in the high Andes. It is a perfect cone covered by a thick blanket of snow which shines so brilliantly at sunset it seems detached from the azure of the sky.

Alexander von Humboldt, 1802

INTRODUCTION The Galápagos islands excepted, this is without a doubt Ecuador's showpiece national park. There are picnic areas, camping sites, huts, and a mountain refuge, making it somewhat similar to the national parks in North America and Europe.

The centrepiece of the park is Volcán Cotopaxi (5897 m) which lies about 55 km south of Quito and whose symmetrical cone can often be seen from the capital on a clear day. This active volcano is Ecuador's second highest mountain and it has long been considered the highest active volcano in the world (although recent claims in favour of Tupungato on the Argentine-Chilean border cannot be discounted).

The history of Cotopaxi's activity is the most dramatic in Ecuador. Although other volcanoes may be more active geologically, Cotopaxi has caused the most death and destruction. Records of its eruptions date back to 1534 though it was undoubtedly active long before then. After a long period of dormancy Cotopaxi erupted three times in 1742, destroying the town of Latacunga and killing hundreds of people and livestock. More eruptions followed in 1743, 1744 and 1766. A major eruption in 1768 again destroyed Latacunga, which had been rebuilt, with much loss of life and property. Almost a century of inactivity followed, but in 1853 Cotopaxi again began to display its awesome power and erupted frequently for several years. Four separate eruptions occurred in 1877 and the one of the 26th of June produced catastrophic lahars (avalanches of ice, snow, water, mud, and rocks), one of which reached Esmeraldas on the Pacific coast, and another which swept down on ill-fated Latacunga, wiping out the greater part of it yet again. This lahar was recorded as having reached the town in 30 minutes. Latacunga lies 35 km southwest of Cotopaxi as the crow flies but the lahar would have followed the lie of the land by a more circuitous route — the concept of a huge wall of volcanic and glacial debris sweeping toward one at some 90 km per hour, or 25 m per second, is impossible to comprehend. As Michael Andrews remarks in *The Flight of the Condor*, "I find it very curious that Latacunga has been rebuilt repeatedly on its old site." Frequent but minor eruptions continued for 8 years after this catastrophe. Since 1885 eruptions have been limited to two minor ones in 1903 and 1904, and a disputed one in 1942. Fumarolic activity continues in Cotopaxi's crater at present, as anyone who has climbed the volcano will know.

Cotopaxi was first climbed in 1872 from the southwest by the German geologist Wilhelm Reiss accompanied by Angel M. Escobar, a Colombian. A few months later the German, Stübel, accompanied by four Ecuadorians (Jantui, Páez, Ramón, and Rodriguez) logged the first Ecuadorian ascent. Edward Whymper with the Carrel cousins spent a night on the summit in 1880 — a somewhat hazardous exercise bearing in mind the restless nature of the volcano at that time. Since then many successful ascents have been made and today the mountain is a popular destination for weekend mountaineers and tourists from Quito as well as foreign climbers. Despite its relative simplicity this is not a climb for the inexperienced, and beginners should avail themselves of professional guides.

The national park surrounding the volcano offers excellent hiking and camping opportunities as well as lesser peaks to climb. Rumiñahui (4712 m) and Morurco (c. 4840 m) lie within the park boundaries and the peaks of Sincholagua (4893 m) and Quilindaña (4878 m) are found just outside the park. There is talk of extending the park boundaries. Hiking a complete circuit around the base of Cotopaxi is a good 6 to 7 day trip and all the above peaks can be seen or climbed.

ACCESS   This describes two ways to reach the administrative centre. Hiking or climbing routes from there are described individually. There are two entrance roads to the park, both of which start from the Pan American Highway and are therefore accessible by any Quito-Latacunga bus. The first entrance is at the old NASA minitrak station, about 16 km to the south of Machachi. The satellite tracking station has recently suspended operations but the turn off is still marked with a huge sign and the tracking equipment is plainly visible. About 9-10 km further south on the Pan American is another turn off with a small wooden sign and a railroad crossing. Both entrances are frequently used and during the weekend there is little difficulty in hitch-hiking into the park but midweek there is almost no traffic. The first turn off is asphalted for the first 2 km until it reaches the old tracking station where it becomes a dirt road. There are signs most of the way; you pass a railway station and then cross the tracks and continue to the Río Daule campsite which is about 1 km beyond the tracking stations. This campsite has plenty of flat tent spaces, two small picnic shelters (unsuitable for sleeping in), and fireplaces. Drinking water is from the river about 100 m past the campsite, beyond a bend in the road. If on foot, this is a good place to spend your first night.

The dirt road continues climbing slowly and 1 to 2 km beyond Río Daule passes a hairpin bend with a camp by it; there is a stable and a thatched hut but no water. After a further 1 to 2 km take an unmarked left hand turn (look for herds of llamas; the animals are being studied in the area) down a road which continues through an entrance gate (where a small fee of less than US$1 is charged) arriving 4 to 5 km further on at the abandoned administration centre. It is about 15 km from this centre, Campamento Mariscal Sucre, to the climbers' refuge.

To reach Campamento Mariscal Sucre from the second entrance road head 5 to 6 km further south on the Pan American to a turn off marked by a wooden 'Parque Nacional Cotopaxi' sign. About a kilometre south on the Pan American past the turn off is a small, rounded, grassy hill on the left this useful landmark is reputedly a preconquest mound but no one seems to know very much about it. Take the entrance road and immediately cross the railway tracks. Ignore a right turn soon after the tracks and go about a kilometre to a T junction where you take the right fork. A few hundred metres further take a sharp left turn and continue towards the park on a road which has signs where necessary. You meet up with the first entrance road by the park entrance gate and continue to the administration centre This is about a 15 km trip from the Pan American Highway. Alternatively you can get off the Quito-Latacunga bus at the railway station in the small village of Lasso and hire a taxi or camioneta to take you into the park.

Drivers charge about US$5 and many hikers opt to go as far as Laguna Limpiopungo. If you're on foot you can arrive anytime but if you're driving remember that the entrance station is open only from 8.00 a.m. to 6.00 p.m. During weekends it is open longer; from 7.00 a.m. to 6.30 p.m. Outside of these hours you must find someone to open the locked gate. You'll need your passport and a small fee is charged.

HIKING AROUND COTOPAXI

This is a beautiful and not too difficult hike which takes about a week and can be combined with ascents of some of the nearby peaks. A dirt road runs more than halfway around the volcano but some cross-country hiking will be involved to complete the circuit. Good maps are available from the IGM; the 1:50,000 topographical sheets of Machachi, Sincholagua, Cotopaxi, and Mulaló will be required. If you're a beginner and not confident of your abilities to hike without trails, you can do the dirt road sections and return the way you came. During weekends you will be able to hitch-hike much of the way but midweek you will probably find the jeep road deserted.

Your first step is to reach the old, unused administrative centre at Campamento Mariscal Sucre by one of the two entrance roads described in *Access*. If you are on foot your first night's camp will probably be at Río Daule. On the second day you should reach the administrative centre in 4 to 6 hours from Río Daule and can continue to one of the several nearby campsites.

The first campsite is some 2 to 3 km along the road beyond Campamento Mariscal Sucre. There is a small sign and a turn off to the left onto a small plain where there are little picnic shelters, an outhouse, a recently built cabin, and water running from a pipe in the gully behind the campsite. On a clear day there are excellent views of Chimborazo about 100 km to the south southwest. This campsite provides one base for climbing Rumiñahui but don't leave your gear here because it is not safe.

About a kilometre further down the road is a second camping site, also signed, but this time to the right. Again picnic shelters and a small cabin are available, but there is no running water.

Just beyond the turn off to the second campsite there is a track off to the left of the road across a large plain to Laguna de Limpios (also known as Limpiopungo) at about 3800 m. Around the lake you should watch for waterfowl and other birds, as well as the black *Atelopus* toad (see *Natural History* in Chapter 3). There is a trail around the back of the lake which will be described in *Climbing Rumiñahui*.

To continue your hike around Cotopaxi go from the campsites, past Laguna Limpiopungo, and along the road as it begins to curve further east around the mountain. Some 2 to 3 km beyond the lake, the hiker will see a signed road to the right leading to the Cotopaxi climbers' refuge some 9 km away (see *Climbing Cotopaxi*).

About 3 km after the turn off for the refuge the road forks. The track going straight on will eventually bring you to Machachi over 20 km away to the northwest. Take the right fork and curve northeast, east, and southeast until you cross a small bridge over an unnamed river about an hour's walk beyond the fork. This point is about 8 km from the lake and you could camp here, although it is rather exposed. It's better to continue southeast a further 8 km on the gently climbing road around Cotopaxi to the next running water which is usually at the stream crossing the road just above the area marked Mudadero on the IGM map. If this fails, head left or west across flat pastureland to the Río Hualpaloma which runs all year. This camp gives good views of the northeastern flanks of Cotopaxi.

(N.B. The bridge mentioned in the above paragraph is the departure point for climbing Sincholagua.)

From this camp continue on the jeep road southeast and then south for about 1 km to the point where (on the IGM map) the road stops and becomes a four wheel drive jeep track heading east. This place is easily identified because the track makes a hairpin bend into a small but steep-walled canyon. Continue into the canyon and you'll soon come to the Río Tamboyacu; good camping is also possible here.

Now you have two choices. You can continue along the jeep road as it curves east, south, and finally back west to Hacienda El Tambo, which is the furthest driveable point and about 14 km away. At about the halfway point there is a fork where you go right. Alternatively, you can forsake the jeep track and head south across country. With the IGM maps and a compass this is quite easy. Head more or less south and pass a small conical hill (Chiguilasín Chico) to your left. Continue south across a plain (you should find a horse track) over a pass to the left of a flat-topped hill (4222 m on the map). On the other side of the pass you look down on the valley of the northwest arm of the Río Tambo. Follow the valley on the right hand side southwards for about 1½ km until you come to a large valley on your right. Here there are good views of Morurco (c. 4840 m) about 1 km to the west. *(Climbers Note: Morurco can be approached from this area using an IGM map; Koerner (1976) writes that Morurco is a minor southern peak of Cotopaxi, has only been climbed once, and is reputed to be easy but interesting, with technical possibilities. Access is from the east and north around Cotopaxi. The snow cover is variable.)*

At this point turn to the southeast and follow the Río Tambo valley for about 5 km. This valley has wonderful views of Cotopaxi behind and

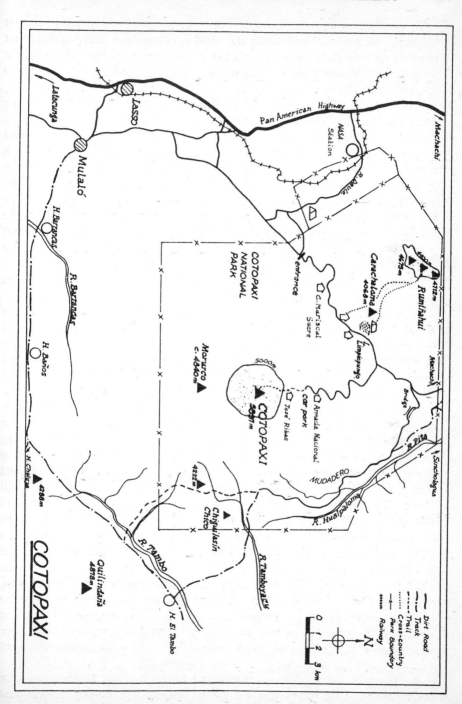

Quilindaña ahead and you can camp anywhere. When you get to the mouth of the valley you will see a snow-capped peak about 40 km to the northeast; this is Antisana.

At the mouth of the valley cross the southwestern arm of the Río Tambo — it is not difficult to ford. The IGM map shows a trail running along the river northeast for about 3 to 4 km to the Hacienda El Tambo, and southwest for about 16 km to the Hacienda Baños. At best this trail is no more than a meandering animal track, but the Río Tambo valley is easy enough to follow. This area is used as a base for climbs of Quilindaña (see page 138).

Heading southwest you will see a mountain with a steep rock face about 7 km away. The trail, or what you can find of it, follows the Río Tambo for 4 to 5 km, and when the river turns northwest to its headwaters, the trail continues southwest and passes this steep faced mountain (identified by its altitude of 4288 m on the map) to the right or north. Here the trail becomes quite visible and easy to follow over the pass to the north of peak 4288. Just before the pass is a large flat area which is the best place for a last camp.

Beyond the pass north of peak 4288 the trail continues clearly to the southwest for 1 to 2 km and then joins a dirt road. This is marked only as a footpath on the IGM map. Turn left and after some 8 to 10 km you'll reach Hacienda Chalupa, which can be used as a base camp for Quilindaña. The right turn takes you out to the Pan American Highway. The IGM maps are not very useful here as the road is not properly marked. Follow the road for some 7 to 8 km past a white stone block marker for Hacienda Baños. A few hundred metres further on take a left fork and after another few hundred metres go straight at a junction. There are no more major turns for the next 3 to 4 hours. Then you descend into the Río Barrancas valley where you could camp. Otherwise climb up the other side and follow the trail another 3 to 4 hours into Mulaló, where you will find buses to Latacunga. There are many forks in the trail beyond the Río Barrancas; take the most used looking trail and ask the many inhabitants for the way to Mulaló. It is possible to walk out on the road to Mulaló in one long, hard day; otherwise camp in the flat valley bottom of Río Barrancas. There are no hotels in Mulaló and buses stop running before nightfall.

CLIMBING COTOPAXI (5897 m)

Not too long ago a German guidebook came out with a description of climbing Cotopaxi that pointedly said it was not a technical climb, therefore no special equipment was necessary. Trying to convince its readers they could *not* climb in running shoes was practically impossible. The climb is not difficult, but *is* considered technical because of the equipment required for the ascent. Ropes, ice axes, crampons and wands are absolutely necessary. Experienced teams don't usually bother with protection, but less experienced climbers may want to carry along a couple of snow stakes and deadmen.

The Cotopaxi area is blessed with the highest number of clear days per year in the Ecuadorian Andes and thus climbs may be attempted year round. Cotopaxi is further west than Cayambe and Antisana, so it experiences the climate of the central highlands rather than the Oriente. June and July are the driest months, but extremely high winds blowing continuously for days on end are not uncommon. December and January are almost as dry and much less windy.

If you are a mountaineering party and want to reach the climbers' refuge quickly you'll need to hire a jeep or pickup truck. This can be done in Lasso some kilometres north of the park entrance (see *Access* in *Hiking Around Cotopaxi*), or in Latacunga's Plaza El Salto where you will find an *estacionamento* where there are various transportation companies. A company which will do the trip for around US$7 per pickup truck is Cooperativa de Transportes Riberas del Cutuchi.

If you have your own vehicle or are on foot, follow directions in the *Access* and *Hiking Around Cotopaxi* sections until you get to the turn off for the climbers' refuge. The turn off is at 3830 m; it is 8½ km to the parking area at 4600 m so you have to climb hard. The road is easy to follow; en route you pass the Armada Nacional refuge at 4400 m. It's old, small, damaged, and rarely used. If you're on foot, the gully behind this refuge offers a short cut to the new refuge; it takes at least an hour with a pack. From the parking lot a trail leads up the sand to the new refuge. Though it looks close, with a heavy pack it will take at least half an hour to walk there.

The José Ribas refuge was built in 1971 and extended in 1977. It has about three dozen bunkbeds and floor space, basic food supplies, running water, kitchen facilities, outhouses, a fireplace, and lock-up facilities for your gear when you climb. It costs about US$3 per night night to stay here.

The standard route (other routes are rarely climbed) takes 5 to 9 hours for the ascent and 2 to 4 for the descent. The snow becomes unpleasantly wet and soft by early afternoon so you should leave the hut between 12 midnight and 3 a.m. The first hour of the climb takes you up a triangular scree slope which is sometimes snow covered. Once you are on the glacier you climb straight up and then towards the right. There is talk of 'subtle ridges' in some accounts, but in fact the climb is rather featureless and mainly a long snow plod once the problem of getting onto the glacier has been overcome. Although the mountain is well crevassed, for the most part the crevasses are spectacularly large and open and thus easy to avoid. A route is usually well marked around the crevasses with wands and footprints — remember this is the most popular high climb in Ecuador. The main feature to look for is a huge rock face called Yanasacha (literally 'large black rock' in Quechua). You ascend across the snow, angling to the right on the glacier below this rock face, and then come back to the left to reach the summit crater. The last 200 m or so are quite steep..

The classic round crater is over half a kilometre wide and a circuit is possible. Steam can be seen escaping from vents in the centre and from the walls. Expeditions into the crater have been undertaken; the first was in 1972 when a Polish-Czech expedition spent 6 hours in the crater and since then several Ecuadorians have repeated the venture.

An alternative route follows the standard climb up the glacier, but then traverses left to below Yanasacha. Here it turns right just below the rock face and climbs a long snow ramp to the summit. Several years ago this was the more commonly used route but a huge crevasse has since made it impassable. The same thing may now be happening on the standard route as a huge crevasse is threatening to cut off the line to the summit. A more direct route may have to be devised in the near future.

CLIMBING RUMIÑAHUI (4712 m)

A geologist would place Rumiñahui in Chapter 4, The Central Valley, but I include it here because it is within the confines of Cotopaxi National Park. This long-extinct volcano is located 45 km south of Quito and only 13 km northwest of Cotopaxi. It is an easy ascent and has often been climbed; surprisingly, I could find no records of ascents prior to the 1950s. Although occasionally sprinkled with snow, it is normally a walk up with a rocky scramble at the top.

Rumiñahui is named after one of Atahualpa's famous generals and means 'face of stone'. Despite the name, one should remember that the stone is heavily laced with metal, so you should descend if an electric storm threatens.

The most well-known route begins from Laguna Limpiopungo (see *Access* and *Hiking Around Cotopaxi*). The lake is quite shallow, and during the dry months may be a bit scummy or even completely dry, but you'll find a path going around its east side and past a boggy area to the north. About a kilometre northwest of the lake you'll find possible camping spots with clean running water. This is not an officially designated campsite and has no facilities.

From here head west up a small steep-sided valley, following the stream around to the northwest to a boggy plain below the mountain. Skirt this plain to the northeast and ascend the grassy ridge coming off the Central Summit. Once on the ridge swing west and head for the Central Summit, which should take 1½ to 2½ hours. To get to the main north summit, a traverse across the summit ridge is not possible. You'll have to descend about halfway down back towards the grassy ridge where you'll see a number of narrow arêtes running up to the summit ridge to the north. Traverse below these across rocky *páramo* until you come to the last major gully of reddish sand which is the route to the summit ridge. This gully is just before the large rockface at the northern end of the mountain. Climb to the top of the summit ridge, cross it, and then drop down the western side. From here you should be able to scramble to the summit; ascents from the eastern side are difficult. Except for the last few metres, which are the usual rotten rock, the ascent is an easy scramble. Even if you don't quite make the top the view is great.

Climbing the south peak (incorrectly marked as Rumiñahui Central on the IGM map) involves an easy grade (about 5.5) of technical rock climbing and the proper technical equipment. Follow the directions below into the gully/valley behind Carachaloma. There is good camping here if desired. Walk north to the end of valley and begin a scramble up the flanks below the south peak. Head directly for the centre of the base where there are a number of rock routes though the rock isn't all that great. For an excellent view into the crater, traverse right from the south summit base and head for the low point on the ridge that separates the south and central summits. There is an obvious grey sand slope leading up to the summit ridge. Up to here only a bit of careful scrambling is necessary. However, the rocky traverse across the ridge to either the south or central summit will require some technical rock climbing. Best to bring rope and some protection if planning the traverse. Not for the unexperienced.

The lake, river valley, plain, and grassy ridge mentioned in the description are all quite easy to find on the IGM maps (1:50,000 series) Machachi and Sincholagua. The positions of the West and Central Summits are inaccurately marked on the IGM maps. From a mountaineer's point of view, the West Peak is the 4615 m one at map reference 770346 (Machachi), and the Central Peak is at 775352.

You may prefer to camp at the official site on the left hand side of the road about 2½ km in from the entrance station. The route from here lies up the gully behind (north of) the the campsite, around the hill called Carachaloma (4068 m) which is about 1½ km to the north, and then northwest up the stream valley to the boggy plain mentioned in the standard approach. This way is rather longer. The climb takes 4 to 6 hours depending on how well you've acclimatized.

Other approaches and routes are possible but less frequently climbed. Approaches are made from the northeast over the Filo Santo Domingo to the bottom of the last sandy gully described in the standard route. The rockface just north of this gully offers a technical rock route first climbed in 1972 by the Ecuadorian climbers Cruz, Reinoso, and Berge. Ascents from the Machachi side (from the northwest) are reportedly possible.

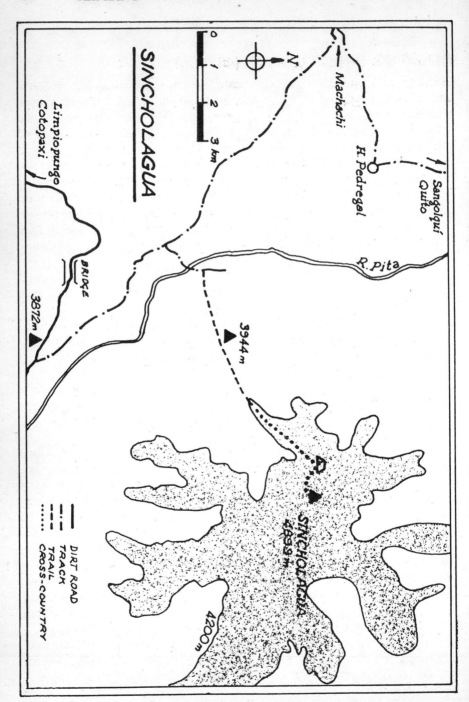

CLIMBING SINCHOLAGUA (4893 m)

Sincholagua is an extinct volcano located 45 km south southeast of Quito and 17 km northeast of Cotopaxi, just outside of the national park boundary. It is one of the many mountains first ascended by Edward Whymper and the Carrels in 1880. They climbed the northwest ridge and this is still considered the normal route. It used to be a well glaciated mountain and the IGM 1:50,000 Sincholagua map shows a permanent ice cap over 1½ km long. In common with other Ecuadorian peaks the permanent snow line has receded over recent decades and today there is no permanent glacier, although after a heavy storm there is some snow cover. The climb is mainly a scramble but the summit pinnacle is of rotten rock which is loose and difficult except after a good snowfall and cold night when the rocks should be solidly frozen together.

Access is most frequently made from the south via Cotopaxi National Park although access from Quito is also possible. Enter the national park as usual and continue around Cotopaxi on the dirt road described in *Hiking Around Cotopaxi*. Go to that point on the road when you cross an unnamed river on a small bridge (map reference 865347). If in a jeep continue beyond the bridge about 3 km until you pass a perfectly cone shaped hill (3872 m) on your right and a hillock to your left. Look for an unmarked jeep trail which goes hard left and northwest. Follow this track for about 4 to 5 km, then turn right on a side track which fords the Río Pita. If on foot you can go north cross-country from the bridge and meet the track just before the right turn about 2 km north of the bridge.

This point can be reached by four wheel drive jeep from Quito. Head south on the Valle de los Chillos freeway to Sangolquí and continue to the village of Selva Alegre. Head south towards Hacienda Patichupamba and continue south towards the Río Pita and Sincholagua. The road is difficult and unsigned so ask everyone you meet for directions. It's 50 to 60 km by bad road from Selva Alegre.

Once you've crossed the Río Pita head northeast up a ridge with vehicle tracks on it, past a survey marker (3944 m), until you meet a ridge running northwest. This will take a half day on foot from the river, but a four wheel drive vehicle will get most of the way. Camp is usually made near the junction of the two ridges in order to make an early start the next day, whilst the rocks are still frozen together. Water is usually available.

From the camp continue up the northwest ridge. There are several peaks. Pass to the right of the second to last one and at the main summit beware of rockfall. After a cold or snowy night the rocks are usually frozen together but otherwise the last few metres are difficult because of the extremely rotten rocks. A descent by rappelling off the summit is sometimes made.

For the rock climber, Pico Hoeneisen is a prominent 'lower peak' below the southeast peak of Sincholagua. It was first climbed by Miguel Andrade and Hugo Torres in 1972. You'll need a rope, obviously, and an assortment of nuts and chocks for this technical rock climb. The approach begins at the same bridge off the Cotopaxi road. From here you'll see the southeast ridge of Sincholagua with the prominent rock outcrop or peak in the centre of the mountain. Cross the *páramo* northeast following a W-shaped *quebrada* as it ascends to the top of the *páramo*. Drop down from here to just below the base of the south ridge where there is good camping with plenty of water. Follow the *páramo* up from the camping area to the scree and continue along the ridgeline to the mountain. You'll come to a prominent wide ledge, highly visible from below, cutting across the south side of the mountain and intersecting the ridge. Follow the ledge around to the right side of the ridge and you'll come to a 15 metre chimney of good rock. A thin crack in the chimney will take small nuts. Ascending this, you'll next reach an overhanging section which is fairly difficult — 5.10 free, or maybe requiring some aid moves. The rock is loose at the top of this section. Here, the route traverses right to another small chimney of about 10 metres. At the top, you'll come to a triangular sand/snow slope which leads up to the summit. The route will have to be descended the same way with several rappels/abseils.

This is the twelfth highest peak in Ecuador but is rarely visited because climbers tend to concentrate on the ten peaks over 5000 m. So much the better! In common with Rumiñahui and Cotopaxi the weather is better than average; the driest months are June through August.

CLIMBING QUILINDAÑA (4878 m)

This extinct volcano lies just outside the park boundaries about 16 km southeast of Cotopaxi and 65 km south southeast of Quito. It is an infrequently climbed, difficult, and technical mountain which offers one of the most interesting rock climbing routes in Ecuador. It was first climbed in 1952 by a large party of Ecuadorians, Colombians, French, and Italians.

The normal base for the climb is the Hacienda El Tambo (map ref. 980199 on the IGM 1:50,000 Cotopaxi map). This can be reached on foot or by four wheel drive vehicle as described in *Hiking Around Cotopaxi*. You may decide to camp near the hacienda the first night. There is a good site just beyond the hacienda near the river or you can continue south toward several prominent *páramo* hills, hiking about an hour. There is no trail but just after dropping down slightly past the hills, there will be a flat area with water, good for camping and with excellent views of Quilindaña. From here you could attempt the summit by leaving at about 5.00 a.m. to allow enough time for the return trip. (Hide any gear left behind.) Otherwise, you can continue the following day across the *páramo* to the obvious central (north) ridge which leads to the base of the mountain. At the top of the ridge on the northwest flank is a small lake near the saddle with suitable camping. It's about 1½ to 2 hours up the ridge from the suggested *páramo* camp. The climb from the lake to the summit will take about 3 to 5 hours.

An alternative access is from the Hacienda Chalupas, which can also be reached by four wheel drive vehicle. The dirt road from Mulaló to the *hacienda* is not marked on the IGM maps so you have to get directions from everyone you meet along the way. From this *hacienda* hike north for about half a day to the lake mentioned above.

The normal route departs from the lake, traversing left to an obvious couloir (which may be either snow or sand depending on the recent weather). The couloir is the only access to the prominent left (northwest) ridge. Begin rock climbing directly up the ridge, slightly difficult at 5.6/5.7. It's easy to pick out the line on the good, solid rock. The technical part ends where the ridge flattens and from here it's only another 150 metres of easy scrambling to the summit. Keep slightly to the right on the ridge as you approach the peak.

A little easier rock route would be to cross the ridge rather than climb directly up, traversing to below the north rock face. The line up the face to the flat part of the ridge is straightforward — easy 5th class.

Koerner describes three routes that I can't comment on, other than to quote him directly: "On the north face you will see two large and rather triangular rock faces. Somewhere, there exists an aid route which ascends here. To the left is a couloir in which runs another route that is roughly class five, but requires only four to eight pitons.

The west face may be climbed also. From the ridge to the south of the lakes, go up any one of a number of small snow gullies to a bit of a snow field. Climb this to the saddle and then go left up the summit ridge to the summit."

(Author's Note: Remember that changing snow conditions in Ecuador mean that most of the snow described above has disappeared.)

THE LLANGANATES

If you've heard of the Llanganates you've probably heard of treasure. From the time of the *conquistadores* it has been believed that treasure was buried here. The story is that when the last Inca, Atahualpa, was murdered by Pizarro, Atahualpa's general, Rumiñahui, hid the treasure from the Spaniards. Many eminent people have been convinced of its existence or have gone to look for it; they include the botanist Richard Spruce, the scientist and evolutionist Alfred Russel Wallace, George Dyott — the man who looked for Colonel Fawcett — and the British climbers Joe Brown and Hamish MacInnes. No one has found the treasure yet but a Swiss-German resident of Quito, Eugene Brunner, has looked for the treasure for almost half a century. He is convinced that he has found its location and the last I heard was that he had organized yet another major expedition (involving the Ecuadorian armed forces) to recover the gold — estimated at 750 tons!! *Vamos a ver.*

If you want to look for the treasure yourself, you'll probably find it the most difficult trip of your life. The following description by Koerner in his *The Fool's Climbing Guide to Ecuador* (which the author freely admits to being a work of fiction and plagiarism!) explains why. I like the succinctness of his description so much that I reprint it here.

"The Llanganates are a mysterious and almost impenetrable range to the northeast of Baños. Part of Atahualpa's gold is said to be hidden there, and people occasionally go off to look for it. You can too if your interest is to get hideously and hopelessly lost in 15 foot high, razor sharp pampas grass and continuous rain.

"The Llanganates also contain El Hermoso, 4571 m, an occasional snow peak, the identity of which will baffle you when first you see it from some other peak."

The Baños Area

INTRODUCTION   This resort town is popular for its thermal springs, splendid scenery, and pleasant climate. Several day hikes can be made and the town is a good base for climbing Volcán Tungurahua and El Altar, as well as being the beginning of one of Ecuador's principal roads into the jungle.

The town's tourist attractions include several thermal baths (*piscinas*), a small museum, a zoo of Ecuadorian animals, and restaurants serving the typical Andean delicacy *cuy* or roast guinea pig. Your hotel manager can direct you to all of these. By strolling down the main street in the morning you'll see the shop-keepers busy making taffy. A glob of the soft mixture is slung onto a wooden hook on the wall, then pulled repeatedly until it hardens. Although you can buy it in bars, it's much nicer to pay a few sucres for a wispy piece of still warm taffy.

One hotel can be especially recommended to climbers and hikers on a budget. Pensión Patty at Eloy Alfaro 554 (less than two blocks from the market) is simple but very clean, friendly, family-run and inexpensive. Cooking facilities are available and many gringos looking for hiking or climbing partners stay here. The landlady's sons, Carlos and José, are both climbers and will give advice and sometimes act as guides. Baños has a broad selection of lodging in most price ranges. Finding something to meet your needs will present no problem.

DAY HIKES FROM BAÑOS

Baños lies at 1800 m in the valley of Río Pastaza which flows from west to east. Good day hikes may be made in the mountains to the north and in the foothills of Tungurahua to the south of Baños, as well as down the river valley to the east.

To reach the steep hills on the north side of town you must cross the Río Pastaza on one of two bridges, the Puente San Francisco or the Puente San Martín. But once on the other side, directions become meaningless. There are so many paths to choose from, it's up to you how high and far.you climb. Just plan to cross one bridge going and the other coming back for variety. The trail to Puente San Francisco leaves from behind the sugar cane stalls by the main bus station, and after crossing the bridge becomes very steep. You can climb to the top of the hill but the trails peter out near the summit. On a clear day you are rewarded with marvellous views of Tungurahua and Chimborazo, as well as of green cultivated fields, passion flowers, waterfalls, and the turbulent Río Pastaza.

The Puente San Martin lies over a kilometre west of town. Walk out on the main west-bound road, cross a bridge, and keep going until you reach a right fork by a blue religious shrine just before the police checkpoint. Take this fork and walk less than a kilometre to the bridge. It crosses an impressive gorge and a few hundred metres to the right is the waterfall known as Cascada Ines María which can be seen if you take a rough trail to the right from near the bridge. The dirt road continues a few kilometres to the village of Lligua and at several points trails climb the hill to the right of the road so you can take your pick.

If you prefer a day hike with clearer directions and well defined trails then head for the hills south of town. The hike to Pondoa on the slopes of Volcán Tungurahua is one idea (see *Tungurahua*). Another possibility is the hike to the village of Runtun, which consists of half a dozen buildings, one of which is a bar with a pool table! There are two trails to Runtun; the shorter of the two will take about 2 hours from Baños. Leave town by heading south on Calle Tomás Haiflans which soon passes Escuela Vicente Maldonado. Just beyond the school the road becomes a footpath which climbs diagonally left up the hill towards a house with a huge cross plainly visible on the sky line. It's the only good trail so you can't miss it. It will take about an hour to reach the cross with excellent views of Baños. The trail now doubles back to the right and towards the top of the hill until it reaches Runtun. Immediately before the village there is a fork; the left goes to the village (50 m) and the right goes down to Baños. This alternative descent is rather longer than returning the way you came. On a clear day the views of Tungurahua from near Runtun are magnificent.

Finally, if you've had enough of running up and down steep mountain sides, you can walk, hitch, or take a bus (marked Agoyan) as far as you like on the road towards the Oriente. There are three major landmarks which are accessible in a day from Baños. Some 2 km from the town centre is San Vicente where there's a small zoo. It houses an interesting collection of Ecuadorian species including the rare harpy eagle and a free-range ridiculously tame tapir. The zoo keeper is interested in his job and will give you plenty of information and perhaps let you into some of the cages for photography.

Once your zoo visit has been concluded you can continue about 6 km to the once-famous Agoyan Falls (where the bus terminates). A new hydroelectric plant above the falls has altered their lovely character, though at times they will still be visible from the road. At the bus terminus you can continue through the tunnel (take the one on the right) walking or hitching a further 10 km to the Río Verde Falls. There are many different cascades along the road, but the ones at Río Verde are the most impressive. The views along the road are wonderful as the steep walled Río Pastaza canyon slowly opens up into the Oriente. Once at the little village of Río Verde, walk through town and over the road bridge until you find a trail to your right, just by the last house in town. The trail leads steeply down to the Río Pastaza which is crossed by a suspension footbridge from where you can view the falls. Better still scramble right up to them on the steep and narrow path immediately before the footbridge. It is an exciting place; the constricted gorge reverberates with power and it is difficult to make yourself heard above the roar. This point is 20 km from Baños and about as far as you can easily reach in a day and hitch back to Baños — further trips into the jungle are included in the Oriente section.

The paths feather-lined and steep.
Overhead a sky of mud.
Then all of a sudden in the air the purest white lily of a tall volcano.

                                                                    Henry Michaux

TUNGURAHUA (5016 m)

Tungurahua is a beautiful and active snow-capped volcano situated about 10 km south of Baños, and now part of Sangay National Park. An eruption in 1711 destroyed several towns and a major eruption was recorded early this century. Present activity is limited to a few fumaroles and steam vents, and is responsible for the natural hot springs found in Baños. The volcano was first climbed in 1873 by the Germans, Wilhelm Reiss and Alfons Stübel.

From a climber's point of view, Tungurahua is rather an anomaly. It has been described both as 'easy to access and to climb' and also 'one of the hardest climbs in Ecuador'. Both descriptions are correct because although the climb is straightforward and easy from a technical viewpoint, it is physically demanding as it involves 3200 m of vertical ascent from Baños at 1800 m.

To get to the refuge you can either go on foot or hire transport up to the park entrance where you'll pay the US$1 refuge fee. A daily milk truck leaves from Pensión Patty at 6.30 a.m. or you can arrange for a *camioneta* to make the trip (about US$10).

If going on foot, start your climb at the western entrance to Baños at a police checkpoint. Across the highway you'll see a dirt road bearing up and to the right. Walk up this road about 100 m and turn right at a sign for Refugio Nicolás Martínez where you'll pick up the trail which is very steep and narrow. It follows a ridge with fine views of Baños and 1 or 2 hours walking are needed to reach the small village of Pondoa. Stop at the Pondoa store and chat with the owner who will tell you how to reach the hut and can introduce you to the local guide, Sr. Angel Perez who has climbed the volcano dozens of times and is very experienced. He doesn't have much equipment to rent but can arrange mule hire and guide you if you wish. Only very basic supplies (beer, sardines, and crackers) are available at the store.

It takes an hour or two to climb from Pondoa to the park entrance. If arriving by local transport, this is the end of the road, and the start of the final approach to the refuge. Often there are mules and horses available to help carry gear up to the refuge (about US$4 per animal), but don't rely on it. If you definitely want to go with pack animals, then arrange it ahead of time.

The trail up to the refuge begins about 100 m past the entrance station to the left. It's quite steep in places and often muddy. At several points the trail goes through 'tunnels' of bamboo and other tropical vegetation. Expect to take from 3 to 5 hours getting to the refuge.

When you reach the refuge (built in the late 1970s) you will find floor space for about eighteen people and a propane cooking stove. Water is obtained from a spring about 200 m beyond the hut. The altitude here is about 3800 m and the view of Chimborazo's east face is impressive.

The climb from the hut to the top is best attempted in the early morning before the summit snow becomes soft and slushy. A dawn start is adequate. Head south southeast to a survey marker at about 4000 m. About 1 or 2 hours above the hut a rockband is reached through which you can easily scramble and soon after you pass an aluminium cross. Here bear a little to the right (south) towards the craters which will take about 2 to 3 more hours to reach.

There are two craters but only the smaller one is presently active. Climbers sometimes camp in here because it is well sheltered — but don't get too close to the steam vents. The inactive south crater is larger and has a more typical crater shape with beautifully coloured rock walls.

About 45 minutes are needed to climb from the craters to the highest point. Walk straight up the snowfield between the craters. Crampons and ice axe are all that are needed as there is no major crevasse danger and the slope is gentle. Indeed, experienced climbers have reached the top merely by kicking snowsteps with their boots. The top is rather featureless, so if there is any hint of fog take compass bearings.

The descent from the summit back to Baños in one day is not easy, especially with heavy packs. It can be hot, depending on the season, and the steep trail makes it hard on the knees. It is, after all, 3200 m of downhill!

WARNING: This is perhaps the easiest snow climb in Ecuador and it is very tempting for beginning climbers to attempt this 5000 m peak. Enough time must be spent acclimatizing in Quito before the climb, as the low altitude of Baños is not sufficient for acclimatization. The apparent simplicity of this climb can fool you — remember climbers have died on Tungurahua.

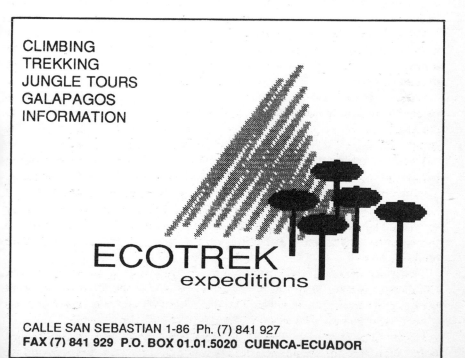

EL Altar (5319 m) Region

INTRODUCTION This, the fifth highest mountain in Ecuador, undoubtedly involves the most technical climbing and has one of the longest approaches. Situated some 170 km south of Quito, El Altar is an extinct volcano which at one time was probably higher than Cotopaxi, but a huge ancient eruption almost totally destroyed the cone leaving a steep-sided and jagged crater, 3 km in diameter. The west wall was destroyed, allowing easy access into the crater but the volcano had never been climbed from within until 1984. Despite repeated attempts by many climbers, including Whymper, the icy ramparts of El Altar withstood all assaults until July 7 1963, when an Italian expedition led by Marino Tremonti conquered the last unclimbed 5000 m mountain in Ecuador.

Indian legend dates the huge final explosion to 1460, but volcanologists agree that it must have been far more ancient. Today, the volcano is inactive. Nine separate sub-summits are recognised on its reversed C shaped crater. They have now all been climbed, although one of the Frailes was not conquered until 1979 by a team of six Ecuadorian climbers led by Luis Naranjo.

El Altar needs no translation into English and its various peaks all bear church related names. The highest is El Obispo (the bishop), 5319 m, but its height is much in dispute, with some authorities suggesting as much as 5465 m. This was the first peak to be climbed. The Italians, led by Tremonti, played an important part in the conquest of El Altar's peaks. They returned in 1965 to conquer the second peak, El Canonigo (the canon), 5260 m, and in 1972 achieved the first ascent of El Fraile Grande (the great friar). The three other Fraile peaks were all climbed for the first time by Ecuadorian teams. Bernado Beate, Jacinto Carrasco, and Rafael Terán were the summit climbers in two of those first ascents. La Monja Grande (the great nun), the third highest peak at 5160 m, was climbed by a US-Japanese team in 1968 and the remaining two peaks, La Monja Chica (the little nun) and El Tabernaculo (the tabernacle) fell to a German team in 1972. The extremely difficult north face of Obispo was climbed from within the crater by a French/Ecuadorian team in 1984. The ascent of this grade VI rock face took six days to complete.

This volcano is obviously not a jaunt for the beginning climber, but a backpacking trip is very rewarding. There is a grey-green crater lake called, curiously, Laguna Amarilla (yellow lake), and from the edge of the crater backpackers can listen to the hanging glaciers crack and rumble and catch glimpses of enormous ice slides. Condors are also seen around here. El Altar is protected as part of Sangay National Park.

The IGM maps available for the area are the 1:25,000 Cerros Negros and Laguna Pintada.

It is rainy most of the year, June and July being the wettest months. The best times to go are from late November through early February, with the majority of successful ascents being made around Christmas and New Year. I have seen one report published in Ecuador which claims that the El Altar region receives 14,600 mm (that's about 48 feet!) of precipitation annually. Although I find this hard to believe, it does indicate that the region is wet ... very wet.

GETTING THERE   From Quito's Terminal Terrestre, take a bus via Ambato to Baños, and continue on to Penipe, about halfway to Riobamba. From Penipe you must make your way to Candelaria, about 15 km away up the Río Blanco valley. It's quite a steep climb.

If you decide to go on foot, and your bus goes into Penipe (rather than passing along the highway), tell the driver you want to go to Candelaria. You will then be let off about a mile past Penipe at the turn-off for Candelaria. The hike takes about five hours and is not bad as far as five-hour hikes go.

The most reliable transport along this route is the *lechera,* or milk truck, departing Penipe at about 6.00 a.m. On Thursday, Saturday and Sunday there is a mid-morning truck. The Penipe market is on Sunday, so all day

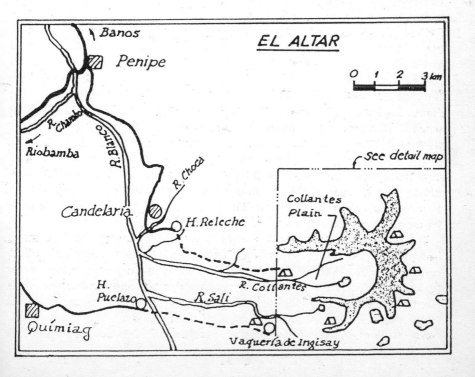

there are various vehicles bound for Candelaria. There is also a driver who will take you in his pickup truck from Penipe to Candelaria and Hacienda Releche. Ask around the main plaza for Ernesto Haro B. He charges about US$5 and will pick you up for the return trip at a pre-arranged time if you wish.

For the return from Candelaria to Penipe you can catch the *lechera* between 6.00 and 7.00 a.m. or ask the teachers for a lift when they leave at about noon.

In Candelaria there is a small store with very basic food supplies and they may be able to suggest somewhere you can sleep. There are also mules available to pack your gear up to the base of the mountain. Return pick up times can be arranged.

HIKING AROUND EL ALTAR

From Candelaria continue along the road for about 2 km until you come to a light green building with a Sangay National Park sign which is the ranger station. Pay your park fee (US$2) and follow this road to the right up a steep hill, across a stream and past the Hacienda Releche. After about 45 minutes the correct trail branches off to the left. This is the only confusing part since there are now only cow paths running up through the meadows. The trail to El Altar goes high on the west facing hillside just below a waterfall but above the cultivated fields. The trail is just behind the trees and is not visible from below, but if you follow the cow paths uphill through the fields you will come to it. Once you connect with the main trail turn right and stride out. There are no other paths to confuse you.

The trail heads east, passing through scrubby woodlands, going gently uphill before rounding a corner and giving you your first views of El Altar and its river valley. A marvellous sight. From there it's a gentle 3 hours of nearly level walking until you arrive at the broad pasture called Collantes (also known as Collanes). This is normally as far as the mules will take you (unless you're going northeast towards Canonigo) and it is often used as a campsite. Too often, in fact, judging by the amount of trash I saw there. This section takes 5 to 8 hours from Candelaria. You can cross the Collantes plain to the trees at the base of the crater to camp out of the wind. Edward Whymper did just that in 1880.

From the Collantes plain there are three basic choices, assuming, that is, you wish to do anything at all. You can go east and visit the crater; you can go south to climb the southern peaks (including Obispo, the highest) or do some backpacking in a beautifully wild and trackless area with many lakes; or you can go north to climb the northern peaks (including Canonigo, the second highest) and do some backpacking in this area which is little explored. A challenging and adventurous hike would be all the way around the back of the mountain — it is rarely done.

The best route from Collantes to the rim of the crater is up along the wooded ridge on the left of the river (follow cow paths), heading toward the deeply incised rock face. Although you can go around the hill at the left of the ridge, the shortest route up is the gully just to the right of the knob at

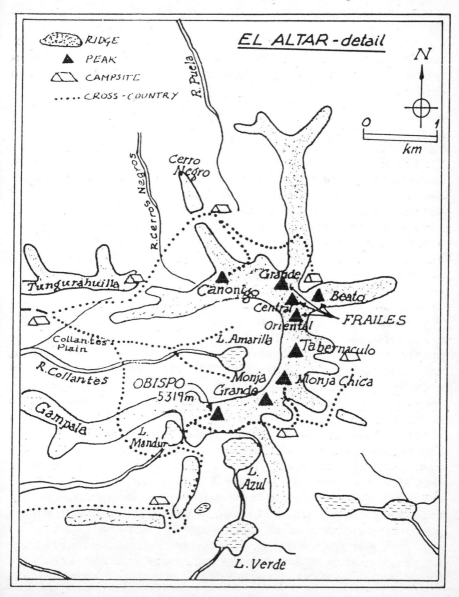

the end of the wooded ridge. The first 5 m are very steep, but not difficult as there is tussock grass to hang onto and flat places where you can regain your breath. If it has been raining you might feel safer (and drier) taking the long route around and up the left ridge, but you'll have to climb much higher. The reward for going this way is that the views are better. It takes about 3 to 4 hours for the round trip.

For the return trip, consider hiking to Hacienda Puelazo via Vaquería de Ingisay (see below).

CLIMBING OBISPO AND THE SOUTHERN PEAKS

From Collantes head south and climb over the Gampala ridge. (I camped on the ridge for spectacular views of Altar, Tungurahua, Carihuairazo, and Chimborazo.) From Gampala ridge drop to Laguna Mandur and climb the Negra Paccha ridge to a small pass near where the Italian camp was situated. Continue north to the lower glacier and cross it to the base of Obispo. The Italian Route climbs the wide and obvious gully and passes through a rock band to the upper glacier. Traverse the upper glacier to the right until you reach the base of a second snow gully, much steeper and narrower than the first. This gully brings you to the summit ridge. Head right and you'll be faced with a difficult 30 m high rock wall which is the final barrier to the summit. This is graded 5.5/5.6, but the extremely rotten rock and severe exposure make it much more difficult. To avoid the first gully, one can climb to the upper glacier on the ridge to the right. To do this, after crossing the lower glacier, go under the ridge and then up and around on the western side. Follow up a snow gully to get on the ridge, staying just below the ridge crest on the snow ledges until you reach the upper glacier, then continue with the Italian Route. This is called the Calvary Ridge route and is used as the standard descent route. Further around the corner from the Calvary Ridge Route is the more difficult Superior Glacier Route. Looking up, you'll see a steep snow slope, with an ice cliff with long icicles on the left and crevasses to the right. The climb begins with three or four pitches of 40 degree climbing but it finishes nearly vertical, topping out onto the upper, or superior, glacier. A bivouac may be necessary. Rappels are usually used for the descent.

An alternative access route is often used instead of the Candelaria-Collantes trail described. From Riobamba get a bus to Químiag and hitchhike or walk to the Hacienda Puelazo. Mules can be hired here and you head east on a trail towards the Vaquería de Ingisay, which is a shepherds' hut a day's journey from Puelazo. Camp is usually made before you reach the Vaquería. The next day continue east on cow paths along the Negra Paccha ridge and make a camp on the ridge. The third day is spent following the ridge to the Italian camp. Fit and acclimatized climbers may be able to combine these two days into one long one. Although this route is longer, it has the advantage that the mules can get closer to the Italian base camp than Collantes.

To climb the other southern peaks, Monja Grande, Monja Chica, and Tabernaculo, you have to continue from the base of Obispo around the south side of the mountain along the foot of the glacier. Approximate positions for campsites are indicated on the map. Half a dozen major and many minor lakes make this an area of exceptional beauty.

CLIMBING CANONIGO AND THE NORTHERN PEAKS

From the Collantes plain head northeast over the Tungurahuilla ridge where there are possible campsites. Continue to the next ridge, Cerro Negro, where a base camp is made. Mules from Candelaria can reach this point in 2 days — or perhaps one long hard one.

From the base camp on Cerro Negro ridge traverse the glacier which lies to the northeast of Canonigo, the second highest peak of Altar. Head towards the base of a small ridge which leads to a minor eastern summit of Canonigo. Difficult mixed climbing takes you up the western side of this small ridge and you then curve around the crater towards the summit west of you. A bivouac is often necessary. Canonigo is less frequently climbed than Obispo and is more difficult.

To climb the other northern peaks, the four Frailes, continue around the bottom of the northern glaciers to a camp in the cirque of the Frailes. These peaks have had very few ascents.

VOLCÁN SANGAY (5230 m)

INTRODUCTION   In many ways Sangay is the most difficult and dangerous mountain to climb in Ecuador. It is said to be the most continuously active volcano in South America and the constant shower of red hot rocks and ash make all attempts to climb it an exceedingly hazardous venture. Furthermore it is situated in a very remote region and several days of hard travel are required to reach its base. The volcano is found in the southern central part of the largely inaccessible Sangay National Park, some 200 km south of Quito.

The height of Sangay is usually given as 5230 m but constant activity periodically alters this. The shape of the cone and the number of craters are also constantly changing. The volcanologist Minard L. Hall recorded three main craters and several smaller ones during investigations in 1976.

The first recorded eruption was in 1628 but it was doubtless active before that date. The next 100 years were apparently quiet but since 1728 the volcano has been erupting almost continuously. In 1849 the Frenchman, Sebastian Wisse, explored the area and counted 267 strong explosions within one hour. A short spell of inactivity occurred from 1916 to 1934 and it was during this time that the volcano was first ascended. The U.S. climbers Robert T. and Terris Moore, Paul Austin, and Lewis Thorne reached the summit on August 4, 1929. Attempts since then have claimed the lives of several climbers, including two British mountaineers who died in 1976 as recorded in the book *Sangay Survived* by Richard Snailham. Despite the constant eruptions and danger several successful ascents by Ecuadorian climbers have been reported in the 70s and 80s. On September 16, 1982, Helena Landázuri, of the Fundación Natura, became the first woman to reach the summit. Since then, the volcano has seen quite a few successful attempts, both by expeditions and individual climbers.

THE APPROACH AND CLIMB   Hiring a guide is practically essential. You could probably get into the base camp at La Playa with no problem, but finding your way across the lower flanks of the volcano at 2.30 a.m. presents some real time-consuming considerations. The route-finding descent is no less difficult. No guide will accompany you to the summit (each will adamantly declare he has a wife and children to think about!) but a guide will get you to the start of the climb and wait there for your return. One well-recommended fellow is José Baño Masa who lives in Alao on the south side of the river. Ask anyone in the village for directions to his house. You can also stay the night there. He charges about US$5 a day, depending on the size of the group. Food must be provided for the guide and any porters that may be hired in addition to the wages paid. Be sure to bring enough for everyone.

The initial stages of the approach are simple: take one of many buses from Quito's Terminal Terrestre to Riobamba. From Riobamba several buses a day go to Licto or Pungala, about 20 km south southeast of Riobamba. From Licto or Pungala occasional trucks go into Alao, which is the starting point for any attempt on Sangay.

Alao is a very small village which nevertheless boasts a few small shops where basic last minute supplies may be purchased. There is also a national park station and two park wardens who will let you sleep in the station for a nominal fee.

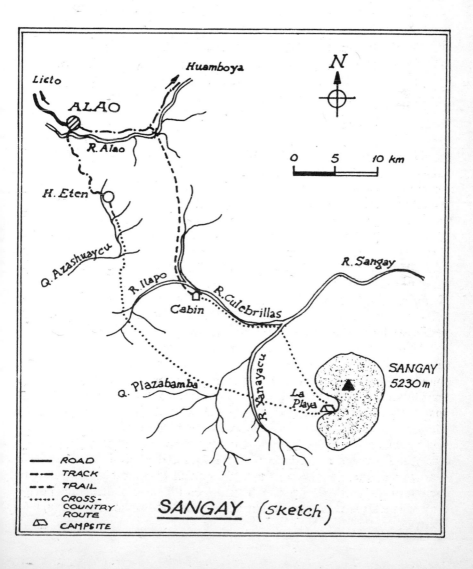

SANGAY (sketch)

There are two routes into Sangay. One is the longer, pack-animal route taking 4 days to get to base camp and requiring some time to arrange the mules in advance. This route begins from Hacienda Eten which is almost a day's hike from Alao. From Eten you head more or less south along the Quebrada Azashuaycu and camp in an area known as Escaleras, continuing the next day in a roughly southeast direction to Plazabamba. The going is very up and down as you constantly climb rises and cross rivers. In one day fourteen river fordings were reported. The vegetation here is not too thick. Plazabamba is a large flat low area which can be seen from quite a distance. There is a simple shelter which is easy to find in the the flat plain. This is as far as the mules will be taken. From here the muledriver/guide will help you carry your gear to the base camp at La Playa, but the going is difficult.

From Plazabamba, there is more vegetation and the terrain becomes increasingly ridged and difficult. There are many streams and small rivers to ford. The base camp is approximately east southeast of Plazabamba. Although you are now close to the mountain, almost constant cloud makes a sighting infrequent.

The other, shorter route requires you to carry in your own gear. Pack animals can go part of the way in, but not far enough to justify using them. Because this route is shorter — only 3 days to base camp — hiring porters to carry extra gear might be more practical than dealing with mules. From Alao the first day's hike goes to the river junction of the Culebrillas, taking anywhere from 8 to 12 hours depending on the trail conditions. The track crosses a watershed which means an ascent (and descent) of almost 1000 m. There are a couple of grass huts for shelter if you don't feel like setting up a tent. If the weather is good, you'll see magnificent views of Sangay.

From Culebrillas the following day gets you to the Yanayacu river camp in about 4 to 6 hours. If the weather conditions were perfect, and your physical condition nearly that, you could probably make it to La Playa base camp in one very long day. However, it's more realistic to plan on camping at Yanayacu after a day of wading through streams and crossing numerous bogs. From here to La Playa, the route goes up and down constantly, through thick, rough vegetation that can cut the hands. A pair of light gloves will provide some protection. The La Playa area, at 3600 m, is reached after about 4 to 6 hours from Yanayacu. On the southwest side of the mountain, this basecamp is an obvious red lava flow flanked by streams. There is a flattish platform of several hundred square metres in size which is used for the camp. Set up tents as close to the mountain as possible. There are signs of previous camps and a plaque commemorating Adrian Ashby-Smith and Ronald Mace, the two British climbers killed in 1976.

At the base camp you can expect to hear explosions every 5 to 10 minutes but clouds often obscure the volcano during the day making night time viewing the best. Although it is hard work to reach this point you are still not in danger from falling rocks. The ascent to the summit can be done in some 8 hours but changing conditions make it impossible to give a standard route. For quite some time there have been three craters on the summit with all three active at different times and to different degrees. One friend who went in to climb was told by an experienced Ecuadorian climber that the north crater was inactive and that rocks only fell down the western face. When he got there, all three craters were active and, though there were a considerable number of rocks being blown down the west side, he found that debris was coming down all visible faces at one time or another. Another couple of friends who climbed the peak reported that red hot rocks the size of Volkswagen Beetles were being blasted out of the volcano on the north and west sides of the cone. To the south and east, only small rocks were coming down and most of these were loosened by the vibration of the eruptions and thawing by the sun. The moral of the story is that it is difficult to predict the conditions. Any descriptions will be out of date by the time you get to Sangay and inaccurate information is more dangerous than none at all. However a few general points can make a summit attempt less risky:

— Find out from your guide where the majority of rocks have been falling lately and take some time to observe for yourself.

— Most recent successful attempts have gone up the southeast face which is smooth and virtually featureless. There is no glacier, only firm, compacted snow in places.

— Remember that all routes to the summit can be dangerous. Some climbers have made it to the top without any rocks falling around them, but the risk is real.

— Move as quickly up and back down the slopes as possible and keep your head up, always looking for missiles coming your way.

An early start, about 2.30 a.m., is essential to minimize the danger from rockfall and to make the going quicker on firm snow.

Your guide will take you to the highest point on the base above a *páramo* ridge. Be sure to have him wait for you there. Carry a compass so as not to get lost on the way down in the invariable morning fog. Crampons and an ice axe may or may not be necessary, but it's best to bring them. The climb is not technical but quite steep in parts and it's difficult to avoid falling on your backside on the way down. Wearing two pairs of old trousers will protect you from the sharp lava rock which rips clothes, and skin, easily. A helmet and sturdy work-type gloves are also advised for safety. A rope is not recommended as it would severely limit your ability to dodge falling rocks. There are no good maps covering the region. The IGM makes two 1:50,000 planometric maps for this area but they show little detail apart from the rivers and the position of the volcano. These maps are 194 Sangay and 201 Lago Tinguichaca.

Even if you're not planning to climb, a hike to the base camp can be a tremendous experience, especially if the weather is good. For both hiking and climbing, a good selection of waterproofs is a must. Attempts on the summit and hikes into the area can be made year round but December to February are the driest months as a rule. July and August are the wettest but other months are also very rainy.

Other routes have been reported as well. Chris Bonington was there in 1966 and records his experiences in his book *The Last Horizon*. He climbed up from the southeast via the Río Upano and Río Volcán. It took him 9 days and he wrote "... every foot of the way had to be hacked from the impenetrable entanglement presented by the undergrowth." Doesn't sound like much fun! He also reports his ice axe turning a dull yellow-green because of the sulphurous fumes.

THE ATILLO AREA

The two hikes described in this section originate in the Atillo area yet are completely different in character. One goes across rough *páramo* past high lakes, the other is a hardy hike to the jungles of the Oriente. Take your pick or invent one of your own using the IGM maps for the area. The region is wide open for adventure and exploration.

This is an area for experienced campers, hikers, and mountaineers who want to get as far off the beaten track as possible.

ACCESS   The following access information covers the various possible routes to Atillo which is approached from the main city of Riobamba.

First to get to Riobamba take one of several buses which leave daily from Quito's Terminal Terrestre. From Riobamba you can either go the Cebadas-El Tingo route to Atillo, or via the new direct Guamote-Atillo road. Transport is scarce beyond both Cebadas and Guamote, hence no clear-cut choice stands out as better than the other.

To get to Cebadas, make your way to the Barrio El Dolorosa section of Riobamba (a taxi will take you there cheaply) to catch the Cooperativa de Transportes Unidos (CTU) bus. It leaves daily at 3.00 p.m. from the intersection two blocks away from El Dolorosa bus terminal. There is an extra bus on Wednesdays and three additional ones on Saturdays going to Cebadas. There are no places to stay in the village but plenty of options for camping. From here you'll need to make your way to El Tingo where the road officially ends. A milk truck leaves every morning at 4.00 a.m. (except holidays) for the trip up to El Tingo. If going on foot, it's about 6 to 7 hours of pleasant road walking. Other options for getting to El Tingo are to hire a camioneta in Riobamba, or to catch a market-day truck from

Guamote (detailed below). The trip from El Tingo to Atillo is covered in the first day's hike in *El Tingo to Macas — Hiking Directions* on page 158.

The other way to get to Atillo is from Guamote which is situated just off the Pan American Highway, about an hour south of Riobamba. You can take a bus direct from Riobamba, or any heading south (to Alausí or Cuenca), and have the driver let you off at the village entrance. The newly-constructed road to Atillo has no regular transport and very few vehicles make the trip. You could hire a truck in Guamote, or walk a day and a half (about 45 km) to Atillo. Thursday is market day in Guamote, and transport much easier to come by, up either the new road toward Atillo, or along the alternative route through Cebadas to El Tingo.

The following two hikes tell you what to do once you've managed to get into this area.

From the Andes to the jungle

In the course of a day, the nakedness of the Interior changed to the luxuriousness of the tropics;... we passed through forest trees rising 150 feet high, mast-like, without a branch, laden with parasitic growth.
                                                        Edward Whymper, 1892.

INTRODUCTION   Walking through windswept *páramo*, passing remote thatched huts and bundled up Indians herding sheep, crossing a high Andean pass, and then dropping down through lush high mountain forest into the jungles of the Oriente — this is an adventurous hike which shows a remarkable cross section of Ecuador's scenery, vegetation, and wildlife.

The locals walk this trail in 3 long days, but I recommend twice this if you are to enjoy the scenery and observe some of the wildlife.

The hike begins in the highlands south of the major town of Riobamba, then crosses a pass in the Eastern Cordillera some 30 km southwest of the continuously active volcano, Sangay, before dropping steeply into the huge wilderness area of the almost trackless Sangay National Park. You finally emerge at the small but important town of Macas, about 1000 m above sea level, situated on the Río Upano on the edge of Ecuadorian Amazonia.

Macas was first settled by the Spaniards nearly 400 years ago and the trail follows the old communication and trading route joining the lowlands with the highlands. Thus the hike is of historical as well as geographical and ecological interest. Today Macas is at the end of an unasphalted road running north-south along the banks of the Upano river. The northbound road to Puyo is now completed. Transportes San Francisco has buses which depart daily from Macas; the southbound road goes through Sucua and then on to Cuenca, the nearest major city, some 12 hours away. A road is projected westwards over the highlands to Guamote and the first section to the Río Abanico, some 20 km west of Macas, has been completed. On the Andes side a road has now been put in all the way to Atillo, and construction continues. It is likely that in the next few years the road will be completed all the way to Macas. For now little transport uses the new sections of road, so the hike is still a pleasing one.

WEATHER AND TIMES TO GO   In the highland section, you are just west enough to experience the weather pattern of the central highlands. The typical dry season is from June through September, with a short dry season in late December and early January and wet otherwise. The lowlands are always wet but the least rainy months are late September through December. We went during the first week in October and more or less avoided rain, but it seems as if most other periods (with the exception of December) will have rain during one part of the hike or another.

EQUIPMENT   By following my route description carefully, you'll find that a shelter is suggested for every night except one. You may decide to take the risk of one night's wet bivvy and leave the tent behind. But a tent is useful for complete independence, so good campsites will also be mentioned. The difficulty, of course, is that the warm clothing needed for the highlands will be unnecessary weight in the lowlands. I partially solved the problem by bringing a very light sleeping bag and sleeping in my clothes in the highlands. (In December/January temperatures in both highlands and lowlands may be cool enough to warrant a medium-weight sleeping bag.) Rain gear is essential. I found ex-army jungle boots the best footwear because regular boots soon became hopelessly waterlogged and heavy in the deep mud of the lowland section. I made a point of always keeping a dry shirt, pair of trousers, and sneakers in a plastic bag. This way I always had warm, dry clothes to put on in the evenings, even if I'd spent hours sloshing through calf deep mud and bogs during the day. (This system only works if you're prepared to dress in your wet and muddy hiking outfit every morning.) Insect repellant is useful, although the bugs are not bad. Very little food is available en route and you should bring enough for 5 to 6 days.

MAPS   Five 1:50,000 IGM maps cover the trail. They are (in the order you will use them) the Guamote, Palmira, and Totoras topographical maps (detailed and useful), and the Zunac 206 and Macas 207 planometric maps which have little detail.

GETTING THERE   Refer to the *Access* directions on page 156.

EL TINGO TO MACAS — HIKING DIRECTIONS

A suitable distance for the first hiking day is from El Tingo to Atillo. You will be following a newly-constructed, yet deserted, dirt road the entire way, but don't let this put you off. This is an extremely pleasant and not difficult 5 to 7 hour walk through gently rising pastureland with starkly beautiful rather than spectacular views. You'll see herds of sheep, cattle, and perhaps semi-wild horses. The people are politely friendly but rather reserved and obviously not used to backpackers. The vegetation is grassy. You are within sight of the river all the way and there is plenty of water.

The road follows along Río Cebadas until the river divides in two, forming Río Osogochi which falls away to the southwest, and Río Atillo which now runs alongside the road. It passes through the straggling community of Colay (a few houses and a schoolhouse) and continues south and southeast through the wide river valley to the village of Atillo, some 7 to 8 kilometres beyond Colay. En route you will change from the Palmira to the Totoras map. Atillo is distinguished by a church, a cemetery, and a schoolhouse in which you can sleep. There are plenty of good campspots in the area before Atillo, or you can continue for about an hour beyond the village to campsites near the lakes.

Past Atillo the road soon curves around to the east and heads along the northern shores of the Laguna de Atillo. There are good campsites with fine views of the lakes and the occasional snowpeaks of Cerros Achipungo (4630 m), Yanaurco, and Sasquín beyond the lakes to the south. Don't camp too close to the lakes as the banks are boggy; it's best to camp on the hillocks just north of the first lake. There are streams for drinking water.

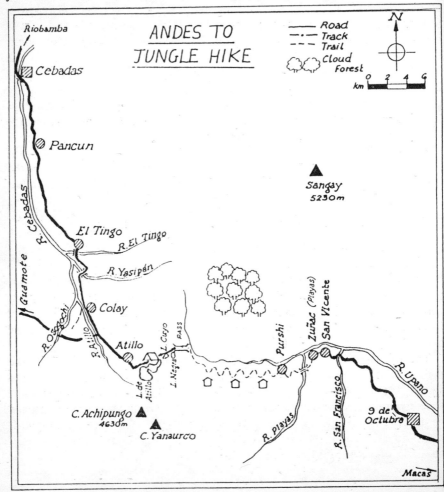

The second day is in many ways the most spectacular of the whole hike as you cross a pass in the Eastern Cordillera and start dropping down into the Amazonian rain forest. The change in vegetation is remarkable. Standing on the pass, you see the stark grassy *páramo* stretching away behind you, while in front huge cloud masses build up from the lowlands as the highlands fall away into incredibly lush cloud forest full of bromeliads and birdsong. Stands of huge trees rear out of the dense carpet of lower foliage and everywhere you look is covered with seemingly impenetrable vegetation. The change from bleak *páramo* to tropical cloud forest is so sudden it stuns your credibility — it has to be seen to be believed.

The road follows along the north sides of the Lagunas de Atillo and then abruptly halts at the third lake, Laguna Negra. At this point, a trail carries on for another 30 m to a cascade of water flowing into the lake. Hike up along the rock-strewn cascade until you meet the trail. Don't attempt to follow the trail which continues straight past the bottom of the cascade. It runs out after about 10 m, and you're left scrambling along steep rocky slopes and thorny bushes. The trail continues through mud above the northern shore of Laguna Negra and reaches the crest of the *cordillera* some 2 to 3 hours from the camp by the Lagunas de Atillo. By now you are passing through a tunnel of thick vegetation but there are occasional gaps in the green walls for you to admire the spectacular views. Here you change to your 1:50,000 planametric map of Zuñac.

At this point you'll have to accept that you're going to get very muddy, say "To hell with it!", and start sloshing on. The steep trail down through the jungle is unmistakable and there are no forks where you could get lost, but it is sometimes used by pack-animals and is usually churned up with thick mud. Occasional slippery logs are a psychological aid, although when you slide off them and end up in the muck you may not feel that they are all that helpful. After an hour of very steep descent the trail flattens out and follows the south side of the deeply cut Río Upano valley. About 2 to 3 hours beyond the divide you'll cross a small stream (with possible but stony campspots on either side). It's better to continue for an hour to a flat, grassy camping area with the remains (4 poles) of a small shelter on the right of the trail. The stream just mentioned is your best water source, but there are also smaller trickles every few hundred metres.

The following day will be an extremely muddy one. Sloshing along the trail isn't really much fun; what we did was made this a half day's walk and then spent the afternoon at the next campsite which boasts good views and the chance to admire the flowers, trees, bromeliads, and thick vegetation and to observe colourful insects and various bird species such as hummingbirds and parrots. Why rush? Relax and enjoy your unusual surroundings — easier to do from a dry camp than along the trail.

From the remains of the first shelter continue about two hours to a second one in similar condition. Another two hours more will bring you to an actual hut with a tin roof and wooden floor which is suitable for passing the afternoon and spending the night. You can't get lost on the trail.

The fourth day will see you continuing eastwards following the slowly dropping Río Upano valley through lush vegetation and ending up at an unusual campsite.... From the hut about three hours of hiking will bring you to the settlement of Purshi which is marked on the map with ten squares and a Sangay National Park sign. You could camp here if you wanted, though there are some rather wild looking cattle which would probably love to rub themselves up against your tent, but about one hour beyond Purshi you come to a covered bridge crossing the Río Playas. This bridge, some 10 m long and 2 m wide and with a tin roof, provided us with a unique campsite where we were lulled to sleep by the rushing rapids below. Be careful not to drop anything though; you certainly wouldn't see it again.

If you don't like the idea of sleeping on the bridge then you could continue for about an hour to the friendly village marked as Zuñac on the map but known locally as Playas after the nearby river. The village consists of about two dozen buildings scattered around a large grass square, and there is a church and a schoolhouse where you can sleep. This is the first settlement after Atillo. Although the distance from Atillo to Zuñac looks relatively short on the map, the extremely winding trail makes it a much longer hike than the map indicates.

On the fifth day you will be walking through more cultivated countryside with plenty of signs of settlement. You'll probably meet a few people driving mules up the trail, or a woodcutter or smallholder. They'll usually stop for a chat and are good sources of information about the trail ahead. The trail beyond Zuñac is blessedly firmer and less muddy. From Zuñac 1½ hours of steep climbing will bring you to two or three huts marking the community of San Vicente. Here is where the hard-packed dirt road picks up once again (or ends if one is travelling from Macas). Follow the road for about 4 to 5 hours until you reach Nueve de Octubre which is the largest community on the hike but unmarked on the maps. You could spend the night in a schoolhouse here, or in the Sangay National Park hut which is staffed by a friendly warden. Buses leave for Macas on Wednesdays and Sundays, or you can hire a truck (US$10) for the 1½ hour trip.

Macas is a gateway town into the jungle. Views of the nearby active volcano Sangay are good on clear days (rare) and it is a useful centre for day hikes into the surrounding countryside (see *The Macas Area* in Chapter 7). There are some mid-priced hotels with private baths as well as the cheap and basic variety and plenty of restaurants. You're back in the twentieth century.

ATILLO TO ACHUPALLAS

INTRODUCTION Very few established hikes in Ecuador combine cross-country navigating across high *páramo* and around remote lakes with isolated villages where simple footpaths provide the only means of access. This 3 to 5 day hike goes into an area rarely visited by any outsider, let alone gringo trekkers. For this reason, it is a unique and spectacular area to explore. On the other hand, it sets up a fragile situation which demands a level of responsibility from the intruder. Practising sound environmental and ecological techniques means not only preserving the natural beauty around you by treading lightly, but treating those cultures with whom you come in contact with equal care. Sweets and loose change tossed out liberally serve no purpose other than to corrupt. As an old-time American hiker once said, "Take only photographs and leave only footprints" and even taking photographs (of people) should be avoided.

MAPS From Atillo, two 1:50,000 topographical maps cover the route — Totoras and Alausí. If coming from Cebadas, you'll also need the 1:50,000 maps of Guamote and Palmira.

GETTING THERE Refer to the *Access* directions given on page 156.

HIKING DIRECTIONS Because of the lengthy approach, you are likely to be arriving in Atillo in the early afternoon. For camping, you can continue past Atillo and look for a suitable spot along Río Atillo. Better still, and time allowing, you could continue another half hour to just below Atillo lake, or another 2 hours to Laguna Iguan.

The route follows the road out of the village for about 5 minutes until Laguna Atillo comes into view. The road will continue up along the north shore, but as soon as you see the lake drop south, crossing a small creek just below the road and head through a pasture toward Río Atillo about a half hour away. From the road you'll spot two prominent hills before Lake Atillo. Head for the righthand hill and you'll find camping possible between the hill and the river. If continuing on, find the best place to cross the river, and then begin the climb up the middle valley (you'll see three valleys coming down into Lake Atillo) to Laguna Iguan about one hour away. There's no trail, but cattle tracks are everywhere. The going is easy up this steep valley, following the left hand side of the creek which flows from the lake. Iguan is beautiful, situated in a big bowl with stunning views looking back northeast to the mountains. There is obvious camping on the southeast side of the lake. A picturesque waterfall at the south end completes the scene. At night the place comes alive with the lights of a million fireflies and noisy frogs singing in chorus.

The next day is a very rugged stretch, heading cross-country along the *páramo*. The going is wet and awkward across tussocks, or spongy clumps of vegetation, heading up to Laguna Pocacocha, 2 hours away. Animal trails will be found occasionally to make the going a little easier, but you can't rely on them. Get a compass bearing before starting out. The route follows up a wide valley with a creek from Pocacocha flowing through it; keep far right on the flanks as you climb up to the lake. The area is lovely around Pocacocha and good for camping.

From Pocacocha, the route climbs up to a pass at 4300m about 1½ to 2 hours away. Again, take a compass bearing before continuing. Stay on the right side of the valley as you skirt Pocacocha lake, and follow alongside the creek as the route ascends. About halfway up the valley, the creek begins to branch out and following it will not be reliable. At this point look up toward the pass and spot a huge rectangular-shaped rock leaning at an angle to the right. Head for this and cross the pass which is about 50 m above.

An interesting side trip from the pass would be to climb Cerro Achipungo, only a mere 360m higher. The climb is easy to the top, following the ridge up to the summit.

From the pass, it's fairly obvious where to go, but it's best to take a compass bearing off the map for the easternmost point of Magtayán lake. You can see two smaller lakes from the pass, and could also get a compass bearing on these. The descent follows a narrow creek through a marshy area which funnels down to an obvious notch. At the notch, you'll see a startling sight — the huge expanse of Magtayán lake and sheer cliffs dropping straight into the water on the opposite side. Way off in the distance is Osogochi.

From here you will see exactly where to aim — toward the eastern point of the lake. Descending at the notch, the last 200 m is a little tricky. A steep grassy chute almost literally drops you down to the lake. Hanging on to the tall grass and sliding on your backside is one method that works. It's about 1½ to 2 hours from the top of the pass down to the lake. Camping near its eastern point is ideal.

The following day, start climbing up from the lake to the rounded plateau at the left about a half hour away. Head to the high point for great views and orientation. You'll begin picking up cattle tracks which skirt right of the small lake you see from the top of the plateau. It's easy walking across (still more) *páramo*, with the trail becoming more distinct as you continue southwest past the small lake.

It follows up a gentle rise, rather flat and easy going, and soon Laguna Cubillín comes into view. Continue alongside a rounded ridge, skirting the flanks and keeping high as you make your way west to the point between the lakes Magtayán and Cubillín. There are spectacular views of the entire area — lots of lakes, and small settlements.

(For the truly adventurous, an extra day or two could be set aside for exploring the southwest end of Laguna Cubillín. From the map it would appear to be an incredible area with lots of little lakes and rocky bluffs.)

The trail heads for a small settlement at the north point of Cubillín lake, but the villagers here have learned to beg from the few strangers passing through. It may be better to keep a little distance, though you'll have to cross a creek and the best place is just near the community. It's about 2 hours to the community from camp and another 1 to 2 hours onto Osogochi.

After passing the community head northwest, following a distinct trail alongside Río Osogochi to the village of the same name, which is visible the entire way. About halfway, you'll cross the river (you can roll up your pants, but your shoes will probably be so watersoaked by this point that it won't matter whether you take them off or not) and continue following it to the town. Just after crossing the river, you'll see a distinct trail leading out of Osogochi, still heading northwest. The villagers here are also unaccustomed to visitors and may be persistent about wanting gifts/money. As with the last community, it might be easier to avoid the village, and skirt south picking up the trail leading out of town. You can camp about 15 min to a half hour out of Osogochi, near a stream, depending on how long or short of a day you choose. Past the stream the trail begins to ascend and go away from the Osogochi river. There won't be much water for camping along the trail until it nears the village of Totoras about 2½ to 3½ hours away. From the stream, the trail is wide, almost drivable. It meanders up and around a marshy area for about an hour, but the going is easy and the road dry. It then levels out for the last part of the way into Totoras, with a short drop as the village comes into view. Visible signs of habitation begin about a half hour out of the village. The town is spread out in a broad area. It is estimated that as many as 5000 live in the environs. Totoras has a small store, cemetery, school, and newly installed electricity. If you don't feel like camping, ask to stay in the schoolhouse.

An infrequently-used road runs from Totoras to Achupallas. On foot it will take about 5 hours. Follow the road as it heads up the left side of the valley. This part of the trek offers some incredible scenery as the road stays quite high, allowing views over the wide expanse of valley below and across the open *páramo* to the east.

In Achupallas there are no hotels, but you can find a place to stay and could even get someone to cook you a meal. Transport is available — you can get a truck to Alausí for about US$6 per hour, or continue along on the Inca road to Ingapirca (see chapter 4).

The Vilcabamba Valley and Podocarpus National Park

INTRODUCTION   The Vilcabamba valley located in the southern province of Loja is an area of rolling hills and lush vegetation that ranges from tropical cloud forest to stark *páramo*. The valley at 1500 m is surrounded by forested mountains nearing an altitude of 3500 m. With the dramatic snow-capped volcanoes attracting the majority of attention in the central and northern parts of the country, this beautiful area is often overlooked by hikers. Access is from the city of Loja which, being the commercial centre of the province, is served by buses from all parts of the country. There is also an airport about an hour away with daily flights (except Sunday) from Quito and Guayaquil. Vilcabamba is about 45 minutes by road south of Loja. Buses leave frequently from Azuay and Guerrero on the west side of Loja across the river.

THE VILCABAMBA VALLEY

Vilcabamba has for many years been famous as the 'Valley of Longevity'. Based on a single anthropological study done some years ago, international attention was drawn to the valley inhabitants who supposedly lived to be well over 100 years old. The excellent climate and simple, unhurried lifestyle in this peaceful valley were said to be major contributing factors. Further scientific research has failed to substantiate the initial research but the legend persists and gives the area a certain claim to fame.

The valley is popular with travellers looking for a place to take it easy. The village of Vilcabamba is a small, 'one-horse town' — in fact horses can be rented for excursions into the countryside. There are some charming places to stay, one of the most popular being the cabañas of Madre Tierra. The simple bungalows, rustic sauna (with mud baths), home-cooked, mostly vegetarian meals, and gardens of colourful flowers make it an excellent base for hikes around the area. Owners Jaime Mendoza and Canadian wife, Durga, are wonderful people and excellent sources of information.

Day hikes and longer excursions are only limited by one's imagination. The IGM 1:50,000 Vilcabamba map shows a number of trails and local 'gringos' can suggest many more. One short trip worth making is to visit the local zoo — called Subcomision Ecuatoriana Centro Recreacional. It's about a 20 minute walk out of the town centre. Follow the road on the north side of the plaza and go east, crossing a bridge and continuing uphill. The road angles to the right (southeast) and you'll follow it until it reaches a junction with a school on the right. Take the smaller dirt road on the right and continue downhill until you see the zoo sign. The collection of animals including monkeys, spectacled bears, ocelots and a variety of large birds is somewhat interesting, but what makes the trip worthwhile is the large greenhouse devoted solely to the cultivation of orchids. There are over 30 varieties, some quite rare, which have been collected from areas throughout the province.

For more demanding excursions, one magnificent hiking area with much potential is found just north of Vilcabamba and bordering it to the east. This is the newly-formed Podocarpus National Park which has seen little tourism so far, but a few hikes are described here.

PODOCARPUS NATIONAL PARK

INTRODUCTION   Podacarpus National Park is the newest in Ecuador, established by the Ministry of Agriculture on December 15, 1982. *Podocarpus* is the scientific name for a type of conifer tree — the only one native to Ecuador. This huge tree can occasionally be found with trunks 3 m in diameter and growing to 40 m in height. However, its fine, rose-coloured wood is highly-prized and the pressure of logging has resulted in the elimination of this magnificent conifer from much of the Ecuadorian sierra. Today the majority of remaining small forests now exist within the park boundaries.

The park spans an area of 146,280 hectares, much of which is unspoiled cloud forest between the highland city of Loja and the city of Zamora in the Oriente. Divided by the Cordillera El Nudo de Sabanilla mountain range, the park ranges in altitude from 1000 m to 3600 m. Six distinct life zones from Amazonian rainforest to high Andean *páramo* provide suitable habitats for a wide array of plants and animals. It is one of the few remaining protected areas for the elusive spectacled bear. Other mammals found in the park include the mountain tapir, the sloth, the Andean wolf (which is actually a fox) and the puma. The birdlife is especially noteworthy with such species as guans, toucans, woodpeckers, flycatchers, swifts, tanagers, hummingbirds, and parrots.

There are two principal entrances into the park. The Cajanuma Park Station is approached from Loja on the western side of the park, and the Bombuscara Park Station is located on the Zamora side in the Oriente. Both have basic refuges at the park entrance where small groups could probably sleep or set up tents nearby. Plans call for an expansion of these facilities, but progress is slow. Short self-guided trails are being developed by Peace Corps worker, Eric Horstman, and ideas for a more detailed information centre are being discussed. A park entrance fee of US$2 is charged and permission should be obtained from the MAG office in either Loja or Zamora. If this proves difficult you could show up at either of the stations and probably pay there. The advantage of going to the MAG office is for a map of the area — quite basic, but nonetheless useful.

WEATHER AND TIMES TO GO   Being so heavily forested, with a broad range of elevations running from the highlands to the edge of the Oriente, the weather within the park is a combination of many climatic zones. This mainly means that when it's raining in the highlands from February through April, it rains in Podocarpus and when it's raining in the Oriente from May through August, it rains in Podocarpus. And of course even during the dry season it can rain! The absolute best month for visiting either side of the park is November, with a somewhat dry period of grace between September and January. On the Cajanuma side the rain is a major impediment; due to the altitude it is quite cold and potentially hypothermic. On the Zamora side this is less of a problem. Here the rain is just wet and the trail muddy (but it almost always is!), and refreshing rather than a major bother.

EQUIPMENT   If it's not already obvious, good rain gear is an essential part of the equipment list, along with the usual tent, stove, sleeping bag, etc. Sturdy, water-proof jungle boots are best, but you can temporarily mistreat you feet and get by with simple rubber boots (botas para agua). Bring plenty of plastic bags to keep spare clothes and other items dry.

MAPS   Along with the rather vague yet functional map of the park available from the MAG office, the 1:100,000 IGM map Gonzanamá gives a good overview of the Vilcabamba side of the park, and the 1:50,000 maps of Río Sabinilla and Vilcabamba will serve for hikes. On the Zamora side the 1:50,000 maps of Zamora and Cordillera de Tzunantza cover a fair bit of the area.

CAJANUMA RANGER STATION PARK ENTRANCE

GETTING THERE   The Loja-Vilcabamba bus passes the Cajanuma park entrance at the top of the pass about 6 km south out of Loja. From here it's a 7 km, 2 to 3 hour walk uphill to the ranger station. Alternatively, you can hire a taxi in Loja for about US$6, and if going only for the day, can arrange with the driver to return and pick you up at a fixed time.

HIKES WITHIN THE AREA   At the ranger station, there are several short hiking trails, one which takes you up through temperate forests full of mountain tanagers to a prominent ridge for some beautiful views over the valley. A longer hike requiring an overnight camp is to head up to Laguna de Compadre which is actually several lakes in a high *páramo* setting. A steep trail leads up from the ranger station, crosses the cordillera and finally gets you to the lakes at 3200 m in about 8 to 9 hours. It's a beautiful place to stay for a day or two, making short hikes in the area. You can return the same way or head cross-country southwest, ending up in Vilcabamba 2 days later. I've attempted this hike twice because it looks so interesting, but, not heeding my own advice about the weather, I was turned back both times by torrential rains. I know it's possible, but can't describe it accurately, not having done it. So if you feel like having an adventure, give it a try.

From Laguna Compadre, with topographic map and compass, head south to Laguna Compana and then continue past the unnamed lake south of Compana to set up camp. This ought to be a fairly full day. From the unnamed lake, there is a trail which will get you back to the main highway a few km north of Vilcabamba in about 6 hours. It's just a question of finding it. I've been on the lower section of this trail and know it exists. It heads up through agricultural land to Quebrada Banderilla and continues up to below Laguna Compana. The terrain throughout is spectacular.

BOMBUSCARA RANGER STATION PARK ENTRANCE

ACCESS   This entrance is located outside of Zamora on the eastern side of the park. The vegetation is much more tropical here and the climate more tolerable. From Loja you can take a bus; Transportes Viajeros or Transportes Loja both make the 3 hour trip several times a day. The ride across the cordillera and the drop down to the Oriente side is spectacular. Zamora has a few places to stay, the new Hostal Seyma (US$2) just off the plaza being the best. You can also go directly to the park entrance (easiest to hire a taxi) and walk 20 minutes into the refuge to camp there. Before leaving Zamora, however, it would be best to stop at the MAG office which is on the main road just as you enter Zamora. Look for a large MAG sign on the right. Here you can get a map, pay your entrance fee and talk with the park guardians.

HIKING AROUND THE AREA   For birdwatchers, the Bombuscara area is especially exciting. You don't have to wander far from the guard station to see an incredible variety of bird species. There is a day hike (4 hours in) along a good trail following the Río Bombuscara. It wanders through semi-tropical vegetation and cloud forest and is not too demanding. The friendly park guards (Luis Tambo is especially knowledgeable) can suggest other outings in the area.

For a longer and more rugged adventure, I heartily suggest the following 4 to 5 day hike from Romerillos. For cloud forest vegetation, this area is unequalled in all of Ecuador, perhaps even in South America. I must, however, admit that our experience in the area was unique and not likely to be repeated by subsequent hikers.

It started when our plans for hiking into the park from the Cajanuma side were literally washed away. We had set aside the time for an extended hike or two and were not to be swayed in our attempts to get out and do something. We decided that if it was going to rain, we might as well be in an area where it wouldn't matter so we headed for the Zamora side of Podocarpus National Park. Looking at the maps in the MAG office and talking with the park guards, we discovered there was a loop trek that appeared to take about 3 days. The guard looked a little sceptical, explaining that going in was no problem but the last section out was a *trocha* (barely-hacked trail) of *puro lodo* (pure mud). It was also an area of the park where mining concessions had been granted by another ministry (such is life in South America) and we had to get permission from the mining company to enter this part of the park. Undaunted by the trocha of puro lodo and with permission in hand, we set off to the settlement of Romerillos for the start of the hike. We discovered the route most of the way was a log trail constructed by MAG several years ago. Despite the explorative mining operation in the area, this part of the forest is virtually untouched and the birdlife prolific. The mountain tanagers became common after the first day, loads of Amazonas parrots flew overhead and we were lucky enough to see the Andean cock-of-the-rock and an umbrella bird among many other colourful species.

Early on the first day we passed a messenger going into one of the mining camps who eyed us incredulously. Evidently three gringo women carrying large packs was not a common sight in that area. (We discovered later that we were the first trekkers to have ever gone into that area.) About the time we were ready to stop for the day we arrived at the make-shift mining camp to find they were expecting us. The messenger had done his job admirably. We were given hot coffee, fed dinner and provided with our own dry tent (compliments of the miners) for the night. Talk around the fire after dinner was entertaining with tales of lost cities and other jungle lore. We also discovered that further along the trail two established camps of wooden buildings had been permanently set up for the mining operation. These we could use along the way.

With thanks for the unexpected hospitality, we set out the next day, planning only to hike the 4 hours or so to the first of the wooden structures called Dos Camas. It was an interesting juxtaposition of concepts to be walking along a well-constructed log trail and to realize at the same time we were deep into a remote area of virgin cloud forest. This was made even clearer when we arrived at Dos Camas and found the two guardians there preparing lunch — for us! Without our knowing, a runner had been sent from the previous camp early that morning with the message that we were on our way and to take good care of us. We were shown to our readied bunkroom, fed lunch and dinner, and breakfast the next morning! It was slightly embarrassing to find ourselves being treated so well on our 'adventurous' trek.

Again we gave thanks for the unexpected hospitality and headed for the second of the mining structures near the top of the cordillera, called La Cumbre. It was an uphill hike, almost 1000 m gain to La Cumbre at 2450 m. The vegetation began to change and the forest opened up from time to time presenting some of the most amazing views I've ever seen — mountain after mountain after mountain of cloud forest. The last hour to La Cumbre was spent in pouring rain not entirely comfortable at that altitude. However, we were greeted at the top by the camp guardian, Ramiro who declared, "Que valiente!" and admitted he didn't think we'd make it. We should have known we'd be expected. Hot coffee was delivered to our bunkroom only a few minutes after arriving, and we were invited to help ourselves to hot showers whenever we were ready! It turned out that La Cumbre was the operations centre for the mining company, and all was provided for, including flush toilets and a generator for electricity. Needless to say, we had lunch, dinner and breakfast provided, along with some interesting conversation with Ramiro who knew the area well.

The next morning we gave the accustomed warm thanks and headed up to the top of the mountain and beyond, to the trocha and puro lodo that awaited us. We were accompanied by Ubaldo, one of the camp guardians, who was leaving for his short vacation. We were hoping to make it the 17 km to Romerillos in one day, but the trocha and puro lodo made moving difficult. We came to appreciate fairly quickly the 3 days spent walking along the log trail. This was work — traversing vertical landslide areas with little more than vines to hang onto, picking our way gingerly around pits of thigh-high mud, slipping down through narrow trails as vines and branches snagged bulky backpacks, and crossing raging rivers on thin logs. The day wore on interminably and Romerillos seemed a distant fantasy. So did the last 3 days of easy living. After 12 hours of *pura lucha* (pure struggle), we found an abandoned shelter, shook out our sleeping bags, and laid down our weary bones without so much as a thought about eating. It was just good not to be stumbling any longer.

The following morning we made it back to Romerillos in time for the 8 a.m. bus to Zamora, but suffered the stares of the other passengers who likely wondered how these gringas came to be so far from home and so completely covered with puro lodo.

THE ROMERILLOS LOOP

It appears that the mining company has since pulled out of the area, not having found the 'mother lode'. It will be interesting to see what MAG decides to do with this area of the park. The buildings along the way are permanent, so even if things are locked up, there's enough covered space to make a suitable shelter.

From Zamora, buses depart from the terminal terrestre for Romerillos twice a day, at 6:30 a.m. and 2:15 p.m. for the 2 hour trip. There is only one IGM map which covers very little of the actual hike — the 1:50,000 Cordillera de Tzunantza — and it's not very useful in the thick forest. Actually you don't really need much more than the MAG map. It's pretty difficult to get lost on the trip in. If you're not on the trail, you're in impenetrable cloud forest and not going anywhere.

At the collection of small houses known as Romerillos, the official road ends. There is a park refuge here where you could pass the night. The hike starts at the bridge — cross it and follow the dirt road which continues to run alongside the river for a short way and then angles left. The road eventually peters out and a track picks up. Stay on the main track which is noticeably wider and more-used than any smaller tracks you may cross. It will make a series of short up and downs for about an hour and half, and then begin a serious ascent of a steep hill just past the bridge. This is the last water until ½ hour past the summit.

The ascent, now along a log trail, takes about 2 to 3 hours, going from 1450 m at Romerillos to 2400 m at the top, and back down to about 1650 m at camp. There are some lovely areas with waterfalls past the summit making a nice lunch stop. Continuing along the trail, you'll eventually cross another bridge and about 45 minutes later will come to some cleared areas suitable for camping. The best is to keep on for another hour to the third bridge and just on the other side there is good camping on a low rise to the right. The river here is also good for a swim. Plan on spending some 6 to 7 hours walking from the roadhead.

From the third bridge camp, the trail continues fairly flatly through splendid vegetation. You'll pass a small farm on the right after about 2 hours. Further on, the trail turns to run alongside a fast-flowing river. Keep an eye out for torrent ducks. Another 2 hours of steady walking will bring you to the wooden buildings of Dos Camas, high on the right as the trail angles left to cross a bridge. La Cumbre camp is only another 3 hours of steady hiking from here, but it seems much nicer to finish walking early in order to enjoy the incredible environment of cloud forest. You'll find Dos Camas a suitable shelter for the night.

The next day is 6 km of steady uphill to La Cumbre at 2465 m and 33 km from Romerillos. Here you'll find quite a set up of several buildings. They may be locked up, but there will be suitable shelter for camping. You may even find that the permanent flush toilets are still working! This is a great area to spend an extra day if you have the time. Leading off to the right, behind the lower building is a trail originally constructed by the Incas. It leads down to an old Incan mine which has seen present-day mining. The round trip from camp would take about 3 hours. For some marvellous views of the whole region, follow the main trail up past La Cumbre about 5 minutes to a cleared area. This was the heliport area for the miners! In fact, if the weather's good and the platform is still there, it would make a nice place to camp.

For the trip back to Romerillos there are two choices. Take the easy way out and go back the way you came in. There's still plenty to see and you'll be able to avoid the struggle of the other choice. That is to continue the loop and find your way along a hacked out trail that is barely manageable. To do this, follow the trail up past La Cumbre to the true summit about 45 minutes away. Along here you'll have to cross three very flimsy bridges which get you from one side of a landslide area to the other. Unfortunately, if these are gone, you'll get no further. After the third bridge, the trail descends to the river following the debris of another landslide. This is a little tricky here as the trail is somewhat lost in the rubble. At the river's edge you'll see the obvious trail continuing on the other side. It ascends and in a short while you come to a mining sign "San Luis" and a very faint trail heading downhill. Continue past and up through wet, *páramo* vegetation climbing up through a gully as the trail seems to disappear.

After about an hour and half from La Cumbre you'll come to a small shelter called Las Dantas camp. The trail continues up from here to El Mirador (the lookout) about 2 hours away. This begins the area called 'El Piñal' for the tundra-like vegetation resembling pineapple tops. Here you are at the watershed: Río Nagantza flows west and the Río San Luis flows eastward. This area is extremely boggy and gets worse a little further up. Keep to the sides of the trail, watching for any vegetation which will support your weight and keep you from sinking in the deep mud. Fortunately the worst is over in about a half hour, and when the mud resumes it's a manageable, ankle-deep level. After an hour, you'll come to the Cueva de Leon. This is a huge overhanging boulder which provides some shelter at its base. Just past is another basic shelter high on the right and beyond the trail begins a steep, difficult descent continuing about 2 to 3 hours to the river. Picking your way through this area is a little confusing as the trail gets lost from time to time as it wanders in and out of several stream crossings. The thing to remember is that the trail will always end up on the right side of the river. If you lose it, follow along downstream as best you can until you see it on the right bank. You'll eventually come to an open pasture area where the trail leaves the river and cuts across the pasture heading right.

There is an abandoned shelter here, suitable for spending the night. The next shelter is another 2 to 3 hours up the trail on the left side of the trail. Romerillos is a thankful one hour from this last shelter.

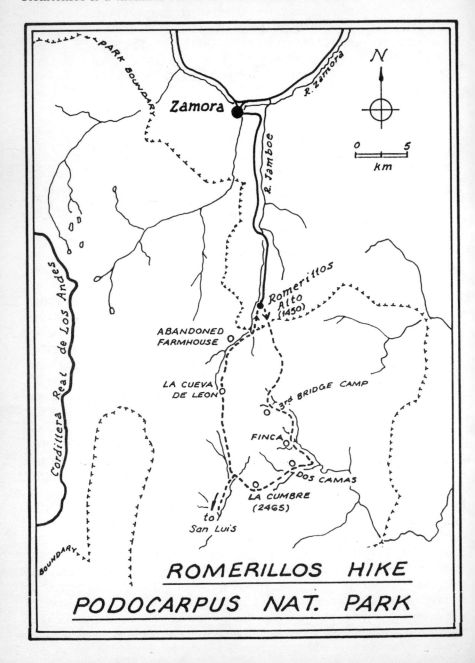

ROMERILLOS HIKE
PODOCARPUS NAT. PARK

CHAPTER 7

The Oriente

If you are wise and know the art of travel, let yourself go on the stream of the unknown and accept whatever comes in the spirit in which the gods may offer it.

Freya Stark

INTRODUCTION

The Oriente is the name given to Ecuador's Amazonia, a huge lowland area east of the Andes and comprising 36% of Ecuador's total territory. Popularly known as 'the jungle', the region is properly referred to as 'tropical rain forest'. Dense, hot, and wet, just as one would expect it to be, the Oriente was largely unexplored and untravelled until the oil boom of the 1960s. Now four roads penetrate the region and access is relatively straightforward.

Without a doubt, the most fascinating aspect of the Oriente is its incredible variety of flora and fauna. This is partly due to the so called edge effect. This means that any region where two different ecological zones are in sharp juxtaposition will have a greater variety of species than a region where two ecological zones gradually merge. The dramatic drop of the Andes to the Oriente is sudden enough to produce this effect. Over 700, or half, of Ecuador's bird species have been recorded in the Oriente; this is roughly equivalent to all the species found in the United States. About 3000 species of butterfly are known in Ecuador; this represents an incredible 15% of the world's butterflies. Sloths, armadillos, and anteaters are present, members of the strange Edentate family which is found only in Neotropica. On a single 10 day trip into the Oriente (admittedly to a remote region) I saw six different species of monkey. And, of course, there are countless insects, many of which still prove to be new to science when classified. The trees and plants are no less varied and interesting; the giant buttressed ceibal tree, the chonta palm covered with thousands of needle sharp thorns over its trunk, and the blossoms muskily scenting the forest all contribute to this fascinating natural wilderness.

Ecuador, land of volcanoes, even manages to produce a couple of volcanoes perched on the very edge of the lowlands. Rearing our of the rain forest, they are the active Reventador (3485 m) and the presently dormant Sumaco (3900 m). Both mountains have slopes dropping within 25 km to high Amazonian forests at 1200 m.

Although roads now penetrate the lowlands, and airstrips occasionally puncture the rain forest, some of the most satisfying journeys into the jungle will be by dugout canoe and on foot. This section describes a variety of trips to different areas with an emphasis on hiking and dugouts.

THE MISAHUALLÍ AREA

For the traveller with a limited amount of time, a trip to the small river port of Misahuallí on the Río Napo will give a good glimpse of the Oriente.

The journey begins at Baños, the prettily situated gateway town to the Oriente (see *The Baños Area* in Chapter 6). From here you take a bus to Puyo which is the capital of the lowland province of Pastaza. Only 66 km away from Baños, it lies just 950 m above sea level. The winding gravel road follows the Pastaza river valley and, as it drops, you can appreciate the rapidly changing vegetation and the many waterfalls (one of which cascades from an overhanging cliff onto the road — a damp experience in a pick-up truck). From the narrow confines of the Río Pastaza gorge, the first sudden sighting of the Amazonian plains is breathtaking. There is an obligatory passport control in Shell-Mera, some 15 km before Puyo.

From Puyo, if the weather is clear, you can view various snowcapped peaks rising over 4000 m above you and only 50 km distant. Sangay is sometimes visible, exploding away some 65 km to the southwest. Several buses a day leave Puyo for Tena. Get off the bus at Puerto Napo, some 75 km beyond Puyo and 7 km before Tena. From Puerto Napo, frequent pick-up trucks act as a bus service to Puerto Misahuallí, at the end of the road 11 km away.

Now you're in the tropical lowlands, just 600 m above sea level. It's amazing to realize that only 80 km away to the northwest Antisana towers over 5000 m above you, whilst the mouth of the Amazon at Belém lies over 3000 km to the east, with no higher ground in between.

Just 20 years ago Puerto Misahuallí was no more than a huddle of a few huts, but the oil boom, the new road, and tourism have enlarged it to over a thousand inhabitants. It is still a very sleepy little port, with only very basic hotels and restaurants. Sometimes gaily painted dugout canoes powered by modern outboard motors arrive at Misahuallí's sandy beach loaded down with cargoes varying from bananas to parrots. Most produce now goes by way of the new Tena-Coca road, however, and river traffic has slowed to a trickle. Nevertheless, occasional gold panners come into town to sell gold dust and hardy colonists may arrive in the port trying to sell their corn, papayas and other produce.

Just a generation ago, the region east of here was the territory of the Indians known as the Aucas, which in Quechua means 'savage'. In 1956 five missionaries were killed by the Aucas. Oil was discovered at about this time and the now important town of Coca founded. Killings by both settlers and Indians continued into the 60s but by the 70s the situation had stabilized with the Aucas withdrawing to remote regions of the jungle, as they have done for centuries to avoid genocidal conflicts. In 1983 a reservation of 66,570 hectares was set aside for them in a remote region where, for the time being, they are able to continue life in a relatively traditional manner. Nevertheless, some Aucas are now undergoing the painful change from their simple livelihoods to a twentieth century society — a process which is so rapid that it proves very traumatic and often fatal to many primitive peoples.

Some 2 to 3 days' walk away from Misahuallí is an Auca Indian village. As often as twice a week local guides take groups of tourists there to gawk. The Indians sit around miserably with little interest in their surroundings or the visitors who have come to see them. Seeing the parade of goods which to us seem basic: shoes, backpacks, sunglasses, cameras, penknives, matches, etc., is a disorientating experience for these people. For the visitors, it is sad to visit a group of bewildered looking Indians who are losing their traditional values and abilities. What promised to be an exciting adventure to see 'real' primitive Indians turns out to be a long, uncomfortable trek with a somewhat shaming conclusion.

If you want to see the Indians — wait until they come to you. A few of the more adventurous and acculturated Aucas usually come into Misahuallí and you can see them and they can see you in an unstrained and uncompromising atmosphere. Recently, the Aucas issued a proclamation that they no longer wished to be visited by groups of tourists because such visits created a negative impact on the Indians. The authors of the book request that travellers heed the Auca's wishes.

Even if you don't normally take organized tours, I feel that some of those offered in Misahuallí are both inexpensive and worthwhile. Many outfitters are available (too many to list here). The SAEC office in Quito or other travellers can tell you of recommended outfitters. Douglas Clarke, Carlos Lastra and Héctor Fialles have been recommended. Tours range from one day walks in the nearby jungles to 10 day trips reaching close to the Peruvian border. Usually a minimum of five people are needed (more for longer trips) but there are plenty of gringos in Misahuallí looking for companions. Food, transportation, and accommodation are provided for US$20 to US$30 a day depending on the difficulty and duration of the trip. It must be remembered that the immediate area has been colonized so you won't see much in the way of monkeys, wild pigs and so on. Local wildlife is limited to birds and insects which are varied and colourful. A trip along the river near Misahuallí often produces sightings of egrets, vultures, wild turkeys, toucans, anis, tanagers, caciques, and oropendulas. A recommended one day walk into the jungle is Douglas Clarke's waterfall trip. Keep your eyes open for well-camouflaged stick insects, fist sized toads, armies of ants, and hosts of colourful butterflies. Ask to be shown the Achiote (*Bixa orellana*), a plant which is crushed to produce a red paint for body decorations, and a vine containing water fit to drink. A good guide will be able to show you much you would have missed on your own, particularly if you ask many questions and convey your interest and enthusiasm.

If you can get a group together and take a longer tour you mill see more wildlife. These tours are not for the soft traveller, but you'll certainly see monkeys, caymans, macaws, and parrots, and with any luck pacas, capybaras, anteaters, armadillos, wild pigs, and... who knows, a tapir or a jaguar?

CONTINUING INTO THE ORIENTE

From Misahuallí you can continue downriver by dugout for the 6 hour journey to the town of Coca, but with the new Tena-Coca road, regular river transportation has all but ceased to exist. It can be costly to hire an unscheduled canoe to make the trip. The Río Napo has long been travelled and settled, so don't expect to see monkeys and wild Indians, but you will see dramatic views of the forest and many birds including parrots. Easier and less expensive is to take the bus from Misahuallí to Coca. With the new road, transport is cheaper and faster to this ramshackle town and many guides have begun to operate trips into the jungle from here. Wymper Torres and Luis García are two native guides well-recommended in the area.

From Coca daily buses head north to Lago Agrio, another jungle town produced by the oil boom. It is the most eastern town of any size in Ecuador and the capital of the new province of Sucumbios. The Sunday market brings in members of the local Cofan tribe, with the men often wearing their typical *kushma*, or knee length smock, and perhaps a headband of porcupine quills around their short hair. They often bring necklaces of feathers, seeds, teeth, and even insect wings to sell to tourists.

From Lago Agrio a dirt road follows the oil line to Quito, some 265 km and 10 hours away by bus. The road passes the active volcano Reventador (3465 m) and the village of Baeza, both described later in this chapter, and continues past Volcán Antisana (5704 m) and the village of Papallacta (see Chapter 6) before reaching Quito.

Regular flights from both Lago Agrio and Coca return to Quito, or a return from Puerto Misahuallí to Quito is by bus via Tena (several a day from Misahuallí). Tena is the capital of Napo province. Good views are often had of the dormant volcano Sumaco (3900 m) about 50 km north northeast. From Tena buses continue on the new dirt road north which runs parallel to the Andes, passing through Archidona and on to Baeza nearly 100 km away. Archidona is famous as being the centre from which you can visit the large cave complex of Jumandi. Unfortunately, the stalactite hunter and phantom spray painter have reached the caves before you, and they are now a rather sorry sight.

A final note about the weather. It can rain year round but June through August seem to be the wettest around Misahuallí. November and December have the least rain. During these times the Río Napo could be either too high or too low to make a boat trip.

REVENTADOR (3485 m)

INTRODUCTION   Reventador lies 90 km east northeast of Quito. Its name means exploder and this volcano has been frequently active as far back as records go — the first recorded eruption was in 1541. For many years little was known about the area and it was not until 1931 that an Ecuadorian, L. Paz y Miño, visited the area to study it and map it for the first time. It remained relatively inaccessible until the building of the trans-Ecuadorian oil pipeline began in the late 1960s. This in turn prompted the construction of a road from Baeza to the new oil boom town of Lago Agrio and it is from this new road that access to Reventador is made.

Reventador consists of a large outer crater some 2 to 3 km across within which is a huge volcanic cone hundreds of metres high. Extrapolating from the outer crater one can assume that it must once have been one of the highest mountains in the country.

During the mid 1970s Reventador was in a highly active phase and its eruptions are said to have equalled those of the famous Sangay. Major activity ceased in the late 70s and today Reventador merely emits fairly continuous but gentle puffs of steam and gases. This situation could change dramatically thus rendering my route description inaccurate. Check with locals before you climb.

MAPS   The IGM topographic 1:50,000 which covers this climb is Volcán El Reventador.

WEATHER AND TIMES TO GO A friend who lives in the Lago Agrio area claims to have driven the Lago Agrio-Quito road dozens of times but has only seen Reventador twice, although it is only 12 km from the road as the crow flies. The area is very wet and usually cloudy. The wettest months are June and July, and the best are September through December — but you can still expect daily showers.

EQUIPMENT A trail of sorts has been hacked out of the forest but a machete is still handy to have along and it can be helpful as the trail is overgrown. During the 'dry' season, insects aren't a major problem but repellent should be brought during the wetter months. A waterproof tent is a must. My preferred clothing is raingear (GoreTex) over tee shirt and shorts, with a dry shirt and pair of trousers kept in plastic bags for camp and tent wear. It's too warm for a heavy sleeping bag; a blanket and dry clothes are fine to sleep in. The trail is extremely muddy and at times you'll be on hands and knees crawling under trees in 3 inches of mud. My favourite footwear is army style jungle boots; sneakers are not really suitable and hiking boots become heavy and waterlogged very quickly. The Ecuadorian knee-high rubber boots (*botas para agua*) are quite suitable, though not entirely comfortable. A spare pair of sneakers for camp and tent wear mean your feet can dry out occasionally. A large selection of plastic bags is a must. Bring extra water bottles because the last camp is waterless.

GETTING THERE Catch a bus from Quito's Terminal Terrestre through Baeza to Lago Agrio. Although you will be going only two thirds of the way to Lago Agrio you may be charged the full fare at the bus station. The bus journey is very interesting and worth a description.

The road descends from Quito through several small villages and is paved for about 60 km. A good way beyond Pifo it changes to dirt and begins the ascent over one of the highest road passes in Ecuador, crossing the Eastern Cordillera at an altitude of nearly 4100 m some 50 km out of Quito. The road then drops to the lake of Papallacta from where an entry may be made to climb Antisana (see Chapter 6). Just before the village of Papallacta, over 60 km from Quito, is a turn off to the left with a sign for thermal baths which are some of the best in the country. The road continues to drop through enchantingly beautiful high mountain forest, with many strange plants and colourful birds. Some 100 km from Quito the road forks; we follow the left fork and proceed through the villages of Borja and El Chaco, from where you may get your first views of Reventador. There are frequent views of the Río Quijos on your right. About 150 km from Quito you cross the Río Azuela on a large steel bridge — this is a major landmark. Some 10 km further a small bridge crosses the Río Malo (the starting point for the 'wrong way' approach). 170 km from Quito you pass a little cement block hut with an INECEL sign at a turnoff to your right. Just beyond this is a little settlement known as Río Reventador (not to be confused with El Reventador some 13 km further down the road). This is where you get off the bus to climb Reventador.

CLIMBING REVENTADOR — THE WRONG WAY

Before giving the directions for this not too difficult climb, let me describe our experiences as pathfinders.

Relatively little information about this volcano was available in Quito — I couldn't find anyone who claimed to have climbed it, and written descriptions were uninviting: "There are reported to be snakes, nasty insects, and 7 metres of rain a year" (Koerner), and "Reventador is still active and potential heroes armed with machetes can try hacking their way through the thick forests which cover its slopes to reach the crater." (*South American Handbook*).

I must admit to certain feelings of trepidation as our little group of three pulled out of the bus terminal in Quito. We had read one route description which told us to go between the two branches of the Río Malo and climb to the rim of the outer crater. From here we could circle clockwise around the rim to the back of the mountain and descend into the crater to make an ascent of the inner cone. Accordingly, we told the rather surprised bus driver to let us off at the Río Malo bridge, and we were left standing in the middle of nowhere looking rather disconsolately at our packs and the trackless jungle around us. We couldn't even see the volcano we had come to climb. There was about an hour of daylight left and no obvious camping places so, remembering a small cluster of houses some 2 km back, I suggested we return there, find the inevitable store/bar, and talk to the locals.

After several beers we felt decidedly better adjusted to jungle life and persuaded the landlady to let us have some water (not exactly a rare commodity around here) and camp in front of the store/bar by the pipeline running along the road. The few people around obviously thought we were insane to be going into that thick jungle to look for an active volcano. One person had volunteered the information that he had been about 500 m back from the road — he seemed to think that was quite far enough. So much for our hopes of obtaining information or hiring a guide.

The following morning we left early and walked back to the Río Malo. On the left hand side of the river we could see a thin path leading off into the jungle, so I dropped my pack and trotted along to investigate. It ran close to the river and was easy to follow for several hundred metres so I trotted back to the group and reported it was worth a try.

About a kilometre from the road the path began to peter out and we started to use the machete. If you've never used a machete before you'll find it's harder than it looks. Try to cut branches at an angle rather than through at 90°. And be careful that the machete doesn't fly out of your muddy and sweaty hands with a particularly energetic swing — I nearly decapitated one of my companions this way. When all signs of the path faded we hacked our way to the Río Malo to try walking up the river, which at this point was knee deep. After several hundred metres of wading we came upon an extraordinarily impressive sight: in front of us was a cirque of cliffs some 50 m high with the river cascading down in a spectacular waterfall. So much for our ideas of wading upstream! We were totally unprepared for these falls but decided to continue upstream right to their base; a rather damp but exciting experience.

Our next move was to consider the best way over the cliffs before us. We thought there was a way up to the right some 300 m before the falls and spent most of that afternoon cutting our way up a steep and muddy slope, holding on with one hand to loose and slippery roots whilst swinging the machete with the other hand. Several hours of hard work almost brought us to the top of the slope, at which point we discovered a 7 m high vertical mud cliff. It looked virtually impossible to climb up the crumbling clay, and the cliff extended a long distance either way. This was obviously not the way to go. It was getting late, so in 15 minutes we stumbled and slid our way back down on the trail we had spent laborious hours cutting and set up a camp on a sandbar by the river.

WARNING. Setting up camp close to an unknown jungle river is risky. Sudden rainstorms high in jungle areas sometimes produce flash-floods, with rivers rising metres in minutes and sweeping away everything in their paths. Our decision to camp on the sandbar was influenced by the fact that the river appeared short on the map and therefore seemed unlikely to flood. Also heavy rains the previous night had not significantly affected the river's height.

The following day we went back to the road which took us less than 2 hours. Although this route is not recommended as an access to Reventador, the trip to the waterfall makes a good day hike. Once back on the road we headed northeast. In about a kilometre we came to a small bridge which we assumed crossed the second branch of the Río Malo, but nowhere between the two branches were we able to find any sign of a trail leading toward Reventador. 10 km of walking brought us to the little cement block INECEL hut on the right hand side. From here a jeep track leads some 2½ km down to a small flat area which has great views of the San Rafael Falls (also known as the Coca Falls) and is suitable for camping. The falls are between 145 m and 200 m in height (depending on your reference source).

A trail leads from the camping area to close to the bottom of the falls; allow about an hour for the round trip, although it may still be blocked by the landslide caused by an earthquake in the mid 1980s. There is water available from a small waterfall by the jeep trail some 500 m before the camping area. The falls are probably the highest and certainly the most impressive I've seen in Ecuador and well worth the visit. Koerner tells of the discovery of earthworms glowing blue under the bark of trees near the falls. I didn't see any but I did find some twigs and grasses with a blue luminescent fungus growing on them. There's no telling what gringos spending a quiet night by the falls will discover next! Certainly the area is extremely rich in bird and insect life.

Walking back up to the road and turning right, you come to the tiny community of Río Reventador. Ignoring the first few houses, you'll see a store on the right side with a sign 'Se Vende Gasolina'. Here you can buy stove fuel, as well as beer and noodles — delicious volcano climbing fare. This is the beginning of your route up Reventador.

CLIMBING REVENTADOR — THE RIGHT WAY

The hike begins immediately north of the bridge which crosses Río Reventador on the Baeza-Lago Agrio road. A few meters after the bridge you come to an abandoned building on the right and an occupied house on the left. This 'village' is what is known by the locals as Río Reventador. Hike up the switchbacking road for about 100 m until you see the black oil pipeline cross the road heading left. Follow the left side of the pipeline over one small rise and halfway up another. The pipeline continues up this steep incline and disappears over a ridge, but you'll stop on the second rise and begin looking for a faint trail in the grass which heads left at 45 degrees back towards the river. If you've found the right trail, you'll cross the river in about 5 to 10 minutes and be heading into cloud forest. If you've gone wrong by following the pipeline too far, you'll likely come to the bottom of the incline and see a small cabin on the left. (The occupant is a deaf-mute, but if you make it plain that you're searching for the trail to Reventador, he can help you. Do not follow the trails that begin at his cabin.)

If you decide to hire a guide for the first (and most confusing) part of this hike, there are some local guides available. The most experienced guide is Guillermo Vasquez who was involved in chopping the original trail and who knows the area well. He lives by the school in the Pampas area some 2 or 3 kms before you get to Río Reventador from Quito.

About a half hour after crossing the river the trail heads up a ridge through a stand of large palm trees. Once in the palm trees you can be sure you are on the correct trail as these are the only ones in the area. You

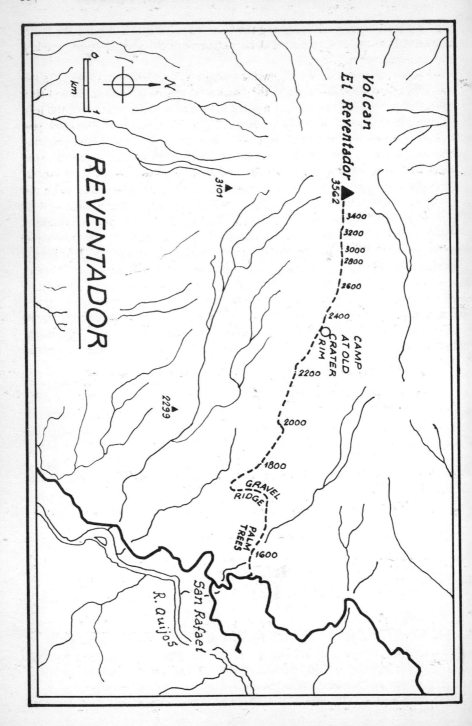

should have no problem following the trail from here; it is not for the faint-hearted however, and you should be prepared for a very slippery, muddy, and at times, steep hike.

All day your compass bearing will rarely vary from west/northwest. As the trail ascends you begin to leave the thick vegetation of the jungle and find yourself on a gravelly ridge with a great view and some exposure on the left. As you reach the end of the ridge, about 1½ to 2½ hours from the road, you will have nowhere to go but down. This section is quite steep and you may find yourself occasionally climbing fallen trees and lowering yourself using vines and roots for help. The trail eventually levels out about ½ to 1 hour from the ridgetop and here you'll come to a muddy stream which may be the last easy water you'll encounter. Extra water containers are a must — 4 or 5 litres per person is not unreasonable, and more likely barely adequate.

Another half-hour or so you'll cross a dry gravel and rock streambed and the terrain begins to change. There are fewer tall trees and the trail is one of slimy (and therefore slippery) rocks and less mud. Between 1 to 2 hours after crossing the rocky streambed the trail once again steepens and within an hour you will come out of the jungle onto mossy rocks and soon on the rim of the old crater. If it is clear you will see the new cone directly ahead of you and the sheer wall of the old crater behind it more than 3 km away. Just over the rim is a good camping area. The trail here could be a little difficult to follow.

The next day it is almost a straight shot across the crater up the cone to the summit. The hike begins with 2 hours or more of traversing mossy, slippery rocks along a vague trail before it begins climbing. You will see an occasional marker flag farther along the way. The trail leads up to a rocky/sandy gully and reaches the summit after a few more hours — some 4 to 6 hours from camp. The view from the top of the desolate, steaming crater is worth the muddy, slippery effort — it is a beautiful, empty, chaotic place which few visit.

VOLCÁN SUMACO (3900 m)

This volcano, lying deep in the jungle some 100 km east southeast of Quito, has been known to Europeans since the Spanish conquest when Francisco de Orellana recorded its presence in 1541 after he saw it from the Río Napo during the first stages of his historic first descent of the Amazon. However, its isolated, forest-bound position and generally wet weather have made it one of Ecuador's least known volcanoes.

Although some sources consider Sumaco to be extinct, the few records we have of it indicate that it is an active volcano. Jiménez de la Espada, who made the first ascent in 1865, found a gullied, 100 m wide crater blown open to the south. In 1925, the British climber George M. Dyott climbed Sumaco and recorded that the crater was 210 m wide with no signs of cracks or gullies. This indicates that an eruption must have occurred between the years 1865 and 1925, but the volcano's isolated position prevented this phenomenon from being recorded by any observer. This theory is supported by the fact that Sumaco has a conical shape which, in an environment promoting severe erosion, indicates that activity must have occurred within the last few hundred years. At present there appears to be no activity whatsoever but volcanologists still consider Sumaco to be potentially active.

The volcano has recently become more accessible with the construction of the new Tena-Coca road along with the newly published IGM 1:50,000 topographical map Volcán Sumaco. The map is not very useful, however, since the vegetation is so thick that identifying contours and physical features is difficult.

After spending a year in Ecuador I had not managed to find any information on how to reach the volcano apart from Koerner's typically laconic "Hire guides and chop east through the jungle for about eight days." My first view of the volcano was from Tena, from the balcony of some Peace Corps volunteers' house. Without any real expectations of hard information, I asked if they had any ideas on how to get up there. "Yeah," they replied, "We climbed it last week." This is what they told me.

Drive down the Tena-Coca road to a point 3 km or so from the Baeza road turn off. Here you'll start looking for the trail on your right hand side heading for the village of Huamani. Finding the trail is the most difficult part of the whole trip. You'll just have to keep looking and asking the occasional person you meet.

Once you're well onto the trail it's difficult to get lost. About an hour from the road you reach a river which must be forded. The trail is muddy with plenty of ups and downs, and the climate hot and humid. Eventually you reach the Río Hollín which is a large river crossed by a bridge. There are areas to camp on the other side. This is almost the halfway point from the road to Huamani. The trail continues clearly to the village and takes one very long hard day from the road. It is better to camp at the Río Hollín and make it two easy days.

Once you get to Huamani you'll find the usual huddle of thatched or tin roofed wooden houses. You will be allowed to sleep in the 'village hall' but don't count on buying food; often there isn't much for sale. The trail ends here and so you should hire a guide. Don Francisco is the man to contact. He will charge US$5-$7 per day. He doesn't have camping equipment so providing him with tent space or at least a large plastic poncho is appreciated. He often brings a friend with him and they hunt monkeys and wild turkeys for food. Bring plenty of your own food if you don't fancy monkey stew, and bring enough for your guides if you want to try to prevent them shooting animals. The men work very hard clearing campsites and starting campfires. About 3 to 5 days are needed for the ascent from Huamani depending on how recently the previous group has been in; the descent along the newly cut trail should take only 2 days. The mountain is thickly vegetated nearly to the summit.

Going to the Galapagos Islands?

The following books are available from Bradt Publications:

A Traveler's Guide to the Galapagos Islands (Boyce)
Galapagos: A Natural History Guide (Jackson)
Galapagos: the Enchanted Isles (Horwell)
Plants of the Galapagos (Schofield)
A Field Guide to the Fishes of the Galapagos (Merlen)
Map of the Galapagos Islands (Bradt/Healey)

For a complete catalogue of books and maps write to:
Bradt Publications, 41 Nortoft Road, Chalfont St Peter, Bucks, SL9 LA, England.

THE BAEZA AREA

Baeza is a small but historical town in the eastern foothills at 1400 m. It was on an ancient trade route even before the conquest. The coming of the Spaniards elevated it to the position of a mission settlement but nowadays no vestiges remain of its past. It is a very quiet place with one basic hotel and a couple of cheap restaurants. It is surrounded by steep hills which could provide days of hiking and exploration. I describe one day hike here, but armed with the IGM 1:50,000 Baeza map you could have several to choose from.

Buses pass through Baeza several times a day to and from Tena. If you are on the Quito-Lago Agrio route you have to walk about 1½ km up the road from the Baeza turnoff. Baeza is about 100 km by road from Quito.

Leave the town plaza on the road going uphill to the right of the church. In a few minutes you will pass the hospital to your left and the cemetery to your right. The trail becomes a stony path. After 15 minutes the trail forks at a foot-bridge. You can go left over the bridge up a steep trail which peters out in fields after about an hour with nice views of Baeza in the valley below. Or you can head straight up the trail (don't cross the river) which takes you through beautiful low mountain pastureland surrounded by trees laden with epiphytes. The birdlife is prolific. I saw hawks and hummingbirds, wrens and woodpeckers, tanagers and thrushes, so bring your binoculars. About 10 minutes past the bridge the trail forks again. Take the right one uphill leaving the stream to your left. A further 10 minutes brings you to a flattish area showing signs of logging. From here the trail becomes increasingly muddy, although stony sections offer relief from the squelch. The trail follows the fence line and then steeply zig-zags over and around a hill. About an hour beyond the logged area it is crossed by a fence and stops suddenly in high pasture on top of a hill. This is a good place for a rest and picnic.

THE MACAS AREA

Though a small town, Macas is the capital of one of the largest provinces in Ecuador, Morona-Santiago. Its history goes back at least four centuries; it was an important Spanish missionary and trading settlement linked with the highlands by a trail still in existence and described in Chapter 6, *From the Andes to the Jungle*. Despite its provincial capital status, Macas had remained a very isolated town until recently. It now has an airport with daily flights to/from Quito, and the recently-constructed road north to Puyo now gives this jungle city two means of access to the sierra. At one time its only link with the rest of Ecuador was the southbound road through Sucua to Cuenca, some 10 hours away by bus.

The Oriente east of Macas is perhaps the least explored region in the entire country. It is the home of the Jívaro Indians, famous for their expertise (now rarely practised) at shrinking the heads of their enemies. Today the Jívaros prefer to call themselves Shuar and are integrating quite rapidly into Ecuadorian society. There is a major Shuar centre in Sucua which is partially run by Indians and plays an important part in both recording and encouraging traditional life styles as well as aiding the Shuar people in the difficult process of entering twentieth century life, which they seem to be doing with more success than many groups. Nevertheless, some semi-wild groups still exist deep in the forests.

From Macas, trails are marked on the maps which penetrate deeply into the Oriente reaching extremely remote villages. The trails are not often used as small aircraft are the main means of communication with Macas, and river travel is used between the villages. I did find, however, one trail which can easily be walked in a day from Macas.

From Macas cross the Río Upano by a simple bridge to Sevilla Don Bosco, a Salesian mission. From here, head south along the road roughly following the eastern river bank. This dirt road slowly deteriorates into a side track impassable to vehicles. You will pass cultivated areas and Indian huts and perhaps be invited to try some of their yucca chicha. This drink is made by the women masticating the yucca and then spitting the contents into a bowl of water which is left to ferment, the process started by the ptyalin in saliva. It takes some time (and a lack of imagination) to develop a taste for this sour, gruel-like drink which is served cold in large gourds. One is normally expected to drink the whole gourd in one or two gulps.

Some four hours from Sevilla Don Bosco you come to the small Indian centre of San Luis where you can buy soft drinks if you're not up to chicha. San Luis is almost the halfway point to Sucua but when I was there a bridge had washed out further along the trail so I returned the way I came. Either way it is a good day hike. If you do get all the way to Sucua you could return to Macas by one of the frequent buses joining the two towns.

190

CHAPTER 8

The Western Lowlands

Here I am, safely returned over those peaks from a journey far more beautiful and strange than anything I had hoped for or imagined — how is it that this safe return brings such regret?

Peter Matthiessen

INTRODUCTION

West of the Andes and stretching to the Pacific Ocean lies some of Ecuador's most valuable agricultural land. Although this is good for the Ecuadorian economy, it means also that much of the lowland forest has been destroyed, along with the accompanying wildlife. The best places to see the western forests are the slopes of the Andes; here the terrain is too rough for agriculture. Few trails have been cut and the area is not really conducive to backpacking trips, being hot, humid, thickly covered with vegetation, and lacking the interest of volcanoes to climb. It is, however, excellent for birdwatching.

For the naturalist, there is the interest of the prolific birdlife and also the ecological changes as one descends from highlands to the coast. A good centre for bird watching in the western lowlands is Tinalandia. Lying about 800 m above sea level on the road to Santa Domingo de los Colorados (some 15 km before the town), Tinalandia is a beautiful guest house run by Tina and Alfredo Garzon. The grounds are extensive and kept in their natural state for optimum birdwatching. There are marked nature trails and over 150 species of birds have been recorded here, including chestnut-mandibled toucans, pale-mandibled araçaris, and a variety of parrots, hummingbirds, motmots, tanagers and other tropical species. The accommodation is comfortable and the food good, so this is not for the

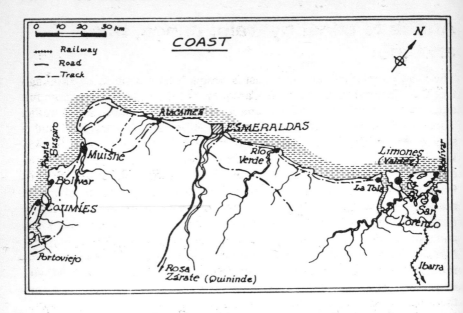

budget traveller. It is also very popular with groups so you may have difficulty in finding a room. (There is no phone so the only way of making a reservation is by writing. Letters addressed to Tinalandia, Santo Domingo de los Colorados, Ecuador will reach there.)

A good variety of sea and shore birds is found on the coast. The southern coast has mangrove swamps but is nevertheless rather scrubby and dry, as is the Santa Elena peninsula west of Guayaquil. Rainfall here is comparatively low and falls mainly from January to April. Further north there is more rainfall, more vegetation, and a longer rainy season, from January to June, and on the far northern coast it sometimes rains during the 'dry' season. Good areas for birdwatching in the south are found at Jambelí, which is a low-lying island off Puerto Bolívar, near Machala, the capital of the province of El Oro. From Machala frequent buses do the short trip to Puerto Bolívar where motor boats can be hired to cruise among the swamps, estuaries, and islands of the area where you can see large flocks of pelicans and other sea birds. In the Santa Fiend peninsula are found many fishing villages and tourist resorts, such as Playas and Salinas. These are often used as bases for walks along the beach although overnight backpacking trips aren't normally done.

The northern coast is perhaps richest in coastal birdlife because of the heavier rainfall and vegetation. I did a hike along part of the coast here. There are also various resort towns you can use as a base.

Andes to coast by train, canoe, bus, and foot

The most popular route to the coast is probably by bus via Santa Domingo to either Esmeraldas or Bahía de Caraquez, but the train is much more fun and passes through remote areas unaffected by a constant stream of traffic. There are two lines; one from Quito via Riobamba to Guayaquil and a shorter one linking Ibarra with San Lorenzo on the northern coast. The 464 km Quito-Guayaquil line is now run in two sections. A bridge was washed out in the '83 floods and has not been repaired. The Andes section runs from Quito to Riobamba, and the coastal section goes from Aluasí. It reaches a height of 3609 m and is a marvel of railway engineering. At one point it climbs nearly 300 m in less than 80 km and includes complex loops and switchbacks — a must for a railway enthusiast. Both the *South American Handbook* and *Ecuador, a travel survival kit* have excellent descriptions of the ride. I personally prefer the 293 km Ibarra-San Lorenzo line because you detrain in a sleepy coastal port with only boat and train connections, rather than in the huge bustling port of Guayaquil.

The train is known locally as *autoferro* and is little more than a converted schoolbus mounted on a railway chassis. When I took it from Ibarra to San Lorenzo the journey, which usually takes 7 hours, lasted 12. We were stopped by two minor landslides, which, by all accounts, was par for the course. The train is accompanied throughout much of its memorable descent by the Río Mira which provides exciting whitewater views.

Once in San Lorenzo (where there are only basic hotels and restaurants) you continue down the coast by dugout canoe through Limones (officially known as Valdéz) to La Tola, some 2 hours away. This is a fascinating trip past mangrove swamps with opportunities to see pelicans galore, as well) as ospreys and frigate birds. The Cayapa Indians live in the area and sometimes come into Limones, particularly at weekends. Unfortunately, they have recently been swept by an epidemic which has affected 60% of the population and leads to blindness. Attempts are being made to halt the spread of the disease, but these have not been very successful because of lack of funds, the isolation of the villages, and the lack of medical knowledge about the causes of the illness.

Occasionally boats go from San Lorenzo directly to Esmeraldas, but normally you have to catch a bus from La Tola for the 4 hour journey on to Esmeraldas. This takes you through lush coastal pastureland with good viewing of egrets, herons, and wading birds. I persuaded the driver to let me sit on the roof which made the hot trip very pleasant — but be careful of sunburn.

Once in Esmeraldas most people continue by bus to Atacames, a popular seaside resort with good beaches and many hotels. A further 30 km by rough dirt road brings you to Muisne, which is a very quiet resort with cabins on the beach and fewer tourists. Muisne is located on an island with a frequent ferry service. From Muisne you can continue south on foot along the beach to Cojimíes; this is a good coastal walk. At low tide, curious open sided buses or pickup trucks speed up and down the hard packed sand. So if you get fed up with walking you can flag one down — they pass every hour or so.

MUISNE TO COJIMÍES

From the cabins at the Muisne seafront walk south along the beach for about 5 km to the end of the island. There will be a motorized dugout canoe to ferry you across the Río Muisne for a few sucres. On the other side of the river go upstream to the tiny settlement of Los Manchas, less than a kilometre away, where there is a huddle of houses and a very small store. Walk through the village and continue along a track on the other side which leads to the coast less than a kilometre away. (If you want to avoid Los Manchas you can just follow the coast.) About 7 km of walking will bring you to the tiny coastal village of Mompiche where there is a poorly stocked store which is often closed. A headland (Punta Suspiro) blocks the beach walk, but a sandy vehicle track goes over the headland and through coastal pastureland which is absolutely teeming with birdlife. You arrive at the Portete Estuary about 4 km away where there will again be a dugout canoe waiting to ferry you across for a few sucres.

Now you have to get to the next town of Bolívar. Dugout canoes will take you there up the Portete Estuary. Or you can just cross the river and walk through a few hundred metres of streams and mangroves to the village of Portete where there is the usual ill-stocked, rarely open store. From here you can walk 6 km along the coast around Punta Bolívar and on to Bolívar. The vegetation is very thick and comes right down to the high tide mark so this section must be done at low tide.

Getting from Muisne to Bolívar involves about 22 km of walking. This can be cut down by taking a boat from Portete to Bolívar or by taking a ride on the occasional vehicles along the beach between Muisne and Portete. Carry plenty of water as the rivers aren't very clean or fresh. Sun protection is essential on the sandy, unshaded beaches. Don't forget problem areas like the backs of your legs.

Once in Bolívar you'll find several small stores where you can buy drinks. I couldn't find a hotel but you could probably persuade someone to give you a place to sleep. The best advice is to leave Muisne at dawn (which gives you a couple of cool walking hours) and arrive in Bolívar in early afternoon. It is then easy to find a boat to Cojimíes, about 8 km due south. (There are passenger boats, but don't charter a boat for yourself unless you are desperate. People will encourage you to do so but this is expensive.) This sea trip takes about 30 minutes. Cojimíes is a fishing village with one basic and unsigned hotel which you will have to ask for. There are simple restaurants and friendly people. It is off the beaten tourist track and a good place to spend the night (or two).

From Cojimíes you can continue south to San Vicente by beach bus. The open sided buses are well ventilated(!), the views are good, and the journey takes about 5 hours. This section is less suited to walking as there are much longer distances between villages and little water. San Vicente is a good beach resort, joined by ferry with Bahía de Caráquez from where you can get buses to anywhere.
(WARNING. Rain during the wet months may cause delays.)

MAPS   There are two IGM maps of this area. The 1:50,000 Muisne topographical map covers from Muisne to just before Mompiche and the 1:50,000 Cojimíes planometric map shows from Mompiche to Cojimíes.

MACHALILLA NATIONAL PARK

Machalilla, located on the central coast between Jipijapa to the north and Manglaralto to the south, is one of Ecuador's newer national parks. It was established to protect the coastal wildlife habitats and to preserve the archaeological remains found in the area. Agua Blanca is the largest present-day settlement within the park and was built over a pre-Columbian site of the Manta culture. Known as Señorio de Salangomé this pre-Columbian capital city served as the political and administrative centre for the area. A large part of this ancient settlement has been excavated and an impressive site museum, constructed with traditional materials, is located in the centre of the modern village. Several families in Agua Blanca are accustomed to taking in people for overnight stays, especially when they are planning to hike or ride up to the San Sebastián cloud forest area of the park. Horses and/or guides can easily be arranged in the village. The official park entrance is 5 km west in the village of Puerto López where the usual fee can be paid (US$2) and transport arranged into Agua Blanca. Many day hikes as well as longer excursions in the surrounding area are possible. The four IGM 1:50,000 maps that cover this area are Puerto López, Jipijapa, Pedro P. Gómez, and Delicias.

GUARANGO TO AGUA BLANCA

Eleven kilometres south of Jipijapa on the main road to Guayaquil is a turn-off for the village of Guarango. Have the bus let you off at the small settlement of San Dimas on the main road. From here it's a short (three dusty kilometres) walk to the small village of Guarango. Beyond (west) the village, along the mostly unused jeep trail, the valley narrows as the track heads north around a steep hill then south again. Two hours after leaving the main road, you'll come to the village of Julcuy. Here there are several examples of pre-Columbian *arroyos* constructed to catch the infrequent rainwater runoff in this semi-desert area.

The trail runs southeast through the village leading up toward a notch in the cliffs. About a kilometre beyond Julcuy, the track drops down to the river valley and enters a deep gorge. Both waterbirds and raptors abound here and the stream has both fish and fresh water shrimp. Once past Julcuy you are in Machalilla National Park.

After about an hour the trail and the riverbed separate, though they will continue to criss-cross regularly. There are a couple of springs along the way and several small clusters of houses. It is possible to hike through to Agua Blanca in one very long hot day (about 9 to 10 hours from the main road), but much more pleasurable to take two leisurely ones looking at the birds and plants. From May to November it's usually dry and this hike can be done without a tent.

The five kilometre walk out from Agua Blanca to the paved road can be done in an hour. Here frequent buses pass going south to the fishing village of Puerto López and north to the village of Machalilla.

CERRO BLANCO

Barely 20 minutes out of Guayaquil, west toward Salinas, is the huge cement operation of Cemento Nacional. The name conjures up images of industrialization with all its negative aspects such as habitat destruction, soil erosion, air pollution, constant chugging of machinery, and the like. Cemento Nacional, however, has done a contrary thing. It has set aside much of its property as an ecological reserve which may eventually become a national park. The lowland vegetation here ranges from dry forest on the northern flanks and scrub and kapok to the south. Despite being practically a stone's throw from the largest city in Ecuador, Cerro Blanco is home to an amazing variety of wildlife. Puma, jaguar, jaguarundi, ocelots, howler monkeys, coatis, and peccaries are representative of some of the mammals. The list of birds in the area is equally impressive — owls, grey hawks, crane hawks, snail kites, chacalacas, and a variety of waterfowl to name a few. You can go in for the day or camp in the reserve.

Permission to enter the area is given by Fundación Natura, D. Sucre 401 and Rosendo Avilés in Guayaquil; tel: 441-793. Eduardo Aspiazu, head of this organization, has considerable information about Cerro Blanco. To get there, take any bus heading west on the main road to Salinas. Have the driver drop you at Urbanización Puerto Azul which is directly across the road from Cemento Nacional. Enter through the main gates of the cement factory and head through the 'works' for about a kilometre up to Cantera 4. Here you'll pick up a four wheel drive track as it ascends a hill. This stretch affords marvellous views across the entire Guayaquil basin. A loop of the area can be followed, starting west/northwest and continuing in a clockwise direction along the jeep track. Numerous trails lead off in various directions from the main path, but extra care should be taken as it's easy to become lost.

One cannot stay on the summit forever —
One has to come down again.
So why bother in the first place? Just this.

What is above knows what is below —
But what is below does not know what is above.

One climbs, one sees —
One descends and sees no longer —
But one has seen!

There is an art of conducting one's self in
*   the lower regions by the memory of*
*   what one saw higher up.*

When one can no longer see,
One does at least still know.

Rene Daumal

Appendices

Spanish vocabulary

With the exception of a few small, remote, Indian groups everyone speaks Spanish in Ecuador, including the Andean Indians, although for them it is a second language after Quechua. Other European languages are rarely understood except in the major tourist agencies and first class hotels. Therefore it is essential that you learn some basic Spanish; take heart, it is an easy language to learn.

Quechua, though widely spoken in the highlands, is a difficult language to learn and dialects tend to vary greatly from area to area. So unless you are an avid linguist you're better off learning some Spanish.

The following list of words and phrases will get you started:

USEFUL PHRASES

Where are you going? . . . . *A donde va?*
Where are you coming from? . . . . *De donde viene?*
I'm passing through . . . . *Estoy paseando.*
Can I camp? . . . . *Puedo acampar?*
Where is the trail to.... ? . . . . *Donde esta el camino por.... ?*
How are you? . . . . *Como esta?*

GENERAL VOCABULARY

Bad	*Malo*	No	*No*
Baggage	*Equipaje*	Pickup truck	*Camioneta*
Bath	*Baño*	Please	*Por favor*
Bus	*Bus, colectivo*	Road	*Carretera*
Good	*Bueno*	Room (in hotel)	*Habitacion*
Good morning/day . . .	*Buenos días*	Thank-you	*Gracias*
Good afternoon	*Buenas tardes*	Train	*Ferrocarril, tren*
Good evening/night . . .	*Buenas noches*	Yes	*Sí*
Goodbye	*Adios*		

Climber's and hiker's vocabulary

Above	*Arriba*	Landslide	*Derrumbe*
Altitude	*Altura*	Left	*Izquierda*
Aqueduct	*Acequia*	Meadow	*Pampa*
Ascent	*Subida*	Moraine	*Morena*
Backpack	*Mochila*	Mountain (without	*Cerro*
Below	*Abajo*	snow)	
Bivouac	*Vivac*	Mountain (snow	*Nevado*
Boots (climbing)	*Botas (de andinismo)*	peak)	
Bridge	*Puente*	Mountaineer	*Andinista*
Camp	*Campamento*	Mule	*Mula*
Carabiners	*Mosquetones*	Muleteer	*Arriero*
Climb (down)	*Bajar*	Needle	*Aguja*
Climb (up)	*Escalar, Ascender*	North	*Norte*
Close (to)	*Cerca*	Pass	*Paso, Abra, Porta-*
Cold	*Frio*		*chuelo, Punta*
Crampons	*Grampones*	Peak	*Pico*
Crevasse	*Grieta*	Plain (plateau)	*Pampa*
(to) Cross	*Cruzar, Atravesar*	Point (minor peak)	*Punta*
Distant	*Lejos*	Rain	*Lluvia*
East	*Este*	Ravine	*Quebrada*
Face	*Cara*	Right	*Derecha*
Fixed rope	*Cuerda fija*	River	*Río*
Fog	*Niebla*	Rock	*Roca*
Forest	*Bosque*	Rope	*Cuerda, Soga*
Freeze	*Congelar*	Route	*Ruta*
Glacier	*Glaciar*	Snow	*Nieve*
Hail	*Granizo*	South	*Sur*
Hammer	*Martillo*	Straight ahead	*Derecho, Recto*
Highlands	*Sierra*	Summit	*Cima, Cumbre*
Hill	*Loma*	Swamp	*Pantano*
House	*Casa*	Tent	*Carpa*
Hut (climbers')	*Refugio*	Trail	*Sendero*
Ice	*Hielo*	Valley	*Valle*
Ice Axe	*Piolet*	Village	*Pueblo*
Ice Screw	*Tornillo*	Waterfall	*Cascada*
Lake	*Lago, Laguna*	West	*Oeste*

ELEVATIONS

The height of a mountain is a constant source of interest to climbers and non-climbers alike. Upon returning from a climb, one is often asked "How high is it?" before being questioned about the difficulty, duration, or equipment needed for the ascent. In lesser known areas, the question "How high is it?" is not easily answered. Maps are often sketchy or inaccurate, and different sources come up with various possible heights for the same mountain. Perhaps one of these is correct, perhaps none.

For the sake of consistency, I have used what appears to be the most accurate source for the elevations in this book. These are from the 1979 Instituto Geográfico Militar (IGM) 1:500,000 map of Ecuador. Many other sources are available, and even different maps from the Institute have a variety of elevations. The following table lists various given elevations of Ecuador's major peaks — take your pick.

SOURCES

1. Instituto Geográfico Militar 1:500,000 map, 1979.
2. IGM 1:1,000,000 map, 1981.
3. IGM 1:50,000 series maps, various years.
4. *Montaña* magazine; Colegio San Gabriel, Quito. No. 11, June 1975.
5. *The Fool's Climbing Guide To Ecuador and Peru* by Michael Koerner, 1976.
6. *El Volcanismo en El Ecuador* by Minard L. Hall, 1977.
7. Kevin Healey's map *North West South America* (1989)

	1	2	3	4	5	6	7
Chimborazo	**6310**	**6310**	**6310**	**6310**	**6310**	6267	**6310**
Cotopaxi*	**5897**	**5897**	5880+	6005	**5897**	**5897**	5891
Cayambe	**5790**	**5790**		5840	**5790**	**5790**	**5790**
Antisana*	**5704**	5705	5753	5750	**5704**	5705	**5704**
El Altar*	**5319**	**5319**		5404	5404	**5319**	**5319**
Iliniza Sur	**5263**	**5263**	5248	5305	5305	5266	**5263**
Sangay*	**5230**	**5230**		5323	**5230**	**5230**	**5230**
Iliniza Norte			**5126**	5116	5116		
Carihuairazo	**5020**	**5020**		5106	5116	4990	**5020**
Tungurahua*	**5016**	**5016**		5087	**5016**	**5016**	**5016**
Cotacachi	**4939**	4937		4966	**4939**	**4939**	4939
Sincholagua	**4893**	4899	**4893**	4988	**4893**	4898	
Quilindaña	**4878**	**4878**	4760+	4919	**4878**	4898	
Guagua Pichincha*	**4794**	**4794**	4784	4850	4839	**4794**	**4794**
Corazón	**4788**	**4788**	**4788**	4810	**4788**	4786	**4788**
Chiles	**4768**	4764	**4768**	4720	4712	4720	**4768**
Rumiñahui	**4712**	**4712**	**4712**	4757	**4712**	4722	**4712**
Rucu Pichincha			4680+	4787	4787	4698	
Sara Urco	**4676**	**4676**		**4725**	4710		
Imbabura	**4609**		4560	4630	4630	4630	
Hermoso	**4571**	**4571**			**4571**		
Puntas	**4452**	**4452**				**4452**	
Atacazo	**4410**	4457	4463	4470	4457	4457	
Pasochoa	**4200**	**4200**	4199	4220	4255	4199	
Sumaco*	**3900**	**3900**		3828	3828	3828	**3900**
Reventador*	**3485**	**3485**		**3485**	**3485**	**3485**	**3485**

All heights are in metres.
* signifies active or potentially active volcanoes.
Elevations used in this book are shown in heavy type.

MEASUREMENTS AND CONVERSIONS

Latin America uses metric measurements and so have I throughout this book. These conversion formulae and tables should help you.

Many people will want to convert metres to the more familiar feet. If you remember that 3 metres is 9.84 feet, or just under 10 feet, you can do an approximate conversion quickly: to convert heights shown in metres to feet, divide by 3 and add a zero, e.g. 6,000 m = 20,000 feet.

The error is only 1.5%.

CONVERSION FORMULAE

TEMPERATURE CONVERSION TABLE

The bold figures in the central columns can be read as either centigrade or fahrenheit

To convert	Multiply by	Centigrade		Fahrenheit
Inches to centimetres	2.54			
Centimetres to inches	0.3937	-18	**0**	32
Feet to metres	0.3048	-15	**5**	41
Metres to feet	3.281	-12	**10**	50
Yards to metres	0.9144	- 9	**15**	59
Metres to yards	1.094	- 7	**20**	68
Miles to kilometres	1.609	- 4	**25**	77
Kilometres to miles	0.6214	- 1	**30**	86
Acres to hectares	0.4047	2	**35**	95
Hectares to acres	2.471	4	**40**	104
Imperial gallons to litres	4.546	7	**45**	113
Litres to imperial gallons	0.22	10	**50**	122
US gallons to litres	3.785	13	**55**	131
Litres to US gallons	0.264	16	**60**	140
Ounces to grams	28.35	18	**65**	149
Grams to ounces	0.03527	21	**70**	158
Pounds to grams	453.6	24	**75**	167
Grams to pounds	0.002205	27	**80**	176
Pounds to kilograms	0.4536	32	**90**	194
Kilograms to pounds	2.205	38	**100**	212
British tons to kilograms	1016.0	40	**104**	
Kilograms to British tons	0.0009842			
US tons to kilograms	907.0			
Kilograms to US tons	0.000907			

BIBLIOGRAPHY

This lists all the books I referred to in preparing this guide and a few more besides. I have tried to give as much variety as possible. Many more books are available if you wish to delve more deeply.

GENERAL SOUTH AMERICAN GUIDE BOOKS

The South American Handbook edited by Ben Box. Trade and Travel Publications Ltd, Bath, England. Updated annually, this 1,000 plus page book is the best overall guide to Latin America. Expensive, but worth every penny to anyone planning on spending a long time in Latin America.

South America on a Shoestring by Geoff Crowther, Rob Rachowiecki, Krzysztof Dydynski. Lonely Planet Publications, Australia. 4th edition. December 1990. A good general guide for the budget traveller, with many city maps.

Ecuador & the Galápagos Islands — a travel survival kit, by Rob Rachowiecki. Lonely Plant Publications, Australia, 3rd edition 1992. The best general guide to Ecuador.

"Mainstream" guides by Frommer, Waldo, Birnbaum and Foder, the US$15 or US$20 a day books etc., are all right as basic guides to the continent.

GUIDEBOOKS FOR THE OUTDOORS

The Fool's Climbing Guide to Ecuador by Michael Koerner. Buzzard Mountaineering, USA., 1976. The first English language guide to Ecuador's mountains. Not particularly detailed but its humorous descriptions make it worthwhile reading.

A Climbers and Hikers Guide to the World's Mountains by Michael R. Kelsey, 1982. Includes about 20 pages of maps and information on Ecuador and over 600 pages on the rest of the world. For the globetrotting mountaineer, this is the book.

Guia Para Excursiones en Automovil a Traves del Ecuador by Arthur Weilbauer. Quito, 1985. Available in Spanish, German and English. An invaluable guide to all the major and most minor roads in Ecuador.

GENERAL MOUNTAINEERING AND EXPLORATION

Travels Amongst the Great Andes of the Equator by Edward Whymper, 1891. Worth getting hold of — this book describes the 1880 expedition which first climbed Ecuador's highest peak, and made seven other first ascents.

Personal Narrative of the Travels to the Equinoctial Regions of the New Continent by Alexander von Humboldt and Aime Bonpland. Various editions. Again, difficult to find, but fascinating reading for anyone interested in the historical aspects of Latin American exploration.

Sangay Survived by Richard Snailham. Hutchinson, 1978 (now out of print). The story of a six man British scientific expedition to the volcano which ended disastrously when an eruption killed or injured most of the members.

The Next Horizon by Chris Bonington. Victor Gollancz Ltd., 1973. This autobiographical book by one of Britain's leading climbers includes two chapters on climbing Sangay.

NATURAL HISTORY AND VOLCANOLOGY

Fauna del Ecuador by Erwin Patzelt, Quito 1978. In Spanish, now out of print. A small but comprehensive book, particularly useful on mammals, though shetchy on birds and other animals.

The Andes by Tony Morrison. Time-Life Books, 1975. A beautiful book covering the whole Andean chain; Ecuador's mountains are not forgotten with superb phonographs of Cotopaxi and Sangay.

Land Above the Clouds by Tony Morrison. Deutsch, 1974. This book also deals with the whole Andean chain with an emphasis on its wildlife. Recommended.

The Flight of the Condor by Michael Andrews. Collins, 1982. Subtitled *A Wildlife Exploration of the Andes* this well-illustrated book contains an excellent chapter on Ecuador.

Ecuador: Snow Peaks and Jungles by Arthur Eichler, English translation, Cromwell, N.Y., 1955. Also bilingual edition by Eichler, Quito 1970. Although some of the information is rather inaccurate, the excellent photographs make thin a book well worth looking at.

Ecuador — in the Shadow of the Volcanoes, Ediciones Libri Mundi, 1981. Available in English, Spanish, German and French. A "coffee-table" book, with many superb photos.

El Volcanismo en El Ecuador by Minard L. Hall. I.P.G.H., Quilo, 1977. In Spanish, mainly of interest to the volcanologist — the best work on the subject.

Neotropical Rainforest Mammals —A Field Guide, by Louise H. Emmons, University of Chicago Press, USA, 1990. A detailed and well illustrated guide to the mammals of Amazonia and the Central American rainforests — recommended.

Tropical Nature by Adrian Forsyth and Ken Miyata, Scribners, New York, 1984. Sub-titled "Life and Death in the Rain Forests of Central and South America", this book is a great introduction to the natural history of the rainforest.

A Neotropical Companion by John C. Kricher, Princeton University Press, USA, 1989. Sub-titled "An Introduction to the Animals, Plants, and Ecosystems of the New World Tropics", this book is just as good as the one listed above. Both are recommended.

ORNITHOLOGY *(My thanks to Paul Greenfield, bird illustrator and expert on Ecuadorian species, for help in preparing this exhaustive list.)*

A Guide to the Birds of Ecuador by R. Ridgely and P. Greenfield. Princeton University Press. Expected c. 1988. One of a series, this definitive book will illustrate and describe every Ecuadorian species, including those on the Galápagos. Other books in this series are:

A Guide to the Birds of Panama by R. Ridgely. Princeton University Press, 1976. An excellent book, of use in the coastal regions of Ecuador.

A Guide to the Birds of Venezuela by R.M. de Schauensee, W.H. Phelps Jr., and G. Tudor. Princeton University Press, 1976. Particularly useful for the Oriente, but has some inaccuracies.

A Guide to the Birds of Colombua by Brown and Hilly. Princton University Press, expected 1984/85. This book will probably cover about 80% of Ecuadorian species.

The Birds of Ecuador and the Galápagos Archipelago by Thomas Y Butler. Ramphastos Agen POB 1091, Portsmouth, N.H. 03801, U.S.A., 1979. Basically a check list with useful tables showing the zones in which each species is found.

A Guide to the Birds of South America by R.M. de Schauensee. Livinstone Pub. Co., Wynnewood, P.A. The only book to cover all of the nearly 3,000 birds of the continent, hence necessarily brief in its descriptions.

South American Land Birds — A Photographic Aid to Identification by John S. Dunning, Harrowood Books, Newtown Square, P.A., 1982. A new book which describes over 80% of the South American species. 1,112 are illustrated. Again, necessarily brief descriptions and does not cover sea, shore and lake birds.

South American Birds — A Photographic Aid to Identification by John S. Dunning, Harrowood Books, Pa, USA, 1987. 1,400 birds illustrated and 2,700 described in this book, which covers water as well as land birds.

Birding Ecuador by Clive Green, Tucson, Arizona, USA, 1991. Detailed account of a birding trip made in June-August 1990. Contains useful checklists, descriptions and access details of many birding hotspots in Ecuador. Available from the South American Explorers Club.

MISCELLANEOUS

Ingapirca edited by Jorge Aravena. Editora Andina, Quito, 1982. A small, Spanish language guide to the ruins, with photographs, poems, and a short playing record.

El Clima y Sus Caracterasticas en El Ecuador by Carlos Blandin Landivar. I.P.G.H., Quito, 1976. A Spanish language book on the meteorology of Ecuador.

Ecuador — A Travel Journal by Henri Michaux, Peter Owen, 1970 (out of print). A book of poetry and prose describing the 1926 visit to Ecuador by a Belgian mystic, poet, and writer.

The Lost World of the Andes by K.D. Gertelmann. Quito, 1977. A multi-lingual book with many colour photographs describing one of the least known and least accessible Indian tribes of Ecuador.

Humboldt and the Cosmnos by Douglas Botting. Sphere Books, London. A biographical account of one of the best known early explorers of Ecuador and South America.

Mountaineering Medicine — A Wilderness Medical Guide by Fred T. Darvill, M.D. Skagit Mountain Rescue, POB 2, Mt. Vernon, WA 98273, USA. A smallbooklet useful for carrying on hiking and climbing trips.

The Conquest of the Incas by John Hemming. Macmillan 1970. Penguin 1983. A thorough and exceptional work on the subject.

In the eyes of my people by Pablo Cuvi, Dinediciones/Grijalbo, Ecuador, 1988. Difficult to find outside of Ecuador, but highly recommended once you get there. Subtitled "Stories and phots of journeys through Ecuador", this book is written by an Ecuadorian who both loves his country and knows how to write. The photos are some of the best I've seen of Ecuador and its people.

PERIODICALS

Montaña The magazine of the San Gabriel Climbing Club, Quito. The oldest established mountaineering magazine in Ecuador, appearing at irregular intervals. (No. 11, January 1975, No. 12, January 1980, No. 13, July 1981, No. 14, April 1983). In Spanish with some English mountain descriptions.

Campo Abierto Quito, Ecuador. A small mountaineering magazine begun in 1982; latest edition No. 5, March 1983. Spanish language.

INDEX

See also Table of Contents